Gothic
Feminism

Gothic Feminism

~

The Professionalization of Gender from Charlotte Smith to the Brontës

Diane Long Hoeveler

The Pennsylvania State University Press
University Park, Pennsylvania

"Vindicating *Northanger Abbey:* Wollstonecraft, Austen, and Gothic Feminism," in *Jane Austen and Discourses of Feminism,* ed. Devoney Looser, reprinted by permission from St. Martin's Press © 1995.

"Charlotte Dacre's *Zofloya:* A Case Study in Miscegenation as Sexual and Racial Nausea" reprinted by permission from *European Romantic Review* 7 © 1997.

"Professionalizing Gender: The Female Gothic, Beating Fantasies, and the Civilizing Process," in *Comparative Romanticisms: Power, Gender, and Subjectivity,* ed. Larry H. Peer and Diane Long Hoeveler, reprinted by permission from Camden House Press © 1998.

Library of Congress Cataloging-in-Publication Data

Hoeveler, Diane Long.
    Gothic feminism: the professionalization of gender from Charlotte Smith to the Brontës / Diane Long Hoeveler.
    p.   cm
    Includes bibliographical references (p.   ) and index.
    ISBN 0-271-01809-7 (alk. paper)
    1. Horror tales, English—History and criticism. 2. Feminism and Literature—Great Britain—History—18th century. 3. Feminism and literature—Great Britain—History—19th century. 4. English fiction—Women authors—History and criticism. 5. Gothic revival (Literature)—Great Britain. 6. Gender identity in literature. 7. Femininity in literature. 8. Sex role in literature. I. Title.
PR830.T3H64   1998
823'.0873809352042—dc21
                                                  98-19611
                                                   CIP

It is the policy of The Pennsylvania State University Press to use acid-free paper for the first printing of all clothbound books. Publications on uncoated stock satisfy the minimum requirements of American National Standard for Information Sciences—Permanence of Paper for Printed Library Materials, ANSI Z39.48-1992.

This book is dedicated
to some of the men
who have made my life so gothic:

to the memories
of my grandfather
and my father
and to my brother—
all named
Vincent Leo Long

and to my husband and son—
both named
John David Hoeveler:

Ourself behind ourself, concealed–
should startle most–

—EMILY DICKINSON,
"ONE NEED NOT BE A CHAMBER"

Contents

Abbreviations

ATQ	American Transcendental Quarterly
BSUF	Ball State University Forum
CA	Current Anthropology
CR	Centennial Review
CI	Critical Inquiry
EC	Eighteenth Century: Theory and Interpretation
ECS	Eighteenth-Century Studies
EL	Essays in Literature
ELH	English Literary History
ERR	European Romantic Review
ESC	English Studies in Canada
JEGP	Journal of English and German Philology
MLS	Modern Language Studies
NCF	Nineteenth-Century Fiction
NCL	Nineteenth-Century Literature
NLH	New Literary History
N&Q	Notes and Queries
PLL	Papers in Language and Literature
PMLA	Publications of the Modern Language Association
PQ	Philological Quarterly
PR	Partisan Review
PsR	Psychocultural Review
SAB	South Atlantic Bulletin
SBHT	Studies in Burke and His Time
SEL	Studies in English Literature
SH	Studies in the Humanities
SNNTS	Studies in the Novel (North Texas State)
SP	Studies in Philology
SR	Studies in Romanticism
TSLL	Texas Studies in Literature and Language
TSWL	Tulsa Studies in Women's Literature
UTQ	University of Toronto Quarterly
VQR	Virginia Quarterly Review
WL	Women and Literature
WW	Women's Writing

It was only important to smile and hold still,
to lie down beside him and to rest awhile, . . .
I held my breath and daddy was there, . . .
I lay by the moss of his skin until it grew strange.
My sisters will never know that I fall
out of myself and pretend that Allah will not see
how I hold my daddy like an old stone tree.

—ANNE SEXTON,
"THE MOSS OF HIS SKIN"

Preface

When last I put down my pen, I was ruminating on Jerome McGann's observation about the highly ideological nature of "Ideal space" in English Romantic poetry.[1] Contemplating such an image enabled me to envision another sort of approach to the literature written by women during the same period. That is, in thinking about what a series of "idealized spaces" would look like—the home, the church, the school—I realized that they were all inversions of other culturally and socially constructed spaces—the prison, the confessional, the madhouse. And in thinking about the confluence or spiraling sense of both types of spaces, I realized that I had excavated not only the very real shape of my own life but the gendered constructions that women traditionally have been consigned to under the protection racket we sometimes call the "patriarchy." Or rather, I discovered that a particular species of "feminism" that has recently been labeled "victim feminism" originated as a Western, white, middle-class ideology, and that a large portion of its rhetoric evolved out of the discourse system we now recognize as the female gothic novel.

When a contemporary writer like Naomi Wolf claims that "victim feminism" is "antisexual," that it "depends on influence or persuasion rather than on seeking clout in a straightforward way," that it "projects aggression, competitiveness, and violence onto men or patriarchy while its devotees are blind to those qualities in themselves," she fails to recognize that all of these strategies originated and were codified in the female gothic novel tradition close to two hundred years ago. In fact, all of those tactics emerge at one time or another in the majority of female gothic heroines who, in thrall to the codes of sentimentality, cannot bare their teeth in anything other than a smile. I would claim that this one particular type of feminism, labeled "victim

---

1. See Jerome McGann, *Romantic Ideologies* (Chicago: University of Chicago Press, 1983): "Ideas and Ideology therefore lie at the heart of all Romantic poetry. Its entire emotional structure depends upon the credit and fidelity it gives to its own fundamental illusions. And its greatest moments usually occur when it pursues its last and final illusion: that it can expose or even that it has uncovered its illusions and false consciousness, that it has finally arrived at the Truth" (134).

feminism" by antifeminists and then critiqued by Wolf, originated in the rhetorical and literary traditions of the female gothic novel.[2] In short, I discovered "gothic feminism."

Focusing initially on such socially and culturally determined configurations seemed for a variety of reasons the most appropriate place to begin this study of female-created ideologies in the female gothic novel. In other words, this volume picks up where my earlier *Romantic Androgyny: The Women Within* (1990) ended. If *Romantic Androgyny* was concerned with the representation of symbolic women in male-authored poetic texts, then *Gothic Feminism* initially attempted to answer the complementary question: How did female authors represent both male and female characters in that peculiarly feminocentric discourse system, the female gothic novel? And, more important, why did their representations of both men and women move much beyond the purely psychosexual into the distinctly social and political realms of female-created economies, the ideological reconstruction of the body, the family and society at large? Female gothic novelists, I believed, did not so much create "masculine" characters as "masculine" spaces; that is, they constructed spaces that they saw as defined, codified, and institutionalized as "masculine" which they then attempted to rewrite into the literature more benignly as "feminine."

In the process of writing this book, however, I discovered that these novelists were not trying to reshape their worlds subversively or benignly through their writings. They were instead constructing a series of ideologies—a set of literary masquerades and poses—that would allow their female characters and by extension their female readers a fictitious mastery over what they considered an oppressive social and political system through the pose of what I am calling "professional femininity." When Terry Eagleton describes the "bourgeois feminization of discourse" during the mid- to late eighteenth century—a movement that he claims "prolongs the fetishizing of women at the same time as it lends them a more authoritative voice"— he is also accurately and uncannily defining the female gothic project. The female gothic novel cannot be understood simply as it has been traditionally seen, that is, as a genre that is primarily concerned with depicting women's achievement of psychic maturity or socioeconomic inheritance or some combination of the two. It is, in fact, more accurate to see the female

---

2. "Victim feminism" as an antifeminist ideology has most recently been discussed by Naomi Wolf in *Fire with Fire: The New Female Power and How It Will Change the 21st Century* (New York: Random House, 1993), 136–37.

gothic novel functioning as a coded and veiled critique of all of those public institutions that have been erected to displace, contain, or commodify
women.[3]

Following Foucault, I read the female gothic novel as one gendered
response to the creation of "woman as subject" by the juridical systems that
dominate the period—the prison, the school, the asylum, the confessional,
and the bourgeois family. But following Hayden White's theory of "metahis-
tory," I also read what has come to be termed "victim feminism," a species of
professional femininity, as a form of gender construction and an ideology
that grew out of the literary discourse systems we have come to identify as
the gothic, the melodrama, and the sentimental and sensibility traditions of
virtue vindicated and rewarded. This book explores how "victim feminism"
or "professional femininity" as ideologies cannot be understood apart from
their origins in the female gothic novel tradition. The fact that Mary
Wollstonecraft wrote two incipient gothic novels both before and after she
wrote *A Vindication of the Rights of Woman* (1792) has not been fully understood or placed within its broader cultural, literary, and historical contexts:
the gothic feminist construction of "femininity" as a professional masquerade. The middle-class woman as "professional victim" was just one of the
many roles that this literary discourse system invented, codified, and promulgated in order to help women adjust to their confusing and often contradictory status in a newly emerging bourgeois culture.

Indeed, the ideology that seems to ground the female gothic novel tradition is the same one that grounds one version of white, bourgeois Western
feminism, the belief that women are victimized and oppressed not simply
by gender politics but by the social, economic, political, religious, and hierarchical spaces that bourgeois capitalism—and by extension the patriarchal
family—has constructed to contain them. The ideological trajectory of the
female gothic novel can be more accurately read as the need to privatize
public spaces, and is very similar to (although historically distanced from)
the claim made by a variety of feminists in the late 1960s and early 1970s
that "the personal is political." The motivation for the women who write
what we now label the female gothic is both simple and complex: they aim
for nothing less than the fictional feminization of the masculine world, the
domestication of all those masculine institutions that exist to define the sexuality, not to mention the sanity, of women. The optimistic dream that most

---

3. Terry Eagleton, *The Rape of Clarissa: Writing, Sexuality, and Class Struggle in Samuel Richardson*
(Oxford: Basil Blackwell, 1982), 13.

often concludes the female gothic novel requires that juridical violence, paranoia, and injustice, figured as the "masculine," can be brought to heel, punished, and contained safely within the confines of the ultimate fantasy home—the female-dominated companionate marriage.

Recent critical approaches to the female gothic novel have tended to problematize the genre and argue, in fact, that women's gothic novels cannot be analyzed or understood apart from the male gothic tradition. I disagree. The earliest critical attempt to define and codify women's specific contribution to the genre was made by Ellen Moers in *Literary Women* (1976). For Moers, the female gothic was embodied in one persistent struggle: a persecuted heroine in flight between a pastoral, bucolic past and a haunted, ominous castle. An absent mother and a threatening father were staples of the genre, which begged to be read as fantasy, wish fulfillment, and potent historical and ideological residue. Following Moers, literary critics in the 1980s began to interpret the female gothic by emphasizing psychological or sexual readings of the female "self."[4] It seems more accurate to observe, however, that the female gothic novel constitutes a genre with its own distinctive and recurrent aesthetic and political strategies, both designed to dramatize the horrors of English patriarchal life safely displaced onto a remote setting.

In addition to placing gothic feminism in a literary context, however, it is also necessary to position the strategy in feminist theory. Naomi Wolf's recent discussion of "victim feminism" is germane here, although it fails to account for the historical evolution of the ideology or to understand that the attitude is rooted in gothic and melodramatic tropes of female victimization. "Victim feminism," like all ideologies, does not exist apart from or above history; rather, it is grounded in the history of a variety of discourse systems like medical and educational treatises, conduct book rhetoric, as well as the female gothic writings of the late eighteenth through the mid-nineteenth centuries. "Victim feminism," like gothic feminism, is a literary ideology and cannot be understood apart from reading its rhetoric within

---

4. In addition to Moers's *Literary Women* (Garden City, N.Y.: Doubleday, 1976), seminal studies here include Claire Kahane, "Gothic Mirrors and Feminine Identity," *CR* 24 (1980), 43–64; Cynthia Griffin Wolff, "The Radcliffean Gothic Model: A Form for Feminine Sexuality," *MLS* 9 (1979), 98–113; Margaret Doody, "Deserts, Ruins, and Troubled Waters: Female Dreams in Fiction and the Development of the Gothic Novel," *Genre* 10 (1977), 529–72; Juliann Fleenor, ed., *The Female Gothic* (London: Eden Press, 1983); Norman N. Holland and Leona F. Sherman, "Gothic Possibilities," *NLH* 8 (1977), 279–94; and Eugenia C. DeLamotte, *Perils of the Night: A Feminist Study of Nineteenth-Century Gothic* (New York: Oxford University Press, 1990).

the originating sources—the gothic novels of Charlotte Smith, Ann Radcliffe, Jane Austen, Charlotte Dacre Byrne ("Rosa Matilda"), Mary Shelley, and the Brontës. All of these novelists, I will argue, participated in their culture's attempts to professionalize gender—specifically what we now recognize as "femininity"—for the women of the growing British middle class. Granted, Mary Wollstonecraft, Mary Hays, Mary Robinson, Fanny Burney, Harriet Martineau, Hannah More, and Maria Edgeworth among others also wrote a variety of works that participated significantly in the broad pattern of feminist writing and conflict throughout the late eighteenth through the mid-nineteenth centuries. But my focus in this study is on female gothic novels that have attained something approaching canonical status in the field.

Using the theories of Norbert Elias and Michel Foucault, as well as the contemporary French feminists, I will claim that the female gothic novels of this period were thinly disguised efforts at propagandizing a new form of conduct for women. This book will focus on what I am calling "professional femininity"—a cultivated pose, a masquerade of docility, passivity, wise passiveness, and tightly controlled emotions—in an attempt to understand how female gothic novelists helped to popularize and promulgate a newly defined and increasingly powerful species of bourgeois female sensibility and subjectivity. Rachel Brownstein has defined "female heroism" in a manner that is similar to my sense of the growing professionalization of bourgeois femininity: "She is a young woman perfectly chaste, dutiful, obedient, religious, useful, orderly, charitable, thrifty, and kind. She acts and requires others to act according to a firm ethical standard. But her essence is aesthetic. In effect the bourgeois Christian Exemplar is an adaptation of the cliché that a woman is a goddess, a convention of courtship, literature, and polite society that, as Richardson knew and Mary Wollstonecraft was soon to say, has long served to enslave women."[5] I contend that female gothic

---

5. Rachel M. Brownstein, *Becoming a Heroine: Reading About Women in Novels* (New York: Viking, 1982), 43. My emphasis on what I am calling the professionalization or institutionalization of femininity is also obviously indebted to the work of Mary Poovey, whose *Proper Lady and the Woman Writer: Ideology as Style in the Works of Mary Wollstonecraft, Mary Shelley, and Jane Austen* (Chicago: University of Chicago Press, 1984) has been influential in shaping our understanding of the ideological dynamics of women's writing. I want further to acknowledge my indebtedness to the work of Kate Ellis, whose *Contested Castle: Gothic Novels and the Subversion of Domestic Ideology* (Urbana: University of Illinois Press, 1989) discusses many of the issues we are still attempting to unravel in the female gothic. I admire Ellis's use of the garden motif and I particularly appreciate her attempt to recognize shame and guilt cultures within this discourse, but I disagree with her on a number of issues, most prominently her emphasis on the gothic as "subversive." Instead I see the female gothic as more

novels adapted the "Exemplar" model of femininity while making such a heroine covertly powerful, thereby maintaining the trappings or at least the illusion of the heroine's original identity as complaisant and malleable. This conflicted heritage fissured the female gothic heroine, whose strategies of resistance tended to degenerate into illusory, often self-destructive forms of idealization. Recognizing this fault line in the female gothic novel tradition has been uncomfortable for contemporary literary critics in thrall themselves to the need to recast our novelistic foremothers in our own image. But until we recognize the contradictions implicit in gothic feminism—or romantic feminism—we will continue to find ourselves caught up in the self-perpetuating ideologies of the past.

Finally, a word about definitions. All discussions of the gothic employ by necessity the word "fantasy," and my work is no exception. I rely on Freud's generalization that "a happy person never fantasizes, only an unsatisfied one," and I will claim that the female gothic novelists examined here were, indeed, very dissatisfied with the lot of women during this period. Like all contemporary gothic theorists, however, I also owe a debt to the writings of David Punter, who reads the fantasy work of the gothic as both a psychic recuperation of loss and as a social and cultural dialogue that rehearses the death of an old order—the ancién regime—along with the anxiety attendant on the birth of a new order—a chastened and superior bourgeoisie. I read the female gothic novel—with its emphasis on external rather than internal enemies among the most prominent of its distinct differences from the male gothic tradition—as an extended fantasy, an elaborate wish fulfillment, a hysterical discourse system. As Freud has observed, all victims of the wounds of memory, "suffer from reminiscences . . . they can not get free of the past, and for its sake they neglect what is real and immediate." The "hysterical conversion" that brings the female gothic tradition into existence relies on the nexus of representation and female subjectivity, or, as Laplanche and Pontalis remind us, "the day-dream is a shadow play, utilizing its kaleidoscopic material drawn from all quarters of human experience, but also involving the original fantasy, whose dramatic personae, the court cards, receive their notation from a family legend which is mutilated, disordered

---

problematic, as both subverting and at the same time reifying postures of complaisancy and acquiescence on the part of women. Finally, I am also immensely indebted to Nancy Armstrong's important *Desire and Domestic Fiction: A Political History of the Novel* (New York: Norton, 1987), for her analysis of the feminization of subjectivity through the cultural work of conduct book rhetoric and novels like *Clarissa* and *Pamela*.

and misunderstood."[6] Like an elaborate and repetitious daydream, the orig-inating fantasy that empowers the female gothic novel is, I would claim, a specifically female oedipal quest, a need to rewrite history from the vantage point of a beleaguered daughter intent on rescuing her mother—and by extension, her future self—from the nightmare of the alienating and newly codifying and commodifying patriarchal family.

In this study I also use terms like "feminism," "gender," and "patriarchy" without implying that there is any clear consensus among critics about these complicated and controversial issues. As Donna Landry and Gerald MacLean have noted, "Feminism looks more homogeneous or heteroge-neous depending on where one stands. And as with other commodities, only a committed user can fully experience the fiercer forms of brand loyalty which can make other positions, other brands just disappear." I find myself drawn equally to what Teresa De Lauretis has recently called "non-denom-inational feminism," or what bell hooks labels "feminism in movement," the notion that there is no one feminism, but only an unending series of cri-tiques, dissents, and renegotiations.[7] Analogously, like many other feminists, I claim that terms like "gender," "patriarchy," and even "feminism" are equally problematic and open to critique from a variety of positions. This study attempts to problematize all three issues by examining how the female gothic literary tradition influenced the evolution of what has sometimes been called "victim feminism," gender politics, and the "patriarchy."

I first read Radcliffe's *Mysteries of Udolpho* as a graduate student in 1971. I was so entranced by the work that I was bold enough to attempt to con-vince my fellow graduate students of its many virtues. After listening to my recitation, they smiled politely and queried, "Don't you think you're just hungry for *plot*?" On the contrary, I have always suspected that plot is the

---

6. See Sigmund Freud, "Creative Writers and Day-Dreamers," and "Hysterical Fantasies and Their Relation to Bisexuality," in *The Standard Edition of the Complete Psychological Works of Sigmund Freud [SE]*, trans. James Strachey, 24 vols. (London: Hogarth Press, 1953–74), 9:146, 9:160. All quotations from Freud are from this edition with volume and page numbers identified in parentheses in the text. See also David Punter, *The Literature of Terror*, 2 vols. (London: Longmans, 1980; reprinted 1996) and *The Romantic Unconscious* (New York: New York University Press, 1989); and Jean Laplanche and Jean-Bertrand Pontalis, "Fantasy and the Origins of Sexuality," in *Formations of Fantasy*, ed. Victor Burgin, James Donald, and Cora Kaplan (London: Methuen, 1986), 22.

7. Donna Landry and Gerald MacLean, "Commodity Feminism," in *Materialist Feminisms* (Oxford: Blackwell, 1993), 54; Teresa De Lauretis, "Upping the Anti (sic) in Feminist Theory," in *Conflicts in Feminism*, ed. Marianne Hirsch and Evelyn Fox (New York: Routledge, 1990), 255–70; and bell hooks, "Thinking Past Censorship: Having the Courage to Criticize Our Allies," *On the Issues* 25 (1992), 4.

least of my interests in the female gothic. This study began, like *Romantic Androgyny,* two decades ago and out of an attempt to answer the same questions that were provoked by my readings in primary gothic/romantic texts.[8]

I must confess, however, that I was drawn to write about the female gothic at this point in my life for a variety of personal and professional reasons. Although I had spent many years reading and teaching and thinking about how men and women define themselves in a society that sexually segregates and differentiates, I finally needed the impetus to write, and that I received from my colleagues at Marquette University. In fact, the insights I have brought both to this book and to *Romantic Androgyny* are owed in no small measure to the strangely gothic atmosphere of Marquette's English Department. I am grateful to the colleagues who have encouraged and supported my efforts there: Frank Hubbard, Albert Rivero, Michael McCanles, Ed Block, and John Boly. As for the others: "Opposition is true Friendship." I also want to acknowledge my financial debt of gratitude to Marquette's Office of Research Support for four summers of financial support while working on this and other writing projects.

There is considerable irony in the fact that this book in part examines female fears of male clergy and, specifically, the Roman Catholic hierarchy: Irony because I am the beneficiary of the professional kindnesses and decency of the many Jesuits for whom it has been my privilege to work at Marquette University. In particular, I want to acknowledge the support of John Piderit, SJ, William P. Leahy, SJ, and Thaddeus Burch, SJ. I am also grateful for the support of my colleagues in the Women's Studies Program, Alice Kehoe and Janet Boles, who have always been there for me, always willing to listen, encourage, and advise. I have also been fortunate to have the professional support of critics as astute as Stephen Behrendt, Eugenia DeLamotte, Tamar Heller, Margaret Higonnet, Greg Kucich, Beth Lau, Jerome McGann, Anne Mellor, Bernard Paris, Alan Richardson, Gene Ruoff,

---

8. Romanticism and Gothicism (or "Dark Romanticism") as two sides of the same cultural and sexual phenomenon have been analyzed by Robert D. Hume, "Gothic Versus Romantic: A Reevaluation of the Gothic Novel," *PMLA* 84 (1969), 282–90; Robert L. Platzner and Robert Hume, "'Gothic Versus Romantic': A Rejoinder," *PMLA* 86 (1971), 266–74; and G. R. Thompson, "Introduction: Romanticism and the Gothic Tradition," in *The Gothic Imagination: Essays in Dark Romanticism,* ed. Thompson (Olympia: Washington State University Press, 1974). More recently, however, Anne Williams has expanded and corrected our understanding of the connection between "romantic" and "gothic" in her provocative and wide-ranging study *Art of Darkness: A Poetics of Gothic* (Chicago: University of Chicago Press, 1995), while all of the essays published in the "Female Gothic" issue of *Women's Writing* (vol. 1, 1994) are devoted to problematizing and correcting early and easy assumptions about the connections between the romantic and the gothic.

Herbert Sussman, William Veeder, Brian Wilkie, and Susan Wolfson—all of whom have been kind enough to help or support me at some crucial point in my work. I would also like to acknowledge the editors of *ERR*, *Jane Austen and the Discourses of Feminism*, and *Comparative Romanticisms* for permission to reprint portions of the introduction and chapter 3 in slightly revised form. And once again it is my pleasure to acknowledge the courtesy and professionalism of Philip Winsor, senior editor at the Pennsylvania State University Press, in my opinion the very best of editors.

As usual, my husband, David Hoeveler, and our children, John and Emily, have been a constant loving presence in my life. Finally, the dedication of this book to the men in my family represents just a portion of my own private melodrama.

Introduction

Gothic Feminism and the Professionalization of "Femininity"

> *I hold, that a Woman has no business to be a public*
> *character, and that in the proportion that She*
> *acquires notoriety, She loses delicacy: I always consider*
> *a female Author as a sort of half-Man.*
>
> —MATTHEW LEWIS

I

On the dark and stormy night of February 7, 1823, Ann Radcliffe, pious and devoted wife, paragon of domestic virtues, died raving mad. Or so rumor had it.[1] Condemned by the critics of the gothic novel as the original "mad-woman in the attic," Radcliffe created what we have come to recognize as the potent, primal versions of the female gothic, only to be consumed supposedly in death by its horrors. Her novels, particularly *The Mysteries of Udolpho* and *The Italian*, established the narrative trajectory that has persisted into contemporary female gothics: a persecuted heroine trapped in a crumbling castle diffused with manic oedipal anxieties and assaulted by the forces of socioeconomic power (often disguised as religion) run amok. The fears that haunt Radcliffe's heroines are as real as they are ephemeral; that

---

1. Rumors about Radcliffe's sanity began during her own lifetime, and her earliest biographer expended a fair amount of energy trying to disprove the medical fact that Radcliffe died of a brain fever. See T. N. Talfourd, "Memoir" to *Gaston de Blondeville* (London, 1826).

is, the author manages to create a fictional world where disinheritance is figured as the equivalent of incestuous rape. And if neither threat actually materializes, the reader vicariously experiences both as if they did through the vivid imaginative fantasies of each of the heroines. As her heroines flee from towers to labyrinthine catacombs to rooms with trick locks, they seem to be running in quick sand. The strange stasis—manifest in the slow motion followed by sudden flurry, the revolving cycles of inertia and mania—is characteristic of the long-winded, hysterical prose of the female gothic. But such devices merely encode and proffer the dominant ideology that lies at the heart of the genre, that lies at the heart of the heroines, that lies at the heart of women in patriarchal society: the ideology I have come to recognize and label as "gothic feminism."

Radcliffe's later novels actually fictionalize the major claims presented by Mary Wollstonecraft's *Vindication of the Rights of Woman* (1792), for if Wollstonecraft condemns the inadequate educations women receive, Radcliffe demonstrates the disastrous effects of such training on her gothic antiheroines. But it is in the creation of what I have come to recognize as gothic feminism that Wollstonecraft and Radcliffe have the most in common. Both authors conspired (albeit unknowingly) in creating this potent ideology that persists even today and undergirds many of the assumptions of what now goes under the name of "victim feminism," the contemporary antifeminist notion that women earn their superior social and moral rights in society by positioning themselves as innocent victims of a corrupt tyrant and an oppressive patriarchal society.

At this point, however, one realizes that one has once again succumbed to generalizing about the genre, lapsing into that old critical trap—the generic laundry list. The gothic has always lured its critics into that quagmire and managed to elude systematic analysis as a result. The challenge in writing about the female gothic would appear to lie in defining and limiting one's terms. And, unfortunately, analysis of the "gothic" has traditionally been accomplished through what Eugenia DeLamotte has called "the shopping-list approach." Listing devices or conventions as the 1801 *Monthly* did ("unnatural parents,– persecuted lovers,– murders,– haunted apartments,– winding sheets, and winding stair-cases,– subterraneous passages,– lamps that are dim and perverse, and that always go out when they should not,– monasteries,– caves,– monks, tall, thin, and withered, with lank abstemious cheeks,– dreams,– groans,– and spectres") was standard in the critical discourse through the 1960s. But during the past three decades literary critics have turned their attention to defining the genre by addressing questions about the "meaning of the Gothic myth."[2] The female gothic novelistic tradition most recently has been subjected to several useful and provocative interpretations by DeLamotte, Poovey, and Williams, but earlier analysts tended to privilege the notion of the "female" "self" in ways that ignored the highly ideological nature of both the gothic "myth" and their own critical approaches.

As critics we cannot afford to indulge the notion—in life or in literature—that women can ever escape their social, political, and economic conditions and thereby create or preserve some sort of pristine ahistorical "self." In a poststructuralist leap of faith, however, I do believe that we can come to some conclusions (albeit tentative) about the female gothic genre and its complicity with the development of "victim feminism" and "professional femininity" as ideologies. Discussions of the female gothic, like analyses of "feminism," have, unfortunately, uncritically participated in the very fantasies that the genres have created for their unwary readers. We, like the characters in the female gothic novel or proponents of a monolithic feminism, want to find something hidden, mysterious, deep, and esoteric behind the black veil, and usually this elusive deep structure is imaged as some sort of sexual or psychic secret. The lure of the gothic has been precisely in this quality, this notion that as readers we have creative or quasi-artistic power by investing empty signifiers with our own self-created meanings.

This book examines instead the voices that dominate the discourse of British female gothic from the late 1780s to 1853. Those voices—and the discourse systems that emerge from them—have been recognized as adhering to the traditions of sensibility and sentimentality, melodrama and the

---

2. See DeLamotte, *Perils of the Night*, 5. The major pre-1960 critics of the gothic include Edith Birkhead, *The Tale of Terror: A Study of the Gothic Romance* (London: Constable, 1921); Eino Railo, *The Haunted Castle: A Study of the Elements of English Romanticism* (1927; reprinted New York: Humanities Press, 1964); J. M. S. Tompkins, *The Popular Novel in England, 1770–1800* (1932; reprinted Westport: Greenwood Press, 1961); Montague Summers, *The Gothic Quest: A History of the Gothic Novel* (1938; reprinted New York: Russell and Russell, 1964); and Devendra P. Varma, *The Gothic Flame* (1957; reprinted New York: Russell and Russell, 1966). The major post-1960 approaches include Coral Ann Howells, *Love, Mystery, and Misery* (London: Athlone, 1978); Elizabeth MacAndrew, *The Gothic Tradition in Fiction* (New York: Columbia University Press, 1979); Eve Kosofsky Sedgwick, *The Coherence of Gothic Conventions* (New York: Arno, 1980) and "The Character in the Veil: Imagery of the Surface in the Gothic Novel," *PMLA* 96 (1981), 255–70; William Patrick Day, *In the Circles of Fear and Desire: A Study of Gothic Fantasy* (Chicago: University of Chicago Press, 1985); George E. Haggerty, *Gothic Fiction/Gothic Form* (University Park: Penn State Press, 1989); Robert Miles, *Gothic Writing, 1750–1820: A Genealogy* (London: Routledge, 1993); David H. Richter, *The Progress of Romance: Literary Historiography and the Gothic Novel* (Columbus: Ohio State University Press, 1996); and Fred Botting, *Gothic* (London: Routledge, 1996).

hyperbolic staging of female suffering and victimization, and finally what is known as female gothic and vindication fiction. I contend, however, that white, bourgeois women writers have not simply been the passive victims of male-created constructions but rather have constructed themselves as victims in their own literature, and that they have frequently depicted themselves, as have men, as manipulative, passive-aggressive, masochist, and sadistic. In short, the female gothic novelist constructs female characters who masquerade as professional girl-women caught up in an elaborate game of playacting for the benefit of an obsessive and controlling male *gaze*. Several of these terms are themselves taken from psychoanalytic ideologies, and my use of them is informed by the conviction that psychoanalysis has participated, as has literature itself, in the rather broad cultural project of diagnosing and curing social and sexual deviancies that it has actually created.[3]

As early as 1769, Elizabeth Montagu's "Essay on the praeternatural beings in Shakespeare" revealed how quickly and thoroughly the gothic had been constructed, according to Harriet Guest, "as the site of a privatized and licensed dissipation" and an articulation of "a gender-specific utopian politics." For Guest, the gothic as constructed by women writers "facilitated the definition of national character in terms that were both wantonly heterogeneous in their embrace of private and diverse individuals, and redeemed in their idealization of chaste and maternal femininity, the sacred power of Britannia." Middle-class women writers of this period were particularly attracted to the female gothic novel because they could explore within it their fantasized overthrow of the public realm, figured as a series of ideologically constructed masculine "spaces," in favor of the creation of a new privatized, feminized world. As an example of a feminized discourse of "political embourgeoisification," the female gothic participates in the paradoxical enterprise of both criminalizing and deifying women, and thus we are presented over and over with the gothic antiheroine and the dead/undead gothic mother. The persistence of both constructions suggests the need that women writers had to expose and at the same time conceal the uneasy slippages that existed between apparently opposed concepts of women during this period: public and libidinal sexuality poised against pri-

---

3. Helpful discussions of feminism's participation in the ideological construction of gender can be found in Judith Butler, *Gender Trouble: Feminism and the Subversion of Identity* (New York: Routledge, 1990); and Denise Riley, *Am I That Name? Feminism and the Category of 'Women' in History* (New York: Macmillan, 1988).

vate and unimpeachable chastity.[4] The valorization of the private, extrapolitical aspects of the female gothic novel suggests that women writers conspired with their culture to position women securely within the home, propping up the edifice of the patriarchal family and insuring its continuance through the fetishization of virginity and marital chastity. But at the same time (melo)dramatic and hyperbolic eruptions continue to be depicted in these fictions—wanton sexuality, adultery, murder, and mayhem—all of which figure a political import that is subversive or ambivalent at the very least.

The female gothic genre was understood before 1970 primarily as a psychological fiction exploring the fears and guilt attendant on sexual maturation, but these works can more accurately be read as elided representations of the political, socioeconomic, and historical complexities of women's lives under a newly codified bourgeois ideology. That is, the female gothic novelistic tradition became a coded system whereby women authors covertly communicated to other women—their largely female reading audience—their ambivalent rejection of and outward complicity with the dominant sexual ideologies of their culture. Female authors ironically inverted the "separate spheres" ideology by valorizing the private female world of the home while they fictively destroyed the public/juridical masculine world. In other words, the female gothic reified the "separate spheres" ideology in such a way that women were no longer victimized by it but fictively took control of it, although only up to a certain point. This point can be located at precisely the creation of the ideology that I am calling the professionalization or masquerade of femininity: women's supposedly passive acceptance of their newly proscribed social and educational identities as wives and mothers of the bourgeoisie. The dominant issue explored in these novels is the professionalization and institutionalization of bourgeois femininity, a code of conduct that spelled out a proper woman's behavior and responses to not simply her everyday routines but also her possible protracted sojourn in a dank stone cavern in the heart of Sicily.

And whereas the ideology of the Eternal Feminine that dominated the writing of the male Romantic canonical poets demanded female submission, economic disenfranchisement of women, and social conformity to their prescribed domestic roles, the female gothic novel depicted its young

---

4. See the provocative discussion of Montagu and early theories of the gothic in Harriet Guest, "The Wanton Muse: Politics and Gender in Gothic Theory After 1760," in *Beyond Romanticism: New Approaches to Texts and Contexts, 1780–1832* (London: Routledge, 1992), 127–38.

female heroines as anything but entrapped, passive, and docile. Or, to be more precise, the female gothic novel represented women who ostensibly appear to be conforming to their acceptable roles within the patriarchy but who actually subvert the father's power at every possible occasion and then retreat to studied postures of conformity whenever they risk exposure to public censure. I have come to recognize and label this ideology as "gothic feminism," a species of the later phenomenon called "double consciousness" by W. E. B. Du Bois and expanded upon by Ralph Ellison, both of whom revealed it as the root of black attitudes toward white hegemony. Although it may seem frivolous to compare the situations of black slaves to white middle-class women, the same enabling strategies and defense mechanisms were used by both groups to survive what each experienced as alienation and objectification.[5] Ellison's nameless hero in *The Invisible Man* is advised to "grin em to death," to smile while he grinds glass into the food that he so obediently serves his master. We cannot be faulted for recognizing much the same strategies employed by the besieged heroines of the female gothic novel.

Writing his *Commentaries on the Laws of England* in 1765, the jurist William Blackstone stated, "The husband and wife are one person in law; that is, the very being or legal existence of the woman is suspended during the marriage, or at least is incorporated and consolidated into that of the husband: under whose total protection and cover, she performs everything." The ideally "covered" woman of the late eighteenth century and early nineteenth century—not unlike a slave—existed only in relation to her male master/husband. But such an identity, said the female gothic author and reader, was a legal and social construct that could be persistently attacked, deconstructed, and dissolved in the female gothic novel. The most common situation in all of these works concerns an inheritance, a property, or an estate whose entail is in dispute. And although she has all of the considerable forces of the patriarchy aligned against her—you guessed it—the young, innocent, naive heroine manages to gain her rightful inheritance,

---

5. Gary Kelly claims that the Radcliffe heroines have no public existence; they "are entirely private and domestic beings or they are the means of transferring property and power from one man to another" (see his *English Fiction of the Romantic Period* [London: Longmans, 1989], 53). On the same subject, see also Mary Poovey, "Ideology and *The Mysteries of Udolpho*," *Criticism* 21 (1979), 307–30, who comes closest to my reading of the female gothic when she observes, "The root of her [Emily's] strength lies in that particularly feminine gesture of passive aggression" (329). On the similarity between female gothic novels and slave narratives, see Kari J. Winter, *Subjects of Slavery, Agents of Change: Women and Power in Gothic Novels and Slave Narratives, 1790–1865* (Athens: University of Georgia Press, 1992).

usually by besting an evil uncle (read: displaced father figure). And to make matters perfect, the heroine further triumphs over the patriarchy by creating an alternative companionate family, marrying a "feminized" man who promises, if not in word then through his sheer incompetence, to be completely malleable.

The female gothic constitutes what I would call a rival female-created fantasy—gothic feminism—a version of "victim feminism," an ideology of female power through pretended and staged weakness. Such an ideology positions women as innocent victims who deserve to be rewarded with the ancestral estate because they were unjustly persecuted by the corrupt patriarch. If the heroines manage, inadvertently of course, to cause the deaths of these patriarchs, so much the better. Montoni and Schedoni, the hapless villains of *The Mysteries of Udolpho* and *The Italian*, respectively, both appear to self-destruct through their own misguided arrogance and egoism, but we know better. The gothic feminist always manages to dispose of her enemies without dirtying her dainty little hands. The position that Radcliffe and her followers advocated throughout the female gothic was one of "wise passiveness" or what we might more accurately recognize as a form of passive-aggression.

In its convergence of psychological and sociopolitical issues, the female gothic—from its inception during the Industrial and French Revolutions through 1853—stands as a distinctive artistic form spawned in reaction to the radical economic, social, and religious dislocations that occurred with the onset of industrialization and the triumph of a capitalist economy. Women now had the opportunity to express themselves in widely disseminated and cheaply printed novels and dramas that became immensely popular with the new reading audience—largely middle-class women enclosed in the newly created and idealized bourgeois home. These women responded to their sudden change in status with an ambivalence that found its expression in one of the dominant ideologies of the female gothic: the fantasy that the weak have power through carefully cultivating the appearance of their very powerlessness. Such an ideology formed not only the message of the female gothic but also accounts for the works' popularity among women readers who covertly wanted to believe that they could challenge or in some way passively subvert their newly inscribed and institutionalized "spaces," while maintaining their identities and roles as the wives and mothers of the bourgeoisie.[6]

---

6. Anne Williams observes in a footnote, "Indeed, the two decades when Gothic was most popular were the 1790s and the 1960s, both eras of revolution that saw the birth of two different stages of

II

If we consider the female gothic novel as a highly ideological signifying system, a discourse system, then we must recognize that we have labeled the genre a literary category only out of desperation, only because we do not know what else to call it. Unlike other neat period distinctions, the gothic is both peculiarly full and empty at the same time. It cannot be approached through any narrow category of meaning that will explain its many permutations or manifestations. Trying to limit the genre to a particular time period (as Maurice Lévy has done) or trying to define it in terms of "conventions" (as Sedgwick does)—all of these are essentially futile attempts to give shape to the intrinsically shapeless.[7] I would claim instead that the only contours or parameters that can be applied successfully to the female gothic novel are the codified "spaces" and "voices" that emerge from its own fragmented discourse system. Stated in the baldest possible terms, the voices that emerge from the works that traditionally have been identified as female gothic are concerned with delineating highly ideological struggles between "reality" (the forces of political power) and "desire" (the forces of libidinal energy). The nature of these struggles—sometimes seen as sexual or psychic, sometimes as social, economic, political, or religious—is less important than the fact that female characters are depicted as constantly struggling against powerful forces that they think are real and that they believe are poised to destroy them. The enemy is not solely within, as is the case with the majority of gothics written by male authors (Walpole, Lewis, Maturin, Hogg). The real and ideological enemies for women—female gothic heroines as well as their avid female reading audience—are without.[8] Such a dis-

---

feminism. Although I would not want to suggest a simple relation of cause and effect, there is surely a connection." See her *Art of Darkness* 275, note 6. Although I hope that I have not suggested a "simple relation of cause and effect," I believe there is every reason to explore the connection.

7. See Maurice Lévy, *Le Roman "gothique" anglais, 1764–1824* (Toulouse: Association des Publications de la Faculté des Lettres et Sciences Humaines de Toulouse, 1968); and Eve Sedgwick, *The Coherence of Gothic Conventions.* More recently Lévy has expanded his attempts to define and delimit the meaning of the "gothic" in "'Gothic' and the Critical Idiom," in *Gothick Origins and Innovations,* ed. Allan Lloyd Smith and Victor Sage (Amsterdam: Rodopi, 1994), 1–15.

8. One of the most important contributions to the criticism of the gothic has been made by recent feminist critics who have countered the assumption of such writers as Leslie Fiedler and G. R. Thompson, both of whom have argued that the great horror in male gothic fiction is the recognition of the evil other as oneself, thereby situating the focus of the male gothic in the psychological rather than in the social or economic realm. In contrast, DeLamotte, Doody, Poovey, and Russ all situate the horror for female gothic writers in the external world of economic exploitation and patriarchal corruption. My analysis—like the more recent one by Anne Williams in *Art of Darkness*—differs from

tinction is crucial for understanding that there is a genre of novels written by women about women who are struggling against alien and powerful forces and who resort for their own self-defense to using a battery of strategies—"gothic feminism"—drawn from the stock situations of popular stage melodramas and sentimental novels.

The typical female gothic novel presents a blameless heroine triumphing through a variety of passive-aggressive strategies over a male-created system of oppression and corruption, the "patriarchy." The melodrama that suffuses these works is explicable only if we understand, as Paula Backscheider has recently demonstrated, that a generally hyperbolic sentimentalism was saturating the British literary scene, informing the gothic melodramas that were such standard fare during the popular theater season. But melodrama, as Peter Brooks has shown, is also characterized by a series of moves or postures that made it particularly attractive to middle-class women. Specifically, Brooks lists as crucial to melodrama the tendency toward depicting intense, excessive representations of life that tend to strip away the facade of manners to reveal the essential conflicts at work, leading to moments of intense and highly stylized confrontations. These symbolic dramatizations rely on what Brooks lists as the standard features of melodrama: hyperbolic figures, lurid and grandiose events, masked relationships and disguised identities, abductions, slow-acting poisons, secret societies, and mysterious parentage.[9] In short, melodrama is a version of the female gothic while the female gothic provides the undergirding for a species of victim feminism, a hyperbolic ideology bent on depicting women as the innocent prey of a corrupt and evil patriarchal system.

But, as Laura Mulvey has observed, "ideological contradiction is the overt mainspring and specific content of melodrama, not a hidden, unconscious thread to be picked up only by a special critical process."[10] The contradiction at the core of the female gothic, at the core of melodrama as a genre, appears to be the middle-class woman's intense ambivalence toward the paternal home and by extension patriarchal capitalism. The paternal home

---

theirs in subscribing to a view of the "self" as shaped by postmodernist assumptions, that is, that what we call the "self" is a series of discursive, shifting postures. Like Williams, I do not privilege the humanistic notion of a "unitary self."

9. See the extremely suggestive discussion of "Gothic Drama and National Crisis" in Paula R. Backscheider, *Spectacular Politics: Theatrical Power and Mass Culture in Early Modern England* (Baltimore: The Johns Hopkins University Press, 1993), 149–234. And for the best discussion of the stock topoi of melodrama, see Peter Brooks, *The Melodramatic Imagination* (New Haven: Yale University Press, 1976), 3.

10. Laura Mulvey, "Notes on Sirk and Melodrama," *Movie* 25 (1977–78), 53.

as the site of patriarchally based, rather than emotionally based relationships, seems to deny women the chance to exercise their subjectivity, and thus their only means of rebelling is to escape, to run away from the paternal domicile. The nightmare in the female gothic novel is that women frequently cannot run toward what they claim to desire, the man they want to marry. They run instead in a large circle that leads them back precisely to the paternal home, but this time the estate has been magically transformed into a maternally marked abode through the efforts of the heroine's circuitous journey. In short, the female gothic novel accomplishes the cultural work of group fantasy for women; it convinces them that their safely proscribed rebellion will result in an improved home for both their mothers and themselves. But in rebelling against the patriarch, they paradoxically reify the power of the home and family to which they will return, all the while justifying their acts of parricide and class warfare by positioning themselves as innocent victims.

According to Brooks, the gothic novel can be most clearly understood as standing in reaction to the tendency toward desacralization and the increasing pretensions of rationalism. Like melodrama, the female gothic represents both the urge toward resacralization and the impossibility of conceiving of sacralization in anything other than personal terms. For the Enlightenment mentality, there is no longer a clear transcendent value to which one can be reconciled. There is, rather, a social order to be purged, a set of ethical imperatives to be made clear.[11] And, we might ask, who is in a better position to purge the new bourgeois world of all traces of aristocratic corruption than the female gothic heroine? Such a woman—professionally feminine, virginal, innocent, and good—assumed virtually religious significance because within the discourse system much was at stake. Making the world safe for the middle class was the goal inscribed in both female gothic texts and late eighteenth-century bourgeois "feminism." But such a task was not without its perils. What I am calling "gothic feminism" was born when women realized that they had a formidable external enemy—the raving, lustful, greedy patriarch—in addition to their own worst internal enemy, their consciousness of their own sexual difference perceived as a weakness rather than a strength.

Consider, for instance, the typical gothic husband. In *The Sicilian Romance; or the Apparition of the Cliff,* Henry Siddons's 1794 adaptation of

---

11. Brooks, 16–17.

Radcliffe's second novel, the frustrated patriarch chains his rejected wife to a stone wall in a cave and feeds her the way one feeds a forsaken pet that will not die. We might legitimately ask, what sort of action is required by women to protect and defend themselves against such evil tyranny? Over and over again, the female gothic novelist proffers professional femininity—a highly codified form of conduct, a gender masquerade—as the only force strong or cunning enough to tame the ravages of a lustful, raving patriarch gone berserk.

We have arrived—paradoxically as it may seem—at Luce Irigaray's notion of the "feminine feminine" as opposed to the "masculine feminine" woman. According to Irigaray's revision of Lacan, young girls never successfully resolve the oedipal phase and instead lag behind in the imaginary realm, a sort of prison house of illusory images and childhood landscapes. But instead of viewing this entrapment in the nursery drama as completely negative, Irigaray argues that it opens up imaginative possibilities for women that men cannot begin to appreciate or experience. Rather than listening only to what men or patriarchal discourse tells women about their sexuality or their fantasy lives, that is, rather than continuing to be "masculine feminine" women, Irigaray suggests that women need to create themselves instead as "feminine feminine." This latter sort of woman is not a male-identified woman but instead has learned to "mime the mime," mimic and thereby explode the gendered constructions that the patriarchy has invented and codified in order to enslave and dehumanize her. But central to the notion of mimicry for Irigaray is the technique of masquerade, an attempt to play the gender game as if one were in the know, self-consciously, self-referentially, almost mockingly deflating the very role one would appear to be assuming. For Irigaray:

> There is, in an initial phase, perhaps only one "path," the one historically assigned to the feminine: that of *mimicry*. One must assume the feminine role deliberately. Which means already to convert a form of subordination into an affirmation, and thus to begin to thwart it . . . To play with mimesis is thus, for a woman, to try to recover the place of her exploitation by discourse, without allowing herself to be simply reduced to it. It means to resubmit herself—inasmuch as she is on the side of the "perceptible," of "matter"—to "ideas," in particular to ideas about herself, that are elaborated in/by a masculine logic, but so as to make "visible," by an effort of playful repetition, what was supposed to remain invisible: the cover-up of a possible operation of the feminine in language.

For Irigaray, only when women bring themselves to a new and unmediated position of selfhood, subjectivity, and language—apart from the patriarchy—will they be able to become "feminine feminine" women, that is, defined by woman-marked codes, values, and beliefs.

Irigaray's notions of mimicry and masquerade, however, are most suggestive for the female gothic's discourse network. She suggests that women can best battle the patriarchy when they mime the mimes that men have imposed on them. If men have positioned women as simply mirrors for a grandiose masculine imaginary, then women can break through that specular appropriation only when they reflect back to men the same images in grotesque, immense proportions. In other words, women can undo the effects of phallocentric discourse only when they act out and hyperbolize those same codes. To break out of the masculine imaginary that went under the name of the gothic required a new discourse system, the hyperbolic female gothic, a miming of the mime, a mimicry of the gigantic mirror we call the Enlightenment or sensibility cultures.

In an analogous manner, Hélène Cixous has observed, "men and women are caught in a network of millennial cultural determinations of a complexity that is practically unanalyzable: we can no more talk about 'woman' than about 'man' without being caught within an ideological theater where the multiplication of representations, images, reflections, myths, identifications constantly transforms, deforms, alters each person's imaginary order and in advance, renders all conceptualization null and void."[12] The female gothic captures this sense of living within a series of interlocking and stifling "networks," each of which demands a certain psychic and linguistic code—the codes we now recognize as psychoanalytic discourse. And in an attempt to control these networks the female gothic heroine resorts to what we can recognize as "the talking cure"; that is, she attempts to talk herself out of her perception of life as prison, confessional, asylum, or maze. Her "talking cure," the "embodied voice" that emerges from the female gothic,

---

12. Luce Irigaray, *This Sex Which Is Not One*, trans. Catherine Porter (Ithaca: Cornell University Press, 1985), 32, 76; and Hélène Cixous in *New French Feminisms*, ed. Elaine Marks and Isabelle de Courtivron (New York: Schocken, 1981), 96. On a similar note, consider the position of Mary Ann Doane ("Film and the Masquerade: Theorising the Female Spectator," *Screen* 23 [1982], 81–82.) on masquerade: "The masquerade, in flaunting femininity, holds it at a distance. Womanliness is a mask which can be worn or removed. The masquerade's resistance to patriarchal positioning would therefore lie in its denial of the production of femininity as closeness, as presence-to-itself, as, precisely, imagistic. . . . By destabilising the image, the masquerade confounds this masculine structure of the look; masquerade is a type of representation which carries a threat, disarticulating a male system of viewing."

can finally be identified as what Kristeva has labeled "purposely perverse hysteria." And the texts that demonstrate the effectiveness of her "talking cure," that embody the hysteria, are the documents that authors call "novels" or "romances."

When the Marquis de Sade first indulged his tastes for the whip, he created not simply the phenomenon we have labeled in his honor—sadism—but also reified its opposite—masochism. Sadism and masochism existed before the marquis so kindly brought them into relief; masochism certainly existed long before one Leopold von Sacher-Masoch (1836–1895) described it in his novels. Moreover, masochism has the dubious distinction of being one of the few characteristics consistently identified by Freud (and his female disciples) as clearly associated with women. Any analysis of the female gothic, unfortunately, has to confront the mystique of female masochism. Feminist literary critics would like to reject any notion of women as inherently masochistic, indeed, as inherently prone to any essentialist quality. But more germane to our discussion is the need to recognize the female author's careful manipulation of the masochistic pose. That is, the gothic heroine indulges in what we would recognize as masochistic gestures for effect. But more important for the female gothic, what we call masochism became a stock characteristic of the situation for the gothic heroine. These young women not only tolerate all manner of abuse; they actually seem to seek it out.[13] If an event or situation is comfortable, the reader can count on the gothic heroine to pursue trouble.

How, for instance, are we to understand the actions of Emily in *The Mysteries of Udolpho*? A virtual prisoner in a desolate Italian castle, Emily finds herself pursued by not one but two potential rapists. Does she stay sensibly in her room at night? Of course not, she is too busy trying to locate her tortured and starving aunt, imprisoned in another tower of the castle. When Emily does find herself in Montoni's chambers, threatened with marriage to the odious and chubby Morano, we are supposed to believe that this evil has just descended, unprovoked, on the innocent and unsuspecting heroine. Such a perception is cultivated by the author in order to conceal the fact that masochism, the deliberate seeking out of pain as pleasure, stands as one

---

13. My reading of masochism differs substantially from the position taken by Michelle Massé, *In the Name of Love: Women, Masochism, and the Gothic* (Ithaca: Cornell University Press, 1992). Whereas Massé sees women in the gothic novel as actually victimized and internalizing that victimization, that is, finding pleasure in their very repulsions, I have taken a poststructuralist position and instead see women as parodically playing with or masquerading in a pose of victimization: miming the mime. I do admire, however, her use of Freud's essay "A Child Is Being Beaten" as a theoretical paradigm.

of the primary devices in the gothic heroine's arsenal of passive-aggressive strategies. By presenting herself as an innocent and suffering victim, by masquerading as the beleaguered heroine, the gothic feminist actually positions herself for the assault, shielded, of course, from the charge or even the impression that she is the aggressor. Playing the victim often simply conceals the fact that one is a much more effective victimizer: we are once again within the territory of miming the mime. The women who populate female gothic novels clearly and unequivocally triumph in the end, morally and financially, but generally they have caused a good deal of havoc in the process. And do we condemn these heroines? Never. They have managed to win their readers' sympathies through conforming to the carefully delineated construction of innocent victim, what I am calling the professionalization or cultivated pose of femininity. Do Emily and Ellena just happen to triumph over all their enemies? Radcliffe would have us believe that they managed these feats by doing nothing much at all. Passivity, it seems, or lying in wait for the oppressor to self-destruct, is its own reward.

All of this brings us to Freud's seminal essay "A Child Is Being Beaten" (*SE* 17:175–204), a source for much recent speculation on the contours of the female gothic tradition. As others before me have noticed, female gothics actually encode in almost uncanny precision the three versions of the female beating fantasy as Freud has delineated them. For a girl the first and the third psychological positions in the beating fantasy are sadistic and voyeuristic— another child is being beaten by an authority figure, and I am witnessing the act. The second position in the fantasy is masochistic, erotic, and deeply repressed—I am the child being beaten by my father. For the boy the psychic transformation is less complex due to the elimination of one stage. For him the first fantasy, "I am loved by my father," becomes the conscious fantasy, "I am being beaten by my mother."

According to Freud, both male and female subjects, generally children between the ages of five and fifteen, appear to shift continually between these three (or two) positions largely through the conscious and unconscious permutations of incestuous desire for the father and its repression. The struggles we see in Radcliffe's novels, for instance, between her heroines and various other women who actually take the beatings from a variety of father substitutes, suggest the compulsions at work here. The gothic feminist is a deeply conflicted subject who fends off the blows and manages to watch voyeuristically other women get punished for her own projected crimes. Consider, for instance, Jane Eyre who watches Bertha beat and get beaten. The beatings that suffuse the female gothic suggest the ambivalent construction of gender that lies just slightly below the heroine's surface pose of complicity and passivity. Gothic feminist authors are angry while their heroines are pointedly controlled and strategically not angry. These heroines are characterized, unlike their creators, by repression and silence, acceptance or at least the pose of complaisancy. Furthermore, these heroines are professionally feminine, while the projected anger of the female author can only be detected in the violence that just happens to plague anyone foolish enough to stand in her heroine's way.

III

This discussion of just one of the stock strategies of the female gothic heroine presupposes a certain psychological and social matrix, a cash/sex nexus, an interrelation between "desire" and "reality" that produces "ideology." It is necessary, however, to also situate my approach to the female gothic within the methods outlined by the theorists who have grounded discussions of sexuality and historicity in the nineteenth century. Gilles Deleuze and Félix Guattari in *Anti-Oedipus* and *A Thousand Plateaus,* volumes 1 and 2 of their *Capitalism and Schizophrenia,* maintain that the "social field is immediately invested by desire, it is the historically determined product of desire, and libido has no need of any mediation or sublimation, any psychic operation, any transformation, in order to invade and invest the productive forces and the relations of production. *There is only desire and the social, and nothing else*" (*A-O* 29). Deleuze and Guattari further claim that "desire produces reality" (*A-O* 30), while that desire is solely defined by historical process. But if desire is energy that produces reality, then ideology is the attempt to contain desire, to give it shape. Furthermore, for Deleuze and Guattari there is a radical distinction between individual fantasy and group fantasy, fantasy as "speaking-playing" and fantasy as "daydream." In the latter phenomenon, analogous to the construction of female gothic novels, the fantasizer "experiences institutions themselves as mortal" because they can be destroyed or changed "according to the articulations of desire and the social field, by making the death instinct into a veritable institutional creativity." Commenting on this pattern, John Brenkman argues that within a capitalist system, "it is reification, the transformation of the exchanging of human activity into a set of calculable relations between things, that reconstitutes the subject as a separated individual, that converts play into the interiorized fantasies of the ego, that binds the death drive to eros and makes self-preservation an act of aggression."[14] And, we might add, no one is more adept at self-preservation and its concomitant acts of aggression than the female gothic heroine.

Although they think they are revising Freud, Deleuze and Guattari are actually merely paraphrasing him when they assert that the only escapes from the spiral of desire/energy/reality/ideology are either repression or death: "For desire desires death also, because the full body of death is its motor, just as it desires life, because the organs of life are the *working machine*" (*A-O* 8). Therefore, in order to escape the wheels of the capitalist body politic, the female gothic novelist and her female reader fantasize a reality that culminates in either repression or death. In a world that has been radically desacralized, the tragic is no longer possible; hence the invention of melodrama, the dilution of tragedy into a flurry of emotions signifying little beyond the purely personal. If instead the novelist employs repression, then we know ourselves to be reading a work in the realm of the "melodramatically comic" female gothic; if she images death as the only escape, then we know ourselves to be reading a work situated in the "melodramatically tragic" female gothic tradition. Radcliffe's novels, Austen's *Northanger Abbey*, and Brontë's *Jane Eyre* stand as archetypal exemplars of what might be called the "melodramatically comic" female gothic, spawning such descendants as du Maurier's *Rebecca*, Margaret Atwood's *Lady Oracle*, Angela Carter's *Nights at the Circus*, and Iris Murdoch's "gothic trilogy" (*The Italian Girl, The Time of the Angels*, and *A Severed Head*). In contrast, Shelley's *Mathilda*, Brontë's *Wuthering Heights*, Gilman's "Yellow Wallpaper," Jean Rhys's *Wide Sargasso Sea*, and the more recent work of Muriel Spark (*Not to Disturb* and *The Driver's Seat*) and finally Joyce Carol Oates (*Mysteries of Winterthurn, Bellefleur*, and *A Bloodsmoor Romance*) represent the "melodramatically tragic" strain in the female gothic.

Central to what I am labeling the "comic" pattern is the ideological construction of a bucolic family, a static paradise like Radcliffe's *La Vallée* or *Jane Eyre's* Ferndean, a locus that cannot be described because it can be imagined only in the vaguest terms. Such a static ideal conforms to and, in fact, endorses the ideology of white, middle-class womanhood prevalent in Britain and the United States during the past two centuries. The female economy operating in the "comic" work valorizes the heterosexual compulsion, presenting the sexes as finally complementary rather than oppositional.

---

14. Deleuze and Guattari, *Anti-Oedipus: Capitalism and Schizophrenia*, vol. 1, trans. Robert Hurley, Mark Seem, and Helen Lane (Minneapolis: University of Minnesota Press, 1983); John Brenkman, *Culture and Domination* (Ithaca: Cornell University Press, 1987), 175.

On the other hand, the female economy operating in the "tragic" female gothic denies the viability of heterosexuality, rejects the reproductive female body, and explodes the work through the imagery of gender warfare.

In order to understand the issues at stake in this dialectic, it is necessary to look briefly at writings by women about sexual difference. From the late eighteenth-century writings of Mary Wollstonecraft to the work of contemporary theorists like Nancy Chodorow and Carol Gilligan, a certain number of female writers have participated in defining the nature of women as "Other" to men. For Wollstonecraft, women's minds were essentially identical to men's, but these minds became more emotional, less reasonable, more prone to excess through the corrupting influences of patriarchal education. What was the solution according to Wollstonecraft? She advised that women would be wise to bury their emotions, become, that is, reasonable "honorary men." Such a position had the effect of reinforcing "feminist humanism" and the domestic ideology, paradoxically maintaining the marginalization of women in the home. By valorizing the autonomous subjectivity of the inner life, Wollstonecraft—despite her overt advocacy of economic independence and rational self-fulfillment for women—ironically ended up advocating a sort of imprisonment for the domiciled woman.

In a similar manner, Chodorow and Gilligan, presenting themselves as writing within one tradition of contemporary feminism, white, Western, and middle class, codify a view of women that valorizes similar essentialist qualities (according to Gilligan women subscribe to "an ethic of care") that tend to infantilize or trivialize women. Both assert that the maturation process for women in Western culture stands in direct opposition to the process for men. Woman's identity supposedly is rooted not in the realities of psychic separation but in resigned acceptance of her inherent teleological destiny as a woman. Both critics further call for a transvaluation of values in which qualities that have been regarded as womanly and therefore inferior are recognized as superior by the society as a whole.[15] Such ideologies, created by women presumably for female consumption, stand in direct contrast to the angrier, more subversive or ambivalent voices that emerge

---

15. For a fuller critique of Wollstonecraft's "betrayal" of women, see Cora Kaplan, *Sea Changes: Culture and Feminism* (London: Verso, 1986), 39, 41, 155; and Diane Long Hoeveler, "The Tyranny of Sentimental Form: Wollstonecraft's *Mary* and the Gendering of Anxiety," in *Re-Presenting Power: British Women Writers, 1780–1900*, ed. Greg Kucich and Donelle Ruwe (London: Gordan and Breach, 1998). Also see Nancy Chodorow, *The Reproduction of Mothering: Psychoanalysis and the Sociology of Gender* (Berkeley: University of California Press, 1978); and Carol Gilligan, *In a Different Voice: Psychological Theory and Women's Development* (Cambridge: Harvard University Press, 1982).

from the female gothic novel. These voices present the two sides of women's attitudes toward the heterosexual compulsion. On the one hand, a woman can accept and survive; on the other hand, she can rage and self-destruct. If the female gothic heroine cannot finally destroy the patriarchy, she can attempt to outsmart it; she can mime it to death. Positioning herself as the deserving and innocent victim of oppression, malice, and fraud, the female gothic heroine exchanges her suffering for money and a man, a means of financial support and security. In the melodramatic scheme of things, a victim is always rewarded because justice always prevails, while suffering (particularly if one is young and pretty) can become a kind of lucre to be exchanged in the strange barter system that women understood (or misunderstood) as the "shadow labor" of gendered capitalism.[16]

IV

There is no doubt that the "body" that emerges from female gothic textuality is a highly gendered one, the product of that greatest of dualism machines, capitalism. And the writing that emerges from such a machine is gender specific, characterized by the female author's contradictory desire both to conform outwardly and to subvert, that is, to be both a body and a machine at odds with itself. In *A Room of One's Own*, Virginia Woolf wonders why women increasingly turned to writing novels during the early nineteenth century, leaving poetry a male-dominated preserve, a bastion of masculine privilege. She proposes some fairly straightforward answers, such as the fact that novels emphasize character and event and can be written with less concentration than can poetry, which requires of its composer a higher degree of attention to details in order to ensure the poem's internal coherence. Woolf goes on to talk about the deadliness of either "manly" or "womanly" styles of writing, but such a notion, seemingly liberal, fails to account for the inescapability of ideological constructions of gender, not to mention the historical conditions that determined women's complicity and participation in both accepting and overthrowing those historical "realities." If the chaos that characterized France from the period prior to and after the French Revolution was not to pollute British society, then female writers had

---

16. I am referring to the discussion of "broken gender and economic sex" in Ivan Illich, *Gender* (Berkeley: Heyday, 1982), 22–66, although I recommend that Illich's position be read in conjunction with the critique provided by Janice Doane and Devon Hodges, *Nostalgia and Sexual Difference: The Resistance to Contemporary Feminism* (New York: Methuen, 1987), 97–113.

to be enlisted in the attempt to spread an ideology that curtailed the transmission of such dangerous notions as equality, fraternity, and liberty. The marketplace, in other words, demanded a highly gendered society in order to protect the very existence of an economy that privileged the middle and upper classes.

Major eighteenth- and nineteenth-century female writers like Smith, Radcliffe, Austen, Dacre, Shelley, and the Brontës all exploited in their works the appearance of their compliance with traditional "female" domestic values. But we should not confuse such a facade with their elided purposes. The female gothic writer attempted nothing less than a redefinition of sexuality and power in a gendered, patriarchal society; she fictively reshaped the family, deconstructing both patrimonialism (inheritance through the male) and patrilineality (naming practices) in the process.[17] In short, she invented her own peculiar form of feminism. And in challenging both codes of masculine privilege, she possessed her rightful fictional birthright: access to the untrammeled desire and energy to reshape her version of "reality." In the female gothic work she creates what she thinks are alternative, empowering female-created fantasies. In her triumphant act of self-creation she rejects her subjugation and status as "other," whether object or absence, and she refuses to subscribe passively to confining male-created ideologies of the "woman as subject." She proffers instead victim feminism as a female-created ideology, mixing one part hyperbolic melodrama with one part Christian sentimentalism, and creating a heady brew that promised its readers the ultimate fantasy: their socially and economically weak positions could actually be the basis of their strength. The meek shall inherit the gothic earth; evil is always destroyed because it deserves to be.

The buried reality that lies not very far below the surface of the female gothic is the sense that middle-class women can only experience the male-identified patriarchal-capitalist home as either a prison or an asylum. A woman is reduced in such a home to the status of an object, decorative or functional depending on her husband's class. Life in such a home and the identity it conferred on a woman constitute the nightmare at the core of the female gothic and victim feminism. But the home created by Emily and

---

17. For a discussion of how the domesticated family functioned as the "cradle" for a new class culture, see Leonore Davidoff and Catherine Hall, *Family Fortunes: Men and Women of the English Middle Class, 1780–1850* (Chicago: University of Chicago Press, 1987); Harold Perkin, *The Origins of Modern English Society, 1780–1880* (London: Routledge and Kegan Paul, 1972); and Ray Porter, *English Society in the Eighteenth Century* (Middlesex: Penguin, 1982).

Valancourt at the conclusion of *The Mysteries of Udolpho*, for instance, is not a patriarchally marked home. Valancourt appears to be living at *La Vallée* on an extremely tenuous basis, having been perceived by Emily and her friends as damaged goods after his disastrous foray in Paris. Acceptably tamed gothic husbands exist on very short leashes, and it is Emily and her sister heroines who hold the power in these new households. Having traced the ravaging patriarch out of existence, the gothic feminist lives in her new domicile with her ritualistically wounded husband, a quasi sibling who, like her, has barely survived his brush with the oppressor and has emerged chastened and appropriately and professionally gendered. When critics puzzle over the final castrated status of Rochester, blinded in one eye and missing one hand, they reveal that they do not appreciate the long heritage of wounded and feminized gothic heroes that foreground Rochester's history. We cannot fail to comment on the two gunshot wounds Valancourt receives in *The Mysteries of Udolpho*, one of them delivered supposedly by accident by his beloved's father, the mild St. Aubert. Beating fantasies emerge in the quite real wounds that every gothic hero is forced to endure in the female gothic canon, and it is tempting to explain these stabbings or worse, as Bruno Bettelheim has, as "symbolic wounds." But gothic heroes all endure very real beatings and wounds, not merely symbolic ones, and in the receiving of these wounds it is as if they have earned the right to overthrow their fathers and establish a new companionate family and a redeemed class—a bourgeoisie that has learned to tame its excesses and perfectly balance reason and the emotions.

I contend that gothic feminism participates, as do sentimentality and Romanticism as intellectual movements, in the broad cultural project of Enlightenment ideology—that is, making the world a safe place for feminized men and masculinized women. Foucault has charted his version of this cultural shift, claiming that it was exploitation rather than repression that characterized the prevailing attitude of the upper classes since the late eighteenth century: "The new procedures of power that were devised during the classical age and employed in the nineteenth century were what caused our societies to go from *a symbolics of blood* to *an analysis of sexuality*. Clearly, nothing was more on the side of the law, death, transgression, the symbolic, and sovereignty than blood; just as sexuality was on the side of the norm, knowledge, life, meaning, the disciplines, and regulations."[18] For Foucault, the bourgeoisie distinguished itself from both the aristocracy

---

18. Michel Foucault, *An Introduction*, vol. 1, *The History of Sexuality*, trans. Robert Hurley (New York: Vintage, 1980), 148.

and the working class by making its sexuality and its health a primary source of its hegemony. Whereas "blood" was the source of the aristocracy's power, "sex" and its control and regulation became the predominant characteristic of the newly professional middle class, both for men and for women. According to Foucault, it was Sade and the first eugenicists who advanced the transition from "sanguinity" to "sexuality." But Foucault fails to reckon with the female gothicists, whose works chart in increasingly graphic detail this shift from status and class based on blood claims to the superior form of class—the regulation, control, and professionalization of one's sexuality, one's body. When Bertha Mason jumps from the roof of Thornfield, we know that we are witnessing an important event in cultural history. In what many critics have recognized as a mad act of suttee, Bertha effectively extinguishes privileges based on blood claims and effectively makes way for her rival, the perfectly controlled and professionally feminine Jane Eyre.

V

Traditionally, critics have asked about the female gothic novel one question, "What does this mean?" As Barthes notes, we continue to read a text because we have bought into its "enigmatic code," we are engaged in trying to decipher those parts of the text that are still unresolved for us as readers.[19] But it is fair to say that the lure in the gothic is that the characters experience an "enigmatic code" that becomes mirrored by our reading process. For the female gothic heroine, that "enigmatic code" generally clusters around questions of properly gendered behavior, power/property, and the relation of both to sexuality. But it is also important to recognize that female gothic heroines are engaged less in an interpretive struggle than in a highly gendered and ideological one. What is at stake here is the war between "masculine" and "feminine" ways of shaping desire/bodies, of containing energy, of controlling ideology. When the female gothic heroine finally creates her own self-serving ideology of the companionate family, she is able to reject those juridically created systems, the home as prison or asylum, that have ensnared her throughout the novel.

The gothic heroine's goal throughout most of the text is to ascertain the "secret" that the patriarchy has managed to keep from her, either through an elaborate system of walls and locked rooms (the prison and the asylum)

---

19. See Roland Barthes, *S/Z*, trans. R. Miller (London: Cape, 1975), 19.

or through the power of language to dissemble, to reveal and conceal at the same time (missing marriage licenses or wills). The female gothic heroine spends most of the text cultivating the posture of passive-aggression through the two extremes available to her: hiding in a room/silence/repression of her emotions and her body, or moving through space in a sort of manic dance/hysterically acting out her assault on the patriarchy. But if the professionally feminine heroine finally is to be embodied in the female gothic text as anything other than passive or aggressive, she must create a social reality that goes beyond merely internalizing the prison, the asylum, the confessional; she must redeem those institutions and mark them as female controlled and female identified. And so each of the male juridical institutions is taken into, incorporated, swallowed up, and reconstituted by the heroine as the newly created female-defined institution.

In commenting on the nature of revolutions in this period, "or perhaps in any period," Ronald Paulson has noted that there are two basic interpretations of the phenomenon: oedipal and oral-anal. As he notes, in the oedipal version the son kills, eats, and internalizes the father, "becoming himself the authority figure, producing a rational sequence of events, although a sequence that might be regarded unsympathetically as prerational," but in which the "effect is sublime or a progression from sublime to beautiful." In the other category, the oral-anal, the revolution is figured as a "regression to earlier stages of being, an ingestion that produces narcissism rather than internalized paternal authority," a sort of descent into the "grotesque, moving toward the undifferentiation of tyrant and oppressed."[20] The female gothic novel clearly exists as a species of group fantasy work for this culture, while it finds its representation and symbolization in repeated dreams of parricide, seduction, and castration. The female gothic heroine, however, ambivalently rewrites the oedipal revolution by positioning herself as the dutiful daughter reluctantly forced to kill her father while she is compelled to swallow and ingest the patriarch's institutions so that they can be reformed in a manner acceptable to her and her newly validated mother.

In her triumphant overthrow of the patriarchy, most gothic feminists finally do battle with that ultimate patriarchal family—institutionalized Christianity. The female gothic heroine most persuasively establishes her pedigree when she confronts, outwits, and destroys a terrifically corrupt monk or priest. I am thinking here not simply of Jane Eyre's rather tame

---

20. Ronald Paulson, *Representations of Revolutions: 1789–1820* (New Haven: Yale University Press, 1983), 8.

duel with St. John Rivers but of the ferocious struggle against Schedoni that occupies both Ellena and her beloved throughout the entire text of *The Italian*. In finally destroying Schedoni and his evil accomplice, Vivaldi's aristocratic mother, Ellena redeems not only her inheritance, her economy, her world but also creates a home and companionate family that installs her (and her long-lost mother) as female quasi deities. She invents, that is, the middle-class family.

The female gothic protagonist as cultural heroine triumphs precisely because she has brought to birth a new class—the bourgeoisie—shorn of the excesses that characterized the aristocracy and that made it unfit to preside over a newly industrialized society. But in destroying and supplanting the aristocracy, the gothic feminist accomplishes nothing less than the resacralization of her world. She excavates the buried body of her real or metaphorical mother, and by doing so she reinstates a fictionalized feminist fantasy: the matriarchy. In redeeming her mother, as Ellena does in *The Italian* or as Emily manages to do for her long-murdered aunt in *The Mysteries of Udolpho* or as Julia does for the long-imprisoned mother in *A Sicilian Romance*, the female gothic heroine reasserts her inheritance in a long-lost female-coded tradition. This act is typically represented in the texts as the rediscovery and magical reanimation of the mother's supposedly dead body.

Further, these novels posit the end of the discourse as located in the rediscovery of a sort of female-marked epistemology embodied in the stories that these women tell each other, the lost and pieced together narratives about mad nuns and bleeding mothers. The biological heritage of suffering and wounded women is transformed through this ideology into a saga of heroic triumph; the gothic feminist text tells us that the world is reborn and purified through the mother's—not the son's—blood. Gothic feminist heroines discover their own bodies and voices only after they redeem their mothers, and they speak in a voice that some contemporary critics of feminism have termed "victim feminism." But that voice is considerably more complex than has previously been recognized, largely, I would claim, because its origins in gothic and melodramatic texts have not been recognized or studied.

Finally, we need to recognize that what is at stake in the female gothic novel is the psychic and linguistic reconfiguration of the parental figures, both as social and historical realities and as ambivalent psychic and emotional constructions of power and powerlessness combined. Female gothic novels are obsessed with trying to explain the absence of the mother, the brute force of the father, and the victimization of the daughter. But rather than simply depict both mothers and daughters as passive victims of the patriarchy, female gothic novelists attempt something more subtle; they reveal the ways in which their heroines, and by extension bourgeois women in general, collude and conspire with their oppressors in a passive-aggressive dance of rebellion and compliance. Juliet Mitchell sees the same phenomenon at work on a large scale: "The longevity of the oppression of women *must* be based on something more than conspiracy, something more complicated than biological handicap and more durable than economic exploitation (although in differing degrees all of these may feature). It is illusory to see women as the pure who are put upon: the status of women is held in the heart and the head as well as the home: oppression has not been trivial or historically transitory—to maintain itself so effectively it courses through the mental and emotional bloodstream. To think that this should not be so does not necessitate pretending it is already not so." If the oppression of women actually resides in our "mental and emotional bloodstream," then we can understand the ambivalence of imagery and action that occurs whenever the female gothic novelist and her heroine confront the mother's dead and yet undead body. Mary Poovey makes an analogous observation about the ambivalence that characterizes the depiction of familial relations in the writings of Fanny Burney. Using Chodorow's theories about young women who continue to identify with their mothers and yet turn to their fathers, hoping that they will offer the mother autonomy, Poovey notes that these women soon realize that, "The promise of social autonomy is in fact false . . . the girl sees that her relationship with her father has been largely idealized; and she intuits, however dimly, that the man she has idealized is, in fact, the tyrant of patriarchal society."

But there is a distinct difference to be drawn between the historical and actual mother of a child and the maternal "imago" that the psyche constructs out of a disparate set of psychological and emotional needs. Drawing on Lacan's distinction between the "actual father" and the "paternal metaphor," Marie Christine Hamon has argued that in order to be understood, the *mother* must be separated into separate and various functions: "The mother of the unconscious is not the 'actual' mother. Freud indicates this on a number of occasions while discussing that quite other reality 'psychical reality.'" Parveen Adams develops the same idea, stating, "Freud's work does not emphasize the individual mother's performance in respect to her child. . . . Freud is speaking of the mother in the unconscious, a mother who introduces the child to lack, to castration, to representation."

In other words, to the body and to death. All of this brings us to Elizabeth

Bronfen's *Over Her Dead Body: Death, Femininity, and the Aesthetic,* a work that speaks to this same concern, the attempt to understand the motivations that compel artists to create and objectify the dead/undead female body. Bronfen's major claim is that psychoanalysis has consistently attempted to foreground the role and importance of the father in the construction of the ego because of an unacknowledged need to root out, displace, and marginalize the mother. But the displacement of the mother from both Freud's and Lacan's accounts of ego formation actually serves simultaneously to aestheticize the woman's body as an object of death and charge that body with intense and diffuse anxiety.[21] And strange as it may seem, the same sort of "fort-da" game described by Freud in *Beyond the Pleasure Principle* is played out repetitiously in the female gothic novel. The female gothic author keeps disposing of the mother, only to reel her body magically back into the text for obsessive view over and over again, revealing that in both the psychoanalytic and the female gothic traditions the same wound, the same psychic trauma is being fingered, not simply once but repeatedly. That wound would appear to be located precisely in the loss of the matriarchy, the destruction of the mother as a figure of power or even a fantasy of power in a society that no longer values her role or importance.

Because the sons of psychoanalysis and the daughters of the gothic both mourn the passing of the mother's body from view and control, they repeatedly construct texts that represent their fantasized construction and reconstruction of the maternal, aesthetically potent, and deadly beautiful body. Somehow the two movements—psychoanalysis and the female gothic— both participate in some profoundly similar manner in delineating an aesthetics of loss that occurs in what I would label the private theater of the wounded female gothic psyche. And both movements find themselves spiraling into and around each other in yet another attempt to salvage the mother's body and by extension her control and power over society—the late eighteenth- and early nineteenth-century ideology that now goes under the name of "feminism."

---

21. My discussion of the mother's construction is indebted to Elizabeth Kowaleski-Wallace, *Their Fathers' Daughters: Hannah More, Maria Edgeworth, and Patriarchal Complicity* (New York: Oxford University Press, 1991), 9–14; Juliet Mitchell, *Psychoanalysis and Feminism* (New York: Random House, 1975), 362; Mary Poovey, "Fathers and Daughters: The Trauma of Growing Up Female," *WL*, ed. Janet Todd, vol. 2 (New York: Holmes and Meier, 1981), 54–55; Marie Christine Hamon, "The Figures of the Mother: A Study," *M/F* 8 (1983), 34; Parveen Adams, "Mothering," *M/F* 8 (1983), 42; and Elizabeth Bronfen, *Over Her Dead Body: Death, Femininity, and the Aesthetic* (Manchester: Manchester University Press, 1992), 28. On the complex issue of whether or not Freud explains the gothic or the gothic explains Freud, see Terry Castle, "Phantasmagoria: Spectral Technology and the Metaphorics of Modern Reverie," *CI* 15 (1988), 26–61.

ONE

Gendering the Civilizing Process

The Case of Charlotte Smith's
Emmeline, the Orphan of the Castle

This desire of being always women,
is the very consciousness that degrades the sex.
—MARY WOLLSTONECRAFT

I

In 1753, the British Parliament passed the Hardwicke Act, a law that was designed to prevent the clandestine or forced marriages of heiresses who were apparently believed to be so besieged by mercenary bourgeois suitors that the law had to step in to protect them. As Lawrence Stone has observed, the aristocracy at this time was so concerned with the fine points of passing on their property that they became incensed at "the ease with which penniless adventurers could entice or seduce their daughters and heiresses and irrevocably marry them without parental knowledge or consent." We can begin our examination of the female gothic novel by situating the texts that were written after the passage of this law as extended glosses on the motif of pursued and persecuted heiress-heroines. But in order to discuss the female gothic writer's impulse to civilize the process of marriage and by extension the newly emerging capitalist, let me briefly examine two works that attempt to explain the invention of the "civilizing process" that bourgeois women, of necessity, experienced: Norbert Elias's *The History of Manners* and Michel Bakhtin's *Rabelais and His World*.[1]

Elias's work traces the creation during the early modern period of what he calls *homo clausus*, an individual who will professionalize his gender and make total biological control of himself a private matter. Such an individual experiences the culturally imposed "standards of shame, delicacy, and self-control" and the "rising threshold of shame and embarrassment" about bodily functions as an endorsement of increasingly extreme forms of personal restraint, as the institution of "a wall, of something 'inside' man separating him from the outside world" (259). And it was, according to Elias, this newly created and controlled "public body" that was given validation by society, and which distinguished itself from the lower social classes by aping the courtly value of self-control, along with its acceptance of shame as the secret sin at its (bourgeois) heart. What Elias calls "manners," highly gendered customs, behavior, and fashions, now were diffused from the court to the upper class, and then to the next class down the social ladder until all classes were ultimately affected by the codes of conduct that were being advocated in the books of courtly behavior now saturating the newly literate population. According to Elias, it was through the imposition of such "manners" and the use of shame as a disciplinary tool that the modern state could come into existence. "Civilizing" the urban space meant that education and recreational activities were now controlled by "moral censorship," while the "new sensibilities" made physical violence, dueling, hunting, and public displays of bodily functions all abhorrent and grossly unacceptable behaviors (126–29).

Bakhtin's writings, on the other hand, privilege the "carnivalesque" body of the early modern period. This body enacts its essentially antibourgeois values through intense releases of emotion, destroys authoritarian strictures, and challenges and inverts imposed political and religious systems. The

---

1. See Lawrence Stone, *Family, Sex, and Marriage in England, 1500–1800* (New York: Harper & Row, 1977), 35. Stone's controversial work charts the "growth of affective individualism" in eighteenth-century English bourgeois families as the expression of "a new sensibility": "The Man of Feeling" embodying a "genuinely moral" movement, an "upsurge of new attitudes and emotions" (247, 238, chap. 6 passim). My emphasis is on how the woman of feeling gendered those moral movements through the topos of virtue in distress in the female gothic genre. On *homo clausus*, see Norbert Elias, *The Civilizing Process*, vol. 1, *The History of Manners*, trans. Edmund Jephcott (New York: Pantheon, 1978), 249–60; and the valuable discussion of "The Civilizing Process and British Commercial Capitalism" in G. J. Barker-Benfield, *The Culture of Sensibility: Sex and Society in Eighteenth-Century Britain* (Chicago. University of Chicago Press, 1992), 77–98. On the carnivalesque body, see Michel Bakhtin, *Rabelais and His World*, trans. Helena Iswolsky (Cambridge: MIT Press, 1968).

lower classes and women, of course, were freest to indulge in such *charivari,* or communal dances, while the obverse of such "harmless" activity would be the carnage and mob violence of the French Revolution. The struggle between these two bodies—*homo clausus* and the carnivalesque—can be seen as one locus of meaning in the female gothic novel, although ironically the carnivalesque possibility is generally associated in these works not so much with lower-class women as with aristocratic practitioners of adultery, gossip, slander, and dueling or poisoning as the preferred means for settling scores. A woman like Radcliffe's Emily is advised by her father on the one hand to conform, to conceal, to privatize, while on the other hand the carnivalesque possibility is always open to her, luring her into sympathizing with and reenacting the history of the rampaging Bacchae Signora Laurentini, aka Sister Agnes. These two bodies, and the warfare between them, characterize the shifting personae of all the polarized women in Radcliffe's novels, or the struggle between the bodies of Jane and Bertha in *Jane Eyre* or Victoria and Lilla in Dacre's *Zofloya.*

Elias concludes that the middle class founded its status—its economic and political power—on the model of *homo clausus,* the retentive, controlled, concealed, and professionally gendered body. Such a body was usually coded as male and gained its power through the ability to distance others, to refuse engagement, and to mimic the scientific values of objectivity and rationality. The female body, on the other hand, was associated in this formula with diffuse energy, subjectivity, passion, and emotionality. As Gary Kelly has observed, the construction of both the sentimental and the reasonable "woman" during the late eighteenth century was part of a larger ideological project, the creation of a professional middle-class discourse system that would supplant the aristocracy at the same time it gained control over the lower classes. "Woman" in this cultural enterprise was crucial as a pawn in issues of property, children, and inheritance; and finally she constituted a certain technology of the self that we now recognize as "virtue" and "reason."[2]

In light of these theories, it becomes evident that the female gothic novel assisted in the bourgeois cultural revolution by helping to professionalize gender, by collaborating in the construction of the professionally middle-

---

2. Gary Kelly, *Women, Writing, and Revolution: 1790–1827* (Oxford: Clarendon, 1993), 3–5. Markman Ellis provides a valuable overview of the relationship among sensibility, history, and the novel in his *Politics of Sensibility: Race, Gender, and Commerce in the Sentimental Novel* (Cambridge: Cambridge University Press, 1996), 5–48.

class woman and the professionally bourgeois paterfamilias. Women who did not conform to appropriately coded bourgeois norms—who reminded the reading audience of long discarded and disgraced aristocratic flaws like adultery, passion, gossip, slander, and physical violence—became themselves the targets of savage beatings throughout the works. Men who were coded as libidinous and aristocratic, like Rochester in *Jane Eyre* or Valancourt in *The Mysteries of Udolpho,* were allowed to survive and marry the heroine only after they had been subjected to a vicious beating or a series of shootings, and thereafter effectively renounced their flawed and anachronistic aristocratic tendencies.

Central to the ideological construction of gender during this period, as I have pointed out, was the emphasis on separate spheres for men and women, the public/private dichotomy that was played out in virtually every conduct book and quasi-religious tract published from the middle of the eighteenth century through at least the lifetimes of the Brontës. One of the best known of these tracts was Thomas Gisborne's *Enquiry into the Duties of the Female Sex* (1796), a companion volume to his *Enquiry into the Duties of Men in the Higher and Middle Classes of Society in Great Britain Resulting from Their Respective Situations, Positions, and Employments.* Gisborne claimed in the former text that men were particularly gifted in "the science of legislation, of jurisprudence, of political economy; the conduct of government in all its executive functions; the abstruse reaches of erudition, the inexhaustible depths of philosophy; the knowledge indispensable in the wide field of commercial enterprise; [and] the arts of defence and of attack." So while men were slashing and wounding each other in the public sphere, women were supposed to be content with ministering "to the comfort of husbands, of parents, of brothers and sisters, and of other relations, connections, and friends, in the intercourse of domestic life." Further, Gisborne specifies that it is the responsibility of women to "form and improve the general manners, disposition, and conduct of the other sex, by society and example," while the final task of a woman for Gisborne was the "modelling [of] the human mind during the early stages of its growth, and fixing, while it is yet ductile, its growing principles of action."[3]

In the artificially constructed world of the conduct book scenario, men and women inhabited tightly demarcated spheres where duties, rights, and responsibilities were codified and thoroughly accepted by all parties. Such a worldview was seductive for an emerging bourgeoisie that wanted, nay

---

3. Thomas Gisborne, *An Enquiry into the Duties of the Female Sex* (London: 1797), 12–13.

needed, to believe that women were properly positioned as pawns in the broader masculine enterprise we call the patriarchy, that is, a codified system of inheritance and property transfer. But women did not quietly acquiesce to the conduct book construction of their nature and destiny. They wrote female gothic novels that proffered another, alternate fantasy, and in this version they emerged from the private domain with a vengeance. They mimed the mime, masqueraded as professionally feminine, and exploded the limited gender constructions that the masters like Gisborne were peddling.

When Ann Radcliffe's early villain the Marquis de Mazzini (in *A Sicilian Romance*) wants to insult his son, he can think of no greater crime than to accuse him of betraying "'the weak mind of a woman . . . Degenerate boy! Is it thus you reward my care? Do I live to see my son the sport of every idle tale a woman may repeat? Learn to trust reason and your senses, and you will then be worthy of my attention.'"[4] In gothic novels the sexes are arrayed along an axis of characteristics, with the extremes coded clearly as evil. Women who are excessively "masculine feminine"—sexual predators like the voracious gothic stepmother in *A Sicilian Romance* or the overly passionate women who find themselves confined to convents in *The Mysteries of Udolpho*—always die by the conclusion of the novel, leaving no heirs to carry on their character defects.

And, likewise, men who are excessively "masculine"—violent, aggressive, lustful, and adulterous, that is, men who refuse to be civilized and domesticated and professionally masculinized—also suffer a horrific punishment by the end of the novel. They invariably die guilt-wrecked deaths, usually by their own hands. Their sons and heirs, if there are any who are worthy of inheriting the always damaged estate, are considerably tamer creatures, having learned from their fathers that such extremely masculine characteristics do not bring happiness or longevity. The compulsion for both sexes formed under the machine of capitalism was to merge, to eliminate radical distinctions of gender and find some sort of moderate middle ground on which both could stand as equals. In the female gothic novel, the man left standing is invariably a man who has been stabbed or shot (usually twice, just for good measure), while the woman left standing is the one who has successfully navigated her way through labyrinthine corridors and out of towers and catacombs, bringing back into the light of day her long-lost mother. In both her first and last gothic novels, Radcliffe has her heroines find their

---

4. Ann Radcliffe, *A Sicilian Romance*, ed. Alison Milbank (Oxford: Oxford University Press, 1993), 48–49.

mothers, thought in both cases to be long dead. Although the two middle novels play with variations on this theme, the daughter as savior of an earlier and gentler matriarchal tradition is clearly a key component to the ideology being promulgated here. The daughter as culture heroine marries the wounded son figure (one recalls Attis), and together they forge a new ideal couple, as moderate in its lineaments as the previous culture's idealized couple was Titan-like. We can observe that this ideology allows both hero and heroine to endure and survive that ultimate beating fantasy we call history.

According to the female gothic trajectory, the heroine, in her new and valorized masculinized role and identity as oedipal detective and reasonable, rational seeker of the family's buried secret, has become acceptable only because she has managed to abject/reject her "naturally" passionate feminine tendencies toward excess and emotion and cultivated in their place a rational and masculinely identified mind. Possessing the mind of a man means that women are first and foremost reasonable, calm, and easily able to control or better yet repress their emotions. "To think like a man" has for the past two hundred years been the highest praise that could be bestowed by the patriarchy on a woman. But what about men? Why would women seek to create a new masculine ideal that demanded that a man be wounded and vulnerable? To put it crudely, a wounded man is a castrated man is a safe (easily manipulated) man. A weak man, that is, a man who has been professionally gendered as "masculine" according to the bourgeois ideology, will not think he can tyrannize over his wife and children; this man will not attempt anything as foolish as adultery or its attendant sins; he will not chain his wife to rocks in a cave. The professionally gendered bourgeois man has had his dangerously masculine spirit tamed and put safely under the control of the professional girl-woman.

Critics of sensibility have long remarked on the enigma of the feminized hero, and most have placed him firmly within the traditions of sentimentality, originating as a Rousseauian creation or a Burkean spectacle of misplaced emotion. Claudia Johnson in her book *Equivocal Beings* has commented on Burke's hyperbolic reaction to Marie Antoinette's precarious state by noting that a man's need to cry out and moan over the fate of a threatened woman would appear to be yet another veiled sadistic scenario, displaced or elided by a fair amount of masochistic posturing by the sentimental male writing the narrative. The sadistic punishment of women, the trope of the besieged heroine, is for the male authors of the 1790s "not the unthinkable crime which chivalric sentimentality forestalls, but rather the one-thing-needful to solicit male tears and the virtues that supposedly flow with them, and the preposterousness of [the women writers'] work emerges from and engages this horrifying realization" (15).

For Johnson it was the female author of the 1790s who felt herself stripped of her traditional gender markings when the sentimental man assumed the characteristics that were formerly ascribed to the "female." As she asserts, the "sentimental man, having taken over once-feminine attributes, leaves to women only two choices: either the equivocal or the hyperfeminine. For if the man Werther is already the culture's paragon of feeling, then any feeling differentially attributed to women must be excessively delicate, morbidly *over*-sensitive" (12). Additionally, Johnson claims that under the sentimental dispensation "gender codes have not simply been reversed. They have been fundamentally disrupted. . . . [T]he conservative insistence upon the urgency of chivalric sentimentality fundamentally unsettled gender itself, leaving women without a distinct gender site. Under sentimentality, all women risk becoming equivocal beings" (11). As Johnson rightly argues, "under sentimentality the prestige of suffering belongs to men" (17), but what do you do about the spectacle of female suffering that marches across the pages of women's literature—particularly the female gothic—throughout the 1790s? Johnson chooses to read this suffering as an ambivalent gesture by women themselves to regain a sense of agency and subjectivity that had been denied to them by their culture. Johnson claims that "sentimentality upsets all markers of gender," while "female subjectivity itself is cast into doubt as culpable, histrionic, and grotesque" (16).[5]

The female gothic novel is certainly one site of gender confusion, one area in which women writers attempted to stake a claim for the power of professional femininity and victimization suffering. But this femininity had a vague political subtext, what we today would recognize as a species of proto-"feminism," in that women were advised in these novels not to trust to the goodwill of men but to manipulate or control those men—weakened by their own emotions—without those men actually being aware of it. The type of feminism that Wollstonecraft advocated was not perceived by her or her contemporaries as a social, political, or economic movement with a clear-cut agenda and principles. Despite her stated injunctions to women that their "first duty" was to themselves, Wollstonecraft initiated a pedagogical program detailing how best to prepare women to serve as loyal and devoted wives and raise judicious and sensible children. The issues that concerned

---

5. See Claudia Johnson, *Equivocal Beings: Politics, Gender, and Sentimentality in the 1790s* (Chicago: University of Chicago Press, 1995).

Wollstonecraft and Radcliffe were fairly simple: they believed in access to education for women; they advocated the importance of the family presided over by intelligent and devoted parents and inhabited by dutiful children; and they understood the importance of marriage and the crucial nature of the choice of an appropriate spouse as a means of determining a woman's future status and opportunities.

What we have come to label one brand of "feminism" began in the fairly straightforward claims of women who were defined by their society as "orphans," that is, disinherited and worthless because the claims of the first-born son were seen as ever so much more significant. Female novelists like Hannah More and Maria Edgeworth may have practiced what Elizabeth Kowaleski-Wallace has labeled "patriarchal complicity," or an "equally strong longing for the father's sanction" in their writings. As popular purveyors of educational and religious tracts, they were complicit in creating the "myth of the benevolent patriarch" and the construction of what Kowaleski-Wallace has called "new-style patriarchy," promulgated by a "daughter whose attraction to her father compels her to seek his approval." But such a phenomenon is substantially problematized in the female gothic novel. Proving one's legitimacy, proving that one is not an "orphan," or fatherless, becomes a persistent refrain in female gothic novels. Why? Clearly, the answer one is forced finally to confront concerns the nature of the "patriarchy" as perceived by the very different white, middle-class women who were reading and writing gothic novels (as distinct from those who were attracted to the works of More and Edgeworth, for instance). To the female gothic consciousness, the patriarchy (or what we might more naively call "society") exists as a huge protection racket, a system of favors and exchanges according to which one's survival depends on having a powerful protector. As Jay Fliegelman has remarked with regard to the period, "neither Locke nor Rousseau believed that daughters should be encouraged to the same spirit of independence as their male counterparts. . . . [W]hereas sons were freed from parental dependence by the development of autonomous reason, daughters, whose virtue must always have a protector, were to find a similar liberation through marriage."[6] But when women were shut out of this system of protection, when their own names did not signal allegiance and ownership by a powerful patriarch, then they experienced life as a gothic

---

6. See Elizabeth Kowaleski-Wallace, *Their Fathers' Daughters*, 9–20; and Jay Fliegelman, *Prodigals and Pilgrims: The American Revolution Against Patriarchal Authority* (New York: Cambridge University Press, 1982), 126. The nature of the "patriarchy" is, of course, a tremendously complicated and controversial subject, and I would claim that women are not by necessity its mindless and powerless vic-

chamber of horrors. Gothic heroines, if they were to survive, were then forced to seek protection from any surrogate protection agency they could find—the church, an educational institution, marriage to a chastened aristocrat, anything that would provide them a form of "cover," a means of protection that they did not possess in their own right.

II

Charlotte Smith's *Emmeline, the Orphan of the Castle* (1788) presents this ideology in pure undistilled form: women actually have been disinherited and hounded out of their rightful estates and properties by odious men who have found perverse pleasure in robbing and swindling them, and then like vultures have fattened themselves on the spoils of ill-gotten female wealth and goods. An intense fear of masculinity pervades *Emmeline,* while the threat of sexual violence—kidnapping, rape, or forced marriage—is always present for the heroine and other female characters unlucky enough to be without patriarchal protection. Scenarios of sexual violence as a theme have also recently been analyzed similarly by Daniel Watkins, who sees the phenomenon as a persistent and powerful leitmotif in canonical romantic poetry. For Watkins, "the romantic portrayal of gender necessarily depends first not upon language but rather upon the decline of feudal, or aristocratic, patriarchy and the emergence of capitalist, or bourgeois, patriarchy, and it therefore is bound up with historical acts of violence and oppression." Attempting to locate "the historically specific *logic* of gender stratification," Watkins explores acts of violence committed against female characters in the name of masculine privilege and out of the male fear of a new capitalistic economy that the poets (and their masculinist culture) felt threatened by. Thus the poets scapegoat women, doling out to them the violence that became one means by which the bourgeois poet could project onto another (helpless) object his own sense of historical displacement and redundancy.[7]

---

tims. Recent contemporary feminists, such as Naomi Wolf and bell hooks, have asserted that women have developed a variety of enabling strategies that have allowed them to circumvent or undermine the patriarchy's power over them. For more detailed discussions of the theoretical and historical aspects of this question, see Gerda Lerner, *The Creation of the Patriarchy* (New York: Oxford University Press, 1986); and Susan Moll Okin, "Patriarchy and Married Women's Property in England," *ECS* 17 (1983), 121–38.

7. Daniel Watkins, *Sexual Power in British Romantic Poetry* (Gainesville: University Press of Florida, 1996), 28, 30.

This same system of gender stratification, however, can be detected in the female gothic novel, in which the bourgeois woman writer punishes sexual women and castrates aristocratic men in the name of the civilizing process. Smith's Emmeline is plagued by her need to balance "sense" (her masculinist tendencies) and "sensibility" (her feminized romantic characteristics) in much the same way the heroines of Austen must a few years later. Both women writers present in their heroines the same diffuse anxiety, the same sense of powerlessness and dispossession, and always with the threat that real violence, real trauma could descend on the heroine who does not successfully navigate the treacherous gender straits. The female gothic heroine is a woman who has learned the lesson her author wants to teach to the general reading public: the patriarchy is a gigantic protection racket; there is no protection for women unless they too get a big stick behind them any way they can. If there is a system of "traffic in women," then sell yourself to the best (read: most controllable) bidder, the man with the most effective system of protection behind him. This may not be a comforting realization, but then the female gothic world was being constructed as an alternate female domain standing in contradistinction to the industrial and "realistic" world that male authors were codifying at the same time. If the male bildungsroman was a masculinist ideological project intended to depict the "patriarchy" as a benign force, the female gothic novel positioned the "patriarchy" as a duplicitous, inscrutable, good daddy/bad daddy. The ambivalence that saturates the female gothic novel can be traced precisely to this cynical and sometimes self-critical portrait of what a woman has to do in order to survive in a patriarchy. Smith, Radcliffe, and Austen's heroines may marry at the conclusion of their novels, but these marriages are less celebrations than they are quiet acceptances of their new keepers.

Just as Wollstonecraft was picking up her pen to attempt to write fiction, she was reading and reacting to the works of her contemporary, Charlotte Smith (1749–1806). And when Wollstonecraft was asked as one of her very first assignments to review Smith's first novel for the *Analytical Review* she did not find much to praise about it. It is significant that she particularly disliked the secondary story line, the adulterous and passionate romance between Lady Adelina and Fitz-Edward. She lashed out against the happy ending of their tortured love affair, condemning "the false expectations these wild scenes excite, [which] tend to debauch the mind, and throw an insipid kind of uniformity over the moderate and rational prospects of life, consequently adventures are sought for and created, when duties are neglected and content despised." But this reaction should not surprise us, because

Wollstonecraft, who signed herself variously as "M," "W," or "T," became well known as a reviewer for her contempt for what she disparagingly called "feminine novels," or unnatural and affected productions. To be "feminine" in Wollstonecraft's lexicon was to be "ridiculous," "childish," full of "folly and improbability," and finally "stupid."[8] But there was nothing stupid about Charlotte Smith. She was a sentimentalist with a social and political agenda; she was an incipient gothic feminist.

From a privileged background, Smith married well and spent the first twenty years of her marriage to Benjamin Smith bearing twelve children, only six of whom would survive their mother. Smith squandered his paternal inheritance and found himself imprisoned for debt in 1784, and for a time Charlotte and the children joined him there; then they fled to France to escape creditors. Finally, she faced the inevitable and separated from her husband, knowing full well that the support of her surviving children would be her complete responsibility.[9] Smith did what she had to do: she wrote novels about women who marry fops, fools, or scoundrels and then try to deal heroically with the situations such incompetent men produce. Smith wrote ten novels, several translations, collections of poetry, and histories in order to support herself and her children over the next fifteen years. She has been largely ignored since the heyday of her popularity, although in the past five years she has enjoyed something of a critical renaissance. Her first novel, *Emmeline, the Orphan of the Castle,* clearly stands as the forgotten urtext for the female gothic novel tradition and deserves to be recognized as such. Read and admired by Radcliffe, the work was condemned by Wollstonecraft and satirized by Austen. So immediately popular that the first printing of 15,000 copies in 1788 sold out within six months, *Emmeline* was the rage of reading London and as such it served an important function in the transmission and transmutation of female-created ideologies.[10]

---

8. *Analytical Review* 1 (May–August 1788), 333. Wollstonecraft's reviews of Smith are discussed by Chris Jones, *Radical Sensibility: Literature and Ideas in the 1790s* (London: Routledge, 1993), 70–77. Also on the subject of Wollstonecraft as a reviewer, see Ralph Wardle, "Mary Wollstonecraft, Analytical Reviewer," *PMLA* 62 (1947), 1000–1007. Of interest, Wollstonecraft wrote a short but very positive review of Radcliffe's *Italian* (see her *Works*, ed. Janet Todd and Marilyn Butler, vol. 7 [London: Pickering, 1989], 484–85).

9. Carroll Lee Fry's *Charlotte Smith, Popular Novelist* (New York: Arno, 1980), 3–14, contains a biographical summary of Smith's life drawn from all the earlier sources.

10. Very little sustained critical commentary exists on *Emmeline*; however, the novel has recently been discussed as a paradigmatic work of sensibility by Janet Todd in her *Sensibility: An Introduction* (London: Methuen, 1986), 110–28. See also Katherine M. Rogers, "Inhibitions on Eighteenth-Century Women Novelists: Elizabeth Inchbald and Charlotte Smith," *ECS* 11 (1977), 63–76; Eva Figes, *Sex and Subterfuge: Women Novelists to 1850* (London: Macmillan, 1982), 56–68; Dale Spender, *Mothers of the*

Emmeline is one of those novels that contains within it evidence of both the dominant prior discourse system and suggestions and hints of the next paradigm shift. *Emmeline,* in other words, is a sentimental novel with a gothic novel buried within it struggling to emerge as a full-blown genre in its own right. How can we characterize the sentimental residue found in *Emmeline?* Suffice it to say that Emmeline and the secondary female heroine, Lady Adelina, cry, weep, sob, or stifle a tear on virtually every occasion and at least once in every chapter of this long-winded novel. The sentimental code of conduct is implicit in the author's every judgment about what constitutes a "good" and what constitutes a "bad" character. We know that Emmeline's aunt, Lady Montreville, is evil when we are told that "her passions were as strong as her reason was feeble" (62). Emotions and displays of emotion are coded as dangerous throughout this text, while reason is lauded as the most valuable trait for human beings. The heroine, Emmeline or the "orphan" of the castle, struggles to prove her legitimacy and hence her rightful claim to her father's estate at the same time she attempts to avoid marrying her rich cousin, who stands in the position of aristocratic usurper of her own estate. We will not spoil too much of this plot by saying that Emmeline does prove her legitimacy. The papers she needed to do so were always in her own possession; she was simply too occupied fending off a variety of unpleasant suitors to read her parents' marriage license and her father's will.

The multiple suitor convention, brought to a fever pitch in sentimental literature by Richardson, is used here to suggest that the dominant and threateningly odious suitor has about him an incestuous air of familiarity. When Emmeline repulses her rich cousin Delamere as a possible husband, she is acting out the drama that Foucault has identified as characterizing the entire late eighteenth-century cultural enterprise. We will see the rejected incestuous suitor again in *Jane Eyre*'s St. John Rivers, *Wuthering Heights*'s Heathcliff, and *Mathilda*'s papa. Moving out of the family kinship clan and into an exogamous alliance, based on the property of one's body rather than one's blood, proved to be an enormously anxious and ambivalent activity for middle-class women and women writers. But Emmeline actually has three other unsuitable suitors in addition to Delamere. The first is a man

---

Novel (London: Pandora, 1986), 21–20; Mary Anne Schofield, *Masking and Unmasking the Female Mind: Disguising Romances in Feminine Fiction, 1713–1799* (Newark: University of Delaware Press, 1990); and Jane Spencer, *The Rise of the Woman Novelist* (Oxford: Blackwell, 1986). All quotations from Smith's *Emmeline, the Orphan of the Castle* are from the Pandora edition, ed. Zoe Fairbairns (London, 1988), with page numbers identified in parentheses in the text.

who has served as the estate's caretaker and had in his possession the documents that proved Emmeline's rightful claim to the castle of Mowbray. This man appears to be motivated by simple greed: a blatant attempt to claim the castle of Mowbray as his own through marriage to the heiress. But Mr. Maloney (meant to be the object of suspicion by the fact of his Irish surname) is rejected by Emmeline as hopelessly beneath her in class, even though she thinks at this time that she is illegitimate and unworthy of any sort of marriage.

The second unsuitable catch snagged by poor Emmeline is a man named Mr. Rochely, an elderly and unpleasantly plump businessman. Rochely reveals a less than sentimental line of reasoning as he contemplates an engagement with the heroine: "He was determined to chuse beauty, but expected also fortune. He desired to marry a woman of family, yet feared the expensive turn of those brought up in high life; and [he] had a great veneration for wit and accomplishments, but dreaded, lest in marrying a woman who possessed them, he would be liable to be governed by superior abilities, or be despised for the mediocrity of his own understanding" (88). Suffice it to say that Emmeline has the good sense to despise him, even though her greedy and self-serving aunt and uncle desperately want to marry Emmeline off in order to get her out of the sight of their precious son and heir, Delamere. Again, even though the match would appear to provide a means of "erasing the blemish of her birth," Emmeline's innate dignity and pride cause her to reject Rochely.

Toward the conclusion of the novel, Emmeline also attracts as a suitor a French aristocrat, Bellozane, when she travels on the Continent with her friend and mother substitute Mrs. Stafford, who has been forced to flee creditors with her husband and children. Mr. and Mrs. Stafford's situation is a slightly veiled portrait of Smith's own financially desperate marriage to an improvident and foolish man. But Mrs. Stafford is the soul of discretion and common sense in this novel, a perfect chaperon and maternal guide to the young and beautiful Emmeline. Whereas Mrs. Stafford married badly, she is determined to see Emmeline married well, to a wise and good man, and she cannot abide the foppish French suitor anymore than she can stand Rochely. Emmeline's rejection of yet another passionate and unprincipled aristocrat at this point in the book is meant to suggest her increasing self-esteem. She knows that she is worthy of the best, and she is willing to wait no matter how many unpleasant suitors she has to reject.

It is this intense self-possession, this extreme sense of her own worth that puzzles bystanders of the gothic/sentimental heroine. How can a woman society has labeled "illegitimate" respect herself? In other words, how can a woman possess self-respect when the forces of the patriarchy have deemed her beneath their contempt and offered her no formal means of protection? The mystery of the gothic heroine's identity—her inwardness, her silence, her extreme control of her emotions in public, her sexual inviolability and purity—puzzles a social system that wants to believe that only it possesses the power to confer value. The villains of Smith's novel are not simply Emmeline's greedy aristocratic relatives, Lord and Lady Montreville, who want to disparage and patronize her. The more effectual villains in this novel are the upstart lawyers, the nouveau riche functionaries who attach themselves parasitically to the aristocrats and exploit whatever opening is presented to them: Richard Croft and his presumptuous son. The Crofts and their vicious allies commit the most unforgivable sin in the gothic/melodramatic universe: they slander the good name of a good woman.

It is in its subtle class distinctions, however, that *Emmeline* provides such an effective mirror of British society circa 1788. E. P. Thompson has noted that the translations of Voltaire, D'Holbach, and Volney into English made each of their "views appear more radical in English than in French." In particular, Volney's *Ruins of Empire* features a dialogue between the "useful labours that contribute to the support and maintenance of society" and the "valueless faction—priests, courtiers, public accountants, commanders of troops, in short, the civil, military, or religious agents of government." Thompson concludes that, "The notion of the parasitic aristocratic estate or order comes through as the more generalised 'class' of the wealthy and idle. From this the sociology of post-war Radicalism was to be derived, which divided society between the 'Useful' or 'Productive Classes' on the one hand, and courtiers, sinecurists, fund-holders, speculators and parasitic middlemen on the other." Croft and his son are meant to signify the ominous growth of the "parasitic middlemen," a new class of supposedly useful people who actually feed off a variety of vulnerable victims, namely, weary aristocrats or besieged women.

But as E. J. Clery has pointed out, political economy and civic humanism dominated Augustan political thought, valorizing the "real" wealth of land as opposed to finance capitalism, which was based on rumors and speculation and "encouraged the spread of a luxury—excessive consumption—which would corrupt individuals and destabilize the social order": "The attacks on novels and novel-reading in this period were part of the wider opposition to consumerism. In the case of supernatural fictions [or female gothic novels], the civic humanist objection to luxury commodities in general was supplemented by the enlightenment objection to a form of writing which perpetuated irrational ideas for the sake of affect. Within these complementary frameworks, supernatural fiction figures as the ultimate luxury commodity, produced by an 'unreal need' for unreal representations."[11] In order to conceal the "luxurious" or frivolous nature of novel reading, Smith cloaks her narrative in moral lessons of utility—maxims riddle the text—while she has her heroine and hero adhere to the strictest norms of civic humanism. Finally, in her validation of the values of Godolphin and his brother, she reinforces the hegemony of land-based wealth against all nouveau upstarts.

Repetitions or the threat of repetitions, the entropic power of history, characterize the plot of *Emmeline*. The secret marriage of Emmeline's parents is almost repeated years later in Emmeline's kidnapping and just-averted-in-the-nick-of-time forced marriage to Delamere. The adulterous affair of Adelina and Fitz-Edward, which produces another illegitimate child, a son, is used to slander Emmeline, who is accused by the upstart Crofts of being the unmarried mother of the child. The swirl of uncontrolled sexuality, fluid class status, and the naked power of the sword reverberates throughout this text in interesting and suggestive ways. The sword is always rattling in this novel, and the duel that is so feared finally does occur at the conclusion of the novel, thereby freeing Emmeline of the claims made on her by the passionate and violent Delamere. The repetitive structure, however, suggests that there are a limited number of scenarios permitted in this world for women. They can be wives, in which case they will either be the cause of disappointment or they will be disappointed. They can be mistresses, in which case the disappointment will be even more severe. Or they can be single and, therefore, sexual prey, in which case they will be kidnapped in the dead of night, slandered, and generally despised until they choose a protector-husband. And then the whole cycle will begin again.

To escape the sentimental impasse, the dead-end of emotions played out to their logical or illogical extreme, Smith presents a hero worthy of her heroine, Godolphin, who lives in a beautiful estate on the Isle of Wight—surely no coincidence, for the implication is that contact with society could only pollute him, and this is a man who has to be as highly principled and "good" as Emmeline in order to be worthy of her. Godolphin is tested when his sister has an adulterous affair with his best friend Fitz-Edward, runs away

---

11. E. P. Thompson, *The Making of the English Working Class* (New York: Random House, 1964), 99; E. J. Clery, *The Rise of Supernatural Fiction, 1762–1800* (Cambridge: Cambridge University Press, 1995), 7.

from her husband, and bears the resulting child in Bath, attended only by the generous and sympathetic Emmeline. Although she dreads her brother's wrath, Adelina and her son are saved when he decides to forgive her and offers her protection on his estate until her husband conveniently dies and she is free to marry Fitz-Edward. Godolphin loves Emmeline to distraction, but again he is "civilized" enough not to speak to her about his feelings until he is certain she does not love Delamere. Godolphin becomes *worthy* to be the hero of this text when he eschews "masculine" codes of conduct—epitomized in that very deadly masculine pastime of dueling—and empathizes instead with the "feminine" fates of his sister and Emmeline. Godolphin *becomes* a hero when he too feels his sister's disgrace so intensely that he sheds tears over her sexual downfall, and thereby proves that he is as "civilized" as the women who surround him.

Godolphin as a sentimental manly hero is contrasted throughout the work with Delamere, an antediluvian form of the hero, emotional, self-involved, passionate, prone to grabbing his sword or pistols and looking around for a duel to settle the score on his many grievances. We see the same sort of selfishly passionate man eradicated in Godwin's *Caleb Williams,* and in many ways Smith was as important an influence on Godwin as she was on Wollstonecraft. Delamere's emotions are sufficiently excessive to frighten Emmeline away from him and later cause him to become so ill with a fever that his life is thought to be in danger. The ideology of this tradition, however, is predicated on eliminating self-involved emotional men, eradicating them in favor of cool heads and benevolent and sentimental hearts like the one possessed by Godolphin. One is tempted to speculate that an emerging bourgeoisie locating its power in industrial capital and production found emotional and violent men to be anachronistic and embarrassing. Emotion in men was not a useful coin in the new capitalistic realm, at least not self-involved destructive emotions that produced the sort of undiffused energy that resulted in duels over issues like "honor."

Even Delamere's doting father, Emmeline's corrupt and usurping uncle, finds his son's excessive emotions a cause for concern. When Delamere tells his father that he will have nothing further to do with the Crofts, his father replies, "'Pooh, pooh! . . . you are always taking unreasonable aversions. Your blood is always boiling at some body or other. I tell you, the Crofts are good necessary, plodding people. Not too refined, perhaps, in points of honour, nor too strict in those of honesty; but excellent at the main chance, as you may see by what they have done for themselves'" (526). Several interesting shifts are revealed in this paternal homily. Lord Montreville senses that his son's "blood," his aristocratic heritage, has actually placed him at a disadvantage in the new social and economic world. People like the Crofts, capable of seizing the "main chance," have a control over themselves that the young aristocrat lacks. Further, in adhering to outdated notions of "honour," Delamere cripples himself and allows the Croft son to rise at his expense.

Indeed, it is a point of "honour" that dooms Delamere, precipitating the final duel that kills him. When his married sister decides to take a lover, she chooses one of Emmeline's spurned suitors, the French aristocrat Bellozane. After attending a play and seeing his sister openly flaunt her adulterous affair with the Frenchman, Delamere challenges him to a duel and he dies at Bellozane's hands. The death is gratuitous and had been foreshadowed since an earlier duel with another man who had the poor judgment to gossip about Emmeline and Delamere's relationship. The spiral here of adultery, dueling, "public scandal," and gossip, all coding behaviors that are strictly condemned by the civilizing sentimental tradition. In the new bourgeois order, very different values will be crucial: fidelity, monogamy, passivity, and decorum. To be sexually loose, violent, and prone to gossip is to be not only self-destructive but destructive of the social and economic fabric. In both codes, however, the issue is one of self-control. The older and aristocratic order, represented by the Montreville family, has lost control of itself, of their libidos as well as their tongues. The new order, represented by the chastened aristocrats, Emmeline and Godolphin, has learned the value of self-possession, restraint, bodily repression, and emotional control. Theirs are the genes that will reproduce and populate the future generation, whereas the violent and emotional genes of Delamere and his sister will be eradicated. The unlucky sister, we are pointedly told, ends her days in a French convent.

But the love stories that fill this text are almost ancillary to the real concerns of this work: inheritance, property ownership, social status, and class membership. This novel is also about how precarious it is for women to navigate and negotiate a social system that defines them always as appendages, dependents, ornaments, or incidental accoutrements to the "main chance," the patriarch. These characters find themselves drawn to France, ostensibly to escape creditors and live more cheaply, but they instead discover that they are led inexorably to retrace the final days of Emmeline's long-dead father. In a ramble through the French countryside, which would later influence Radcliffe's depictions of the landscape in *Udolpho*, Emmeline literally stumbles on her father's faithful servant Le Limosin, the only man alive who can testify to her parents' legitimate marriage in France. The human witness is as important in this culture as are the documents, the written records that testify to the marriage and the disposal of the estate. This is an important point and again reveals how decisively Smith captured the ideological strains of her culture. The older era—feudal, Catholic, and European based—relied on orality and human witnesses to verify truth. The new era—Protestant and technologically more sophisticated—relies instead on the veracity of written documents to prove claims and assert ownership of the estate. Emmeline's case was not complete without both modes, and these she was able to claim only by going back into the Old World of Europe and recovering, albeit vicariously, her father's history.

When Emmeline learns the truth, that she is the legal and legitimate heir to her father's estate, her first concern is that she has been deprived by her uncle of "education and affluence" (387). This statement is interesting for the priority it gives education in Emmeline's value system. By 1788 women understood the value of education in the social scheme of things. We know, of course, that Emmeline had largely educated herself by reading the moldy books left in her father's castle library: "Spenser and Milton, two or three volumes of the Spectator, an old edition of Shakespeare, and an odd volume or two of Pope" (7). We also know that Emmeline can play the harp, speak French, and sing very prettily, so we wonder exactly what sort of an education Emmeline thinks she has forfeited. It would appear that Emmeline is all too aware of not having the polish that either Mrs. Stafford or Lady Adelina possesses. And yet both of these women, raised with every advantage and educated in a way not allowed Emmeline, have married badly and lived to regret their choices. Smith's ideological purpose here appears to be subversive or at least ambivalent. On the one hand, she appears to advocate some form of formal education for women. On the other hand, even the best educations available to women of her day cannot and will not protect them from marrying foolish and improvident men (hence the necessity for the Hardwicke Act).

With an eyewitness in tow and papers that prove her parents were married not simply once but twice (by both Protestant and Catholic clergy), Emmeline descends on London and embarks on the most practical course she can imagine: she hires a lawyer and asks Godolphin's brother, Lord Westhaven, her rich and aristocratic future brother-in-law, to represent her claims against her uncle. This is interesting in itself, since Godolphin's brother has married Delamere's sister, Emmeline's cousin. The familial interconnections in this text come thick and fast; everyone it would appear is remotely related to everyone else, all of which makes the settlement of the estate a tricky business. In fact, at one point Emmeline exclaims that she thinks it best to drop the suit and conceal her growing love for Godolphin in the interest of family peace and harmony. Her words to Mrs. Stafford express the sense of powerlessness experienced by a woman in the grip of two generations of patriarchal power: "'I dread the mortified pride and furious jealousy of Lord Delamere on one hand; and on the other the authority of my uncle, who, 'till I am of age, will probably neither restore my fortune nor consent to my carrying it out of his family'" (452). Emmeline becomes acceptable in the eyes of the Montrevilles only when she possesses wealth and property in her own right. Only then will they consider her marriage to their son, but by then it is too late for this family to survive. Avarice, lust, greed, adultery, violence, and stupidity have doomed it. The Montrevilles have begun to resemble dodo birds, unable to evolve to the point of surviving a new, more reasonable, rational order.

When Emmeline produces the documents that prove her claims, the Montrevilles and their legal accomplices in crimes, the Crofts, are furious. The senior Mr. Croft had concealed the document in the first place, thinking his duplicity would never be discovered. And when it is, he is neither embarrassed nor contrite; he is furious. His psychology, the pathology of evil, is presented in some of the clearest lines of any female gothic text: "But as the aggressor never forgives, [Crofts] had conceived against Emmeline the most unmanly and malignant hatred, and had invariably opposed every tendency which he had observed in Lord Montreville to befriend and assist her, for no other reason but that he had already irreparably injured her" (455).

To be injured by someone places one in the position of being damaged goods in the eyes of the aggressor, and so women by their very status in such a society can only operate out of various positions of weakness. Emmeline cannot understand why the Crofts have constructed such a vicious slander campaign against her. Because she was seen holding Adelina's baby once by Delamere, she is vulnerable to being constructed by the Crofts as a fallen woman. Delamere believes the gossip on no evidence whatsoever, and from that mischief much misery ensues. But by the time Emmeline has learned about the gossip against her, she also has in her possession the documents that allow her to approach the patriarchy from a position of strength (read: money and land).

Emmeline is actually redeemed, however, not by the wills and eyewitnesses, but by her alliance with the aristocrat Lord Westhaven. It is his status as a reasonable and respected aristocrat that ensures the success of her claim. In Lord Westhaven, Emmeline knows that she has "found a protector too intelligent and too steady to be discouraged by evasion or chicanery—too powerful and too affluent to be thrown out of the pursuit, either by the enmity it might raise or the expense it might demand" (455).

Lord Westhaven becomes the surrogate father Emmeline never had standing in the place of the missing phallic signifier; he becomes the stick, the "protector" she needs if she is to reclaim her rightful inheritance and the Castle of Mowbray. When she marries Westhaven's brother Godolphin, she closes the new and purged family circle around her. She and Godolphin move off the Isle of Wight and to Emmeline's remodeled family castle, where they live in blissful harmony with Mrs. Stafford and her children (sans husband) and Lady Adelina, her son, and the chastened Fitz-Edward.

Much was made at the time of its publication of the fact that Smith failed to punish Adelina and Fitz-Edward for their steamy adulterous affair (the one that Wollstonecraft condemned for "debauching the mind"). Living well appears to be the best revenge these characters are allowed, while the evil Crofts and the corrupt Montrevilles are punished by having to witness their children's blasted futures. Smith dealt finally in the coin of her sentimental realm, tears. Adelina and Fitz-Edward both shed their fair share of tears and are rewarded with a happy marriage—finally—to each other. Tears, the external indication of purified and purged emotion, appear to wash away all sins, including the most fearsome, adultery.

But tears actually stand as the reification of the new civilizing process that Elias has charted during the period. Tears signify one's membership in a new class of benevolent and tender-hearted bourgeoisie. Condemning a corrupt aristocracy was just one aspect of the larger social and cultural enterprise engaged in by women writers such as Smith. Violent outbursts of destructive emotion—dueling, adultery, gossip, and scandal mongering—were all characteristics of a flawed social and class system that no longer served the needs of a growing industrial economy. This crude and highly gendered social system coded dueling as masculinity run amok and gossip and adultery (verbal and sexual excess) as flamboyant femininity run rampant. In eradicating both extremes of behavior, the sentimental writer participated in her culture's attempts to write into existence a new gendered ideal: the womanly man and the manly woman. Godolphin cries and restrains himself as effectively as Emmeline cries and aggressively pursues the truth about her inheritance. He waits passively for her; she adventures until she is worthy enough to be his wife, because she has first been declared an heiress.

III

In this early female gothic work, the heroine sets the pattern that will be followed in the works of Radcliffe, satirized in Austen, hyperbolized in Dacre and Shelley, and finally canonized in the Brontës. The gothic feminist gains her property and bests the corrupt patriarchy, not alone but in allegiance with her accomplice: the feminized gothic hero and his patriarchal power base. *Emmeline* appears to present the "patriarchy" not as a monolithic power but instead as a contested space, with those contestants being first a corrupt aristocracy and the old, kin-based order it implies and second the rising bourgeoisie characterized by its commitment to exogamous marriages. Godolphin and his brother allow Emmeline to defeat her uncle, just as Rochester and a dead uncle allow Jane Eyre to have an estate and a properly chastised husband, "feminized" by his maiming and partial blinding. The wounds inflicted on the gothic hero are physical; the wounds inflicted on the gothic heroine are invariably emotional and psychological. But make no mistake: no one escapes unscathed in the gothic universe. To civilize a class and make a new social and cultural order requires ritual maiming, wounding, and testing. The construction of a "civilized" class of bourgeoisie required nothing less than the drastic purging and pruning of excessively gender-coded behaviors, characteristics, and emotions.

As we have seen in this text, dueling and physical violence are defined as extreme masculine behaviors, while the men who engage in such activities are eradicated by the end of the novel. And the appropriately masculine figure who emerges here as culture hero is a version of what I would call the sentimentally feminized man: Godolphin. But it is in the territory of the feminine that the real cultural work of this text occurs. *Emmeline* constructs a newly "feminine feminine" woman (in Irigaray's sense), a woman who has abjected out of her all "masculine feminine" tendencies, all excessively gender-coded behaviors like adultery, gossip, and diffuse libidinal energy. It would appear that the female gothic novel actually presents another version of the impulse that Kristeva has identified as operating primarily in male texts: intense abjection, a compulsive casting out of all those qualities that the social system defines as unclean. Kristeva defines the abject as that which "disturbs identity, system, order": "'subject' and 'object' push each other away, confront each other, collapse, and start again—inescapable, contaminated, condemned, at the boundary of what is assimilable, thinkable abject."[12] And the "boundary" that haunts the gothic is, I would claim, the amorphous construction of appropriately gendered behaviors. When a woman author holds female characters up to fictional scrutiny and then sub-

---

12. Julia Kristeva, *Powers of Horror: An Essay on Abjection*, trans. Léon S. Roudiez (New York: Columbia Universitiy Press, 1982), 4, 18.

jects them to literal and metaphorical beatings, she does so because she is operating out of a potent cultural force field, a coded system by which women warned other women how to behave and survive, how to masquerade as "feminine feminine" women in a man's world.

Irigaray builds on this notion when she defines masquerade as a form of male mimicry, a hysterical renunciation of authentic female desire because the woman can only know man's desire, not her own. That is, she can only become real in her own eyes by objectifying and positioning herself as an object of the obsessive male *gaze*. For Irigaray:

> Masquerade has to be understood as what women do in order to recuperate some element of desire, to participate in man's desire, but at the price of renouncing their own. In the masquerade, they submit to the dominant economy of desire in an attempt to remain 'on the market' in spite of everything. But they are there as objects for sexual enjoyment, as those who enjoy. What do I mean by masquerade? In particular ... 'femininity' ... a woman has to become a normal woman, that is, has to enter into the *masquerade of femininity* ... [has to enter] into a system of values that is not hers, and in which she can "appear" and circulate only when enveloped in the needs/desires/fantasies of others, namely, men.[13]

Throughout the female gothic novel, woman paradoxically positions herself as the image of femininity in order to conceal that she has masculinized her subjectivity in a desperate bid to attract and hold the authenticating male gaze. The female gothic presents woman as spectacle rather than spectator precisely because the woman as author and reader has come to believe that she has no legitimate and independent existence in her own eyes; for the female gothic author and reader, woman's only reality can be found within the male signifying system she recognizes as the gothic, and in which she participates as both object and costume.

In the elaborately coded textual universe of the female gothic, professional femininity became very much a masquerade, and I use the term with

---

13. Luce Irigaray, *This Sex Which Is Not One*, 133–34. For a discussion of Irigaray's theories in relation to film, see Mary Ann Doane, "Film and Masquerade: Theorising the Female Spectator," *Screen* 23 (1982). 74–87: "For Rivière, as well as for Lacan and Irigaray who take up the concept within their work, masquerade specifies a norm of femininity—not a way out, a 'destabilization' of the image, as I argued.... But it is a curious norm, which indicates through its very contradictions the difficulty of *any* concept of femininity in a patriarchal society" (42–43). See also her "Masquerade Reconsidered: Further Thoughts on the Female Spectator," *Discourse* 11 (1988–89), 42–54.

not simply Irigaray's meaning in mind but also with Joan Rivière's seminal essay in view. For Rivière, "the mask of womanliness" and "authentic womanliness" are identical because femininity itself is an elaborate construction, a costume, a form of cover that shielded one from the blast furnace of the patriarchy. For Rivière, women who "wish for masculinity may put on a mask of womanliness to avert anxiety and the retribution feared from men." As Rivière observes, "Womanliness therefore could be assumed and worn as a mask, both to hide the possession of masculinity and to avert the reprisals expected if she was found to possess it—much as a thief will turn out his pockets and ask to be searched to prove that he has not the stolen goods. The reader may now ask how I define womanliness or where I draw the line between genuine womanliness and the 'masquerade.' My suggestion is not, however, that there is any such difference; whether radical or superficial, they are the same thing."[14] Rivière's thesis about femininity as an elaborately constructed and gendered masquerade has led to two alternate readings of the phenomenon: on the one hand the masquerade is seen as a "submission to dominant social codes," while on the other hand it has been read as a disruptive, subversive "resistance to patriarchal norms."[15] We are approaching once again the terrain of reading the conflicted female gothic text: is the genre socially subversive or does it actually encourage women to assume subject positions of acquiescence and passivity? As I will argue throughout, the female gothic, like masquerade as a guise of femininity, does both, and that bifurcated posture, ironically, has resulted in the very real basis of its continuing cultural power.

In an analogous manner I would contend that the British middle class built itself on the shorn backs of the aristocracy, taking wealth and property where they could and justifying the rout by exposing the emotional and spiritual inadequacies of the class they were replacing. It is no fluke that Emmeline is an aristocrat through her weak father and a member of the middle class through her beautiful mother. She is the embodiment of a society in transition, and thus unable to understand the rapid social and

---

14. Joan Rivière, "Womanliness as a Masquerade" (1929), reprinted in *Formations of Fantasy*, 35, 38.

15. Theories of femininity as masquerade, along with its association with gendered spectacles, spectatorship, exhibitionism, self-display, voyeurism, and woman as the object of an obsessive male *gaze*, have been crucial in redefining cinema theory as well as eighteenth-century literature. A useful overview of the issues here can be found in Catherine Craft-Fairchild, *Masquerade and Gender: Disguise and Female Identity in Eighteenth-Century Fictions by Women* (University Park: Penn State Press, 1993); and Terry Castle, *Masquerade and Civilization: The Carnivalesque in Eighteenth-Century English Culture and Fiction* (Stanford: Stanford University Press, 1986).

cultural changes occurring all around her. Her trip to France, a France on the verge of a violent revolution and political upheaval, suggests the political and social nature of her struggle to define herself. Just as the last residues of a strong feudal aristocracy were evaporating in France, so did Britain feel itself poised on the verge of cataclysmic transformation. The role and identity of women in this new social and political order were vague and amorphous at best. The fight to be a gothic heroine, to seize power and money and property in one's own right against the corrupt forces of an old regime, this was the central concern of the gothic feminist. To be a heroine in one's own right, however, led quickly to the realization that women finally could not act alone. They needed male allies; they needed a protection system behind them; they needed feminized husbands. But finding such a husband, a man who could be controlled, who could be trusted and safe, that was the challenge.

TWO

~

Gendering
Victimization

Radcliffe's Early Gothics

By the by, about Women,
it has bothered me often—why do women never
want to write poetry about Man as a sex—
why is Woman a dream and a terror to man and
not the other way around? Is it mere convention and
propriety, or something deeper?

—JANE HARRISON

I

In May 1794, the most popular drama of the season, playing to packed
houses at Covent Garden, was Henry Siddons's *Sicilian Romance; or The
Apparition of the Cliff,* loosely based on the second novel published by Ann
Radcliffe four years earlier. One of the more interesting changes in the play
concerns the villain of the Siddons piece, who keeps his inconvenient wife
chained to solid stone in a rocky cave in the forest, a place he visits only
when he needs to feed her and then blame her for inflicting wounds of guilt
on his heart. And although the gothic villain would later metamorphose
into the Byronic hero, consumed by unspeakable guilt over illicit sins, the
villain of the Siddons play is a bit more prosaic. He simply desires to marry
a younger and more beautiful woman, one who will further improve his
social and political status, because his first wife, the mother of his children,
has become redundant. The young woman he desires, whom we would

recognize as a future trophy wife, is pursued from castle to convent to cavern, aided by the hero, the villain's son-turned-outlaw.[1] As the above synopsis makes obvious, female gothic novels like Radcliffe's *Sicilian Romance* provided the subject matter, techniques, and melodramatic formulae, first on the stage in England, then in French theaters, and later in the Hollywood "women in jeopardy" films like *Silence of the Lambs*, that have continued to promulgate the primal gothic tradition of good or "professional femininity"—a carefully crafted masquerade of passivity, victimization, and docility—triumphing over evil or "masculinity"—phallic and aggressive violence.

Before we can begin close examinations of Radcliffe's early gothic novels—*A Sicilian Romance* and *The Romance of the Forest*—it is necessary to sketch out the formulae that came to dominate the female gothic tradition during the 1790s. In examining Radcliffe's early gothic novels, we can discern a number of conventional repetitions that deserve closer scrutiny than they have previously received. The first and most peculiar concern in these early female gothics is the anxiety that a young, nubile woman faces when confronted with the central novelistic dilemma: whether to marry an odious man of her father's choice or be forced into a convent. The Roman Catholic Church and its network of abbeys, convents, and secret tribunals (captured in its most extreme manifestation in *The Italian* as the Inquisition) runs as a sort of leitmotif throughout the gothic novel, reifying British and Enlightenment dread of medievalism, superstition, and uninformed prejudice.[2]

---

1. See Bertrand Evans, *Gothic Drama from Walpole to Shelley* (Berkeley: University of California Press, 1947), 90–115, for a discussion of Ann Radcliffe and her relationship to gothic drama. Evans's book also contains a helpful chapter entitled "Gothic Drama and Melodrama," 162–76, which discusses William Dimond's *Foundling of the Forest* (1809) and Samuel Arnold's *Woodman's Hut* (1814), both of which are indebted to Radcliffe's *Romance of the Forest*. Michael Booth's observation on melodrama is relevant here: "Essentially, melodrama is a dream world inhabited by dream people and dream justice, offering audiences the fulfillment and satisfaction found only in dreams." See his *English Melodrama* (London: Herbert Jenkins, 1965), 14. More recently, Jeffrey Cox has surveyed the subject in the introduction to his edited collection, *Seven Gothic Dramas, 1789–1825* (Athens: Ohio University Press, 1992). He has analogously observed that gothic drama demanded only two positions from women: "either terrorized and mad or stoic and indomitable, but they were always passive" (53).

2. The motif of secret societies and tribunals in gothic fiction is analyzed by Mark Madoff, "The Secret Chief of Conspiracies," *ESC* 6 (1980), 409–20. Madoff sees the source for the motif in Edmund Burke: "the more powerful, complicated, obscure, secretive, and extensive an artificial structure—whether an imaginary prison or a fictional conspiracy—the more admirably sublime it was" (416). On the same theme, see Pamela Kaufman, "Burke, Freud, and the Gothic," *SBHT* 13 (1972), 2178–92. Anti-Catholic sensibilities are blatant in gothic fiction, and have been discussed by S. Mary Muriel Tarr in her *Catholicism in Gothic Fiction: A Study of the Nature and Function of Catholic Materials in*

Poised against the church as an option for women is forced, dynastic, and loveless marriage, with such a choice effectively positioning women in the virgin/whore dichotomy as a lived reality. Radcliffe and her family were themselves deeply conservative—socially and politically—as well as staunchly Protestant. The Catholic Church, which is featured prominently in each one of her major novels, holds a certain ambivalent allure for Radcliffe, largely because of what we can detect as an attraction to the notion of all-female communities that were possible for women through the church. Women are never happier in Radcliffe's works than when they are living in small groups together and apart from men. A tremendous fear of male sexuality obviously motivates a good deal of the action in these novels. The daggers and swords, frequently "rust-stained," that are swashbuckled and flung around in these novels speak in not very subtle terms about male tools of all sorts. The first characteristic of the female gothic novel is that it is based on the premise that men are intrinsically and inherently violent and aggressive, and as such, to be feared by women.

The second characteristic of the Radcliffean gothic heroine concerns her strangely convoluted relationship with her parents. Either she is an orphan or thinks she is (but is not), or she finds out her father has been murdered by one of her odious suitors or her mother has been imprisoned by her father. Tremendous anxiety bordering on the pathological characterizes the heroine's attitude toward her parents. Traditionally we have read this anxiety as a manifestation of oedipal dynamics, and surely there is some basis for concluding that the inability to form realistic conceptions of the parents is caused by some form of what Freud has labeled "the family romance." More recently, however, we have followed Foucault in reading this peculiar fixation in social and historical terms—as class anxiety about exogamous marriage outside the basically incestuous familial clan. But before we can understand the compulsions that drive the gothic heroine, that propel her from one near disaster to another, we need to realize that she was devised as a cultural construct composed of many disparate discourse systems. An amalgam of melodramatic proportions, she spoke to religious, sexual, social, and political anxieties that assailed middle-class British women in large numbers for the first time. Forced into the newly constructed and codified bourgeois home and domicile, she had no choice but to participate in her

Gothic Fiction in England (1762–1820) (Washington: Catholic University of America Press, 1946); Alok Bhalla, *The Cartographers of Hell: Essays on the Gothic Novel and the Social History of England* (New Delhi: Sterling, 1991); and Kate Ellis, "Ann Radcliffe and the Perils of Catholicism," *WW* 1 (1994), 161–69.

culture's creation of the bourgeois ideology, and at the center of that ideology was the identity and role of woman as wife and mother.[3]

In the female gothic version of the bourgeois ideology, a woman becomes
a wife and mother only after a terrific struggle; she succumbs only after we
have witnessed an intensely toxic and protracted erotic agon. And the only
man deserving of such a wife is a man who has been as ritualistically
wounded as she has been psychically wounded. In other words, both men
and women are victims of both real beatings and beating fantasies in
Radcliffe's novels. The Radcliffean gothic heroine is never actually attacked,
beaten, by any of the many daggers and swords that fill the pages of Radcliffe's
novels. She is merely continually threatened with attack and thereby terrified. But each and every hero in Radcliffe's novels is wounded seriously in the
course of the struggle to gain the beloved, usually by the beloved's father or
father substitute. No one gives or gives in easily in these works.

We can identify the Radcliffean heroine as primarily characterized by her
masquerade of playing the role of the overly feminine gothic victim, a veritable professional girl-woman, a construction that was the creation of the
fertile but bored brain of Ann Radcliffe, bourgeois wife of a man who stayed
late at the office almost every evening. He was entertained, we are told, by
his wife's reading of her day's work to him—amusing little tales of corpses,
poison, and adultery—when he returned home. We also have it on no other
authority than his that the marriage was an extremely happy one.[4] Be that
as it may, we recognize the Radcliffean gothic heroine (hyperbolically feminine, posed in all manner of sexually threatening escapades) as a creature
of her culture composed of two parts Richardsonian sentimentality (with
about equal measures of Clarissa and Pamela thrown in), one part popular
melodramatic heroine (virtue under siege), and one part Enlightenment
rationality (reason triumphing over superstition). This particular brand of
the gothic heroine did not, however, spring full blown from Ann Radcliffe's

---

3. For a provocative reading of the social context of bourgeois ideology and the development of
the female gothic, see Kate Ellis, *The Contested Castle*, as well as the earlier analysis of the subject by
Wylie Sypher, "Social Ambiguity in a Gothic Novel," *PR* 12 (1945), 50–60. For more recent treatments,
see the theoretically informed discussion by Stephen Bernstein, "Form and Ideology in the Gothic
Novel," *EL* 18 (1991), 151–65; and E. J. Clery, "Women, Luxury, and the Sublime," and "The Supernatural
Explained," in *The Rise of Supernatural Fiction, 1762–1800*, 95–114.

4. The early biographies of Radcliffe are usefully summarized in E. B. Murray's *Ann Radcliffe* (New
York: Twayne, 1972). The most important recent study of her life and career is in Robert Miles's *Ann
Radcliffe: The Great Enchantress* (Manchester: Manchester University Press, 1995). Theoretically
informed and provocatively argued throughout, Miles presents valuable discussions of all of Radcliffe's
novels, as well as descriptions of her literary, historical, and political milieus.

head; instead her heroine evolved from Julia (*A Sicilian Romance,* 1790) to Adeline (*The Romance of the Forest,* 1791) to Emily (*Mysteries of Udolpho,* 1794), and finally to Ellena (*The Italian,* 1797). But as several critics have noted, these women are all the same woman; only their dress style slightly distinguishes one from another. So we are forced to ask ourselves, does the meaning of the female gothic reside in the character and destiny of the heroine or her trials? I think not. The female characters in female gothic novels appear to be as mechanical as the setting, the conflict, and the villains. In order to discover the ideological impetus of these texts we have to look for meaning in the entire network of cultural discourses that swirl around the heroine, a sort of black hole of meaning herself, oblivious almost all the time of the social, political, religious, and economic issues pulsating in all directions around her.

The female gothic novel as a genre became highly refined in the works of Radcliffe when one bored and neglected housewife decided to translate her personal and social anxieties into words that could be read by other presumably bored housewives, also anxious about the general political and social unrest plaguing England at the end of the eighteenth century. We know that Radcliffe had, from the few biographical accounts we possess, a relatively privileged childhood and formal education. She is said to have been a student at Sophia Lee's establishment for young ladies at Bath; Lee, of course, was a sentimental novelist, best known as author of *The Recess* (1785), a novel about the sad fates of the two apocryphal daughters of Mary, queen of Scots, raised in a hidden cave and brought into the light of day only for dynastic reasons. The Scottish context suggests the social marginality that has come to characterize the female gothic throughout its history. But the other interesting aspect of *The Recess* is the motif of two daughters, both forced to marry against their will for reasons of political gain by a corrupt aristocratic patriarchy. The theme of social marginality coupled with corrupt or absent parents exerting unjust power over a powerless daughter struck a deeply resonant chord in the general female reading public.[5] We can only conclude that the origins of the ideology spoke to some repressed desire, fear, or anger among middle-class women.

---

5. Discussions of Sophia Lee's *Recess* can be found in Ellis, *The Contested Castle* (68–75); J. M. S. Tompkins, *The Popular Novel in England, 1770–1800* (Lincoln: University of Nebraska Press, 1961); and James R. Foster, *History of the Pre-Romantic Novel in England* (New York: MLA, 1949). For background information on the Lee sisters, see also Harrison Steeves, *Before Jane Austen: The Shaping of the English Novel in the Eighteenth Century* (New York: Holt, Rinehart, and Winston, 1965).

If the heroines of female gothic novels seem almost to seek out incestuous situations, it is less because of any attraction to their fathers or uncles or brothers than because of an infantile desire to remain within the paternal and protective domicile of childhood. The known and familiar is tremendously attractive to the female gothic heroine, the source for her nostalgia about home and hearth. The known and familiar is also a crucial component of the bourgeois ideology. The known and familiar—the lure of what I would recognize as toxic nostalgia—can also be recognized as the status quo, the world as the middle class knew it before the Industrial Revolution, before the threat of the French Revolution, before the economic and political realities of the 1790s totally transformed the England the bourgeoisie wanted to preserve—a cozy rural world that had ceased to exist more than a hundred years earlier. In contrast, the objects of fear in the female gothic novel are amorphously associated with the foreign, the continental, the Catholic (with its ties to a primitive past England would have liked to forget). The unknown in the female gothic novel is always fearful, and usually figured as a castle in the furthest point of southern Italy or even Germany.

But in addition to the fictional works of Charlotte Smith, the stock female gothic situation began to be delineated in such rudimentary texts as *The Recess*, Clara Reeve's *Old English Baron* (1777), and Anne Fuller's *The Convent; or The History of Sophia Nelson* (1786). All of these works reveal much the same impulse and originating fantasy: the notion that young women are the innocent prey of their parents' evil designs on them. This rather simple and straightforward statement of theme actually conceals a much larger allegorical and hermeneutical struggle, played out in virtually melodramatic form as the Manichaean struggle between the forces of good and those of an active, virulent evil. The ideological fantasy goes something like this: history, imaged as the power of an aristocratic past, will cannibalistically consume the present and future, represented by the potential fertility of young women, unless these women and their allies ("castrated," wounded men) rise up and create a new bourgeois world free from the corrupt trappings of the past—the aristocracy and its "spiritual" arm, the Catholic Church. The new bourgeois class, plagued by the guilt they feel for destroying the aristocracy, carries the stigma—the mark—of its parricide of the aristocracy in the ritual wounds it ultimately inflicts on itself.[6]

---

6. Ritual genital woundings are analyzed by Bruno Bettelheim in his *Symbolic Wounds: Puberty Rites and the Envious Male* (New York: Collier, 1962). Bettleheim sees these real and symbolic wounds (circumcision and male initiation ceremonies) as the means by which "pre-literate man masters fear by trying to make woman's power his own." On a more prosaic level, it should be noted that during

These compulsions appear to motivate the parricide motif, actually a reification of the beating fantasies we see throughout Radcliffe. But what of the incest that creeps through these novels like a pernicious nightmare? If not actually sexually pursued by their fathers or uncles or stepuncles, or cousins, gothic heroines are frequently robbed of their rightful inheritances by the evil machinations of the same cast of characters. And the stepmothers who populate female gothic novels are frequently as evil, if not more so, than the male characters. Parents in the female gothic universe are fairy-tale parents, allegorically doubled, who are either ravening, gluttonous, sexual depraved, adulterous, incestuous—altogether not the sort of people virtuous heroines even wish to know, let alone be related to by blood—or ideally good and unfortunately dead. The fear that paradoxically underlies this fantasy speaks to a deep-seated fear of separation and boundaries. That is to say, one way to understand the female gothic is to understand projection and introjection. The genre expresses not what it claims to assert but the exact opposite. Parents are villains because they are so fearfully and frighteningly loved and needed by these heroines. The only way a gothic heroine can separate from hearth and home, leave mommy and daddy behind and marry someone else, someone outside the clan, is to imagine that mommy and daddy have done something so evil that they absolutely deserve to be deserted, in fact actually must be destroyed. In other words, incest lies at the heart of the female gothic project. The heroine does not want to leave her father and marry another, a usurper in her own eyes. Therefore, she fancies that her father has attempted to rape her *(The Romance of the Forest)* or her father is an adulterer *(Mysteries of Udolpho)* or her father has tried to kill her *(The Italian)*. Only if she can convince herself that she exists in such a super-charged moral universe, with the stakes at a fever pitch, can she agree to separate from the paternal abode and form a new family of her own. Needless to say, tremendous anxiety about the future is reflected in this scenario. These fin de siècle anxieties express not only personal and psychological fears but social and economic anxieties about the nature and survival of bourgeois culture as it approached the next century.

All of this brings us to what Barthes has labeled the phenomenon of "neither-norism," which he defines as a consistent attempt by the bourgeoisie to

---

the eighteenth century it was commonly admitted that the widespread practice of beating in public schools was sexual in nature, a realization that was repressed during the Victorian era. See Roy Porter, "Mixed Feelings: The Enlightenment and Sexuality in Eighteenth-Century Britain," in *Sexuality in Eighteenth-Century Britain*, ed. Paul-Gabriel Bouce (Manchester: Manchester University Press, 1982), 12; and I. Gibson, *The English Vice: Beating, Sex, and Shame in Victorian England and After* (London: Duckworth, 1978).

distinguish itself from both the aristocracy above it and the lower class below it. The bourgeoisie essentially defined itself by declaring what it was not; it was neither aristocratic nor plebeian. In an analogous but more literary observation, Neil Hertz has noted the presence throughout texts written during this period of what he calls "double surrogation." This phenomenon is practiced when an author's investments in her characters are split between "good" and "bad" versions, while the valued imaginative activity of the "good" surrogate is purchased by the exiling of the "bad."[7] The doubled parental figures who recur throughout Radcliffe's works suggest a compulsion to erase the "bad" and reify the "good," while the Sister Agnes/Signora Laurentini split in one woman suggests a similar need to eradicate the virgin/whore dichotomy operating on the margins of this discourse system.

Parricide, matricide, incest, and fantasies of multiple rape obsess the female gothic heroine, but we need always to keep in mind that she is not simply the victim of these crimes but oftentimes the displaced perpetrator of them. At times *The Mysteries of Udolpho* reads as barely disguised pornography, which the Marquis de Sade would later make explicit in his own tedious attempts to unmask the sexual hypocrisy of the gothic heroine in *Justine* and *Juliette*. It would appear that the female gothic genre has been largely misunderstood because critics have been all too willing to take the texts in a straightforward manner. For the most part, taking them straight has allowed critics simply to dismiss them or ridicule their absurdities or pretensions. But reading them as paradoxically both subversive and accommodating documents allows us to see the tremendous rage and fear that existed at the heart of middle-class women, hemmed in as they were (and are) by a tremendous reliance on their families for their survival. One fears losing what one loves intensely, and so the ambivalence that characterizes much of women's literature begins with this simple equation. To kill and then displace the father and mother out of love became the defining work of the female gothic heroine.[8] Radcliffe's four major gothic heroines all define their identities, such as they are, in opposition to their parents. Siblings, if they exist (in *A Sicilian Romance,* for instance), are allies against the parents, and if siblings drop out of the later novels, it is because their roles have been assumed by the "lovers," who play in these works a sibling-

---

7. Roland Barthes, "Neither-Norism" in *Mythologies*, trans. Annette Lavers (New York: Hill, 1972), 81–83; and Neil Hertz, *The End of the Line* (New York: Columbia University Press, 1986), 224.

8. The gothic has been subjected to several sessions on the psychoanalytical couch, most of which are usefully summarized in David Punter's *The Romantic Unconscious*. For an orthodox Freudian reading of the Radcliffe oeuvre, see Leona F. Sherman, *Ann Radcliffe and the Gothic Romance: A Psychoanalytic Approach* (New York: Arno, 1980).

like role in relationship to the heroines. The generational struggle in these novels is paramount, with a life and death agon ensuing as to who will seize the accoutrements of power—money and property—that ensure the survival of the class.

II

Ann Radcliffe married in 1787 and spent her childless marriage producing books about the struggles and anxieties young women encounter as they seek to find suitable spouses. We know little to nothing about her marriage, but one of the very few biographical facts we have about her is that she was inconsolable about the deaths of her parents. No letters in her own hand survive. In many ways such a woman—faceless and without individuality—was perfectly situated to be one of the founders of the female gothic novelistic tradition. She spoke not about herself, at least we are unable to locate any biographical resonances in her works, but about bourgeois women as a class. We can draw, fairly or unfairly, our initial conclusions about this group of women from her four major gothic novels.

The heroine of *A Sicilian Romance,* Julia de Mazzini, has been raised in a castle in Sicily toward the end of the sixteenth century. It is appropriate that this woman should be a fin de siècle heroine, as she, like all Radcliffe's heroines, is self-dramatizing, extreme, hyperbolic, and given to excesses of emotion and imagination befitting her situation. But even Julia could not imagine the horror that lives at the heart of the southern most edge of her family's property. There, in a deserted and crumbling wing of the estate, her supposedly dead mother lives, held as a prisoner by her father who was motivated to dispose of his first wife because he wanted to marry a younger woman, the evil Maria de Vellorno. Julia's innocence and naïveté are such that much of the novel is taken up with her poking around the south wing trying to figure out what the mysterious light and strange sounds at night signify. And there is the usual bizarre complication with the heroine's proposed marriage, only this time the conflict occurs because the evil stepmother herself lusts after the suitor, the duke de Luovo. In this early work Radcliffe relies on the conventions of the sentimental novel tradition, trying in a similar manner to delineate and contrast the nature of "true love" of Julia and Hippolytus—disinterestedness, *"virtu,"* and mutual esteem—to that of the "false love" of the marquis and second marchioness—violent and self-destructive lust and adultery.

Briefly, the plot is straightforward melodrama: virtuous mother and daughters are persecuted by evil father, who is under the influence of the even more evil seductress. Good triumphs just as surely as evil destroys itself. Or rather than label the plot a melodrama, we might say that the fairy-tale elements of this story dominate to the extent that the work reads as moral allegory. The heroine represents an early embodiment of the bourgeois ideology as it was being constructed in the female gothic novel. She is "good," that is, professionally feminine and victimized: self-effacing, obedient, loving, passive, silent, and long-suffering; in other words, she is a younger version of her mother, and by the end of the text she sees all too clearly how such behavior has been rewarded. The evil stepmother, motivated by jealousy toward her two beautiful stepdaughters, virtually imprisons them in the castle, fearful that their beauty will draw suitors away from her. She is, like the other evil second wives in *The Mysteries of Udolpho,* an adulteress: "She allowed herself a free indulgence in the most licentious pleasures, yet conducted herself with an art so exquisite as to elude discovery, and even suspicion. In her amours she was equally as inconstant as ardent" (10). Sexual passion in women can usually be found only among the aristocracy or the lower class, and always it is a characteristic that causes punishment. Maria is the first of many evil or openly sexual women we might identify as "gothic antiheroines." Always destroyed by the conclusion of the novel, these women represent the antithesis of the feminine bourgeois ideology. Their extreme libidinous emotions, adulterous passions and lusts, and intense desire for power and status doom them to a life of desperate and thwarted designs. "Wise passiveness," reasonableness, tamed emotions, and rational and disinterested love instead characterize the true gothic heroine, who proves her worth by controlling and professionally commodifying her emotions in even the most harrowing of situations.

Julia as an early gothic heroine also possesses a trait that was to become even more dominant throughout the later novels. She plays the lute and sings sweetly her favorite airs all day. This capacity for *virtu*—the ability to be touched by music and art—characterizes all of the good, sentimental characters in the gothic universe. Evil characters do not, indeed they cannot, possess the taste to appreciate music or art; their sensibilities are as stunted as their moral consciences.[9] What Elias has called "the civilizing

---

9. The restrictive and conservative code of conduct expected of gothic heroines is helpfully discussed in Nelson C. Smith, "Sense, Sensibility, and Ann Radcliffe," *SEL* 13 (1973), 577–90; David Durant, "Ann Radcliffe and the Conservative Gothic," *SEL* 22 (1982), 519–30; and Barbara Benedict, "Pictures of Conformity: Sentiment and Structure in Ann Radcliffe's Style," *PQ* 18 (1989), 519–31. The bourgeois

process" is again at work here, for the bourgeoisie distinguish themselves from the aristocracy precisely in this ability to produce and emotionally respond to music and art, rather than merely the capacity to view or consume the arts (as patrons, for instance). As the arts spread through this culture they humanize or "civilize" the larger public in ways that a system of elitist aristocratic patronage never made possible. The gothic feminist becomes a heroine because music or art, as well as nature and its reification in the "sublime," lead her to her rightful identity or destiny. By being able to read art like a text, by following the strains of music or identifying the face in the portrait, Julia—like the later Emily St. Aubert—is led to solve the mystery of her own puzzling parentage and her own identity.

In addition to her mastery of the lute, we know that Julia is a gothic heroine because she is the one who stumbles on the appropriate clues that enable her to solve her familial mystery. Gothic heroines are forever rummaging through chests of papers, just happening to stumble on some secret, long-lost document that explains a hidden and unsolved crime. So it happens that one day Julia, stumbling on "some papers in the small drawers of a cabinet that stood in her apartment," "found a picture which fixed all her attention. It was a miniature of a lady, whose countenance was touched with sorrow, and expressed an air of dignified resignation" (27).

Finding the portrait of the dead mother is always a talismanic moment in Radcliffe's novels. One recalls the theories of the anthropologists Arnold van Gennep or Victor Turner, who both identify the stages that occur in rites of passage as separation, threshold, and aggregation.[10] Gothic heroines are always already separated from their parents or inheritances fairly early in each book so that most of the texts concern their various threshold or liminal experiences, or strange encounters under "arched" doorways that

---

ideology is also treated by John Garrett, *Gothic Strains and Bourgeois Sentiments in the Novels of Mrs. Ann Radcliffe and Her Imitators* (New York: Arno, 1980). All quotations from *A Sicilian Romance* are from the reprint of the 1821 edition, edited by Alison Milbank (Oxford: Oxford University Press, 1993), with page numbers identified in parentheses in the text. Milbank's valuable introduction to this edition reads the novel as concerned "with the power of the masculine order, sexual difference, and the interrelation of the aesthetic and the political" (ix).

10. For an anthropological discussion of the meaning of threshold motifs, see Arnold van Gennep, *The Rites of Passage*, trans. Monika Vizedom and Gabrielle L. Caffee (Chicago: University of Chicago Press, 1960); Victor Turner, "Betwixt and Between: The Liminal Period in *Rites de Passage*," in *The Forest of Symbols: Aspects of Ndemnbu Ritual* (Ithaca: Cornell University Press, 1967), 93–111; and "Liminal to Liminoid, in Play, Flow, Ritual: An Essay in Comparative Symbology" in *From Ritual to Theatre: The Human Seriousness of Play* (New York: Performing Arts Journal Pub., 1982), 20–60. And for a discussion of the motif of "the haunted portrait" in the gothic genre, see Theodore Ziolkowski, *Disenchanted Images: A Literary Iconology* (Princeton: Princeton University Press, 1977).

dominate in virtually all of the texts, particularly *The Italian*. But crucial to any threshold experience is what Turner calls "the communication of the *sacra*," or the use of sacred symbols such as mirrors, portraits, masks, or veils to send secret or hidden messages about identity and purpose to the hero(ine). The arcane knowledge or gnosis that the heroine receives in the gothic universe typically concerns her mother's fate, which we may conclude represents a muted version of the heroine's sense of her own future. When Julia sees the portrait, we are given our first clue that the mother is not dead and that it will be the heroine's task to unearth and restore her to the land of the living: "The mournful sweetness of [the portrait's] eyes, raised towards Heaven with a look of supplication, and the melancholy languor that shaded her features, so deeply affected Julia, that her eyes were filled with involuntary tears. She sighed and wept, still gazing on the picture, which seemed to engage her by a kind of fascination. She almost fancied that the portrait breathed, and that the eyes were fixed on her's with a look of penetrating softness" (27–28). At this moment Julia does not know she is looking at her mother's portrait (she discovers that later), but there is an almost palpable exchange of energy between the portrait and the viewer. Julia is able to commune with and mimic exactly the emotions of the woman in the portrait; the daughter actually embodies the very core of the melodramatic sensibility and as such is the embodied essence of the rite of passage itself. The gnosis was typically delivered through sacred ritual ceremonies such as the Eleusinian Mysteries of the Great Mother and involved the recognition of the "Other" as the sacred force of life and the contrasting and immortal complementary force of opposition in the life cycle. Excavating the buried mother and returning her to the surface of the earth reenacts just such a mythic paradigm (one recalls the Greek myth of Demeter and Persephone, although in the Greek version it is the mother who redeems her daughter from an underworld burial every spring). The female gothic heroine is most decidedly a daughter whose task concerns a rewriting of the mythically heroic: she must redeem her good but missing mother, kill her evil and false father and stepmother, and reinstitute a new world with an appropriately and professionally bourgeois hero-husband. *A Sicilian Romance* is the first version of this tale.

But who exactly is the mysterious mother? The only historical information we obtain about the mother comes from Julia's mother substitute, Madame de Menon, the mother's former best friend and confidante. From Menon we learn that the mother, Louisa de Bernini, had the great misfortune of growing up under Mount Etna, which erupted one day killing both her mother and brother. Unable to marry the man she truly loved, the brother of Madame de Menon, she married instead the man her father forced on her—the infamous Mazzini. We get the rest of her story not from Menon, who thinks Louisa is dead, but from Louisa herself much later in the text. This device of the partial narrative—aborted, fragmented, pieced together by gossip, hearsay, innuendo, and secreted documents—continues throughout all of Radcliffe's works, and indeed throughout the genre as a whole. The difficulty of ever knowing anyone's "true history" stands as the basis for such a device, although we are also reminded that the epistemological writings of John Locke and David Hume were preparing the late eighteenth-century reader for the vagaries of perception that we encounter over and over again in the gothic.

What is most interesting about the mother's early history, however, is the overlooked clue to her misery—she wanted to marry the brother of her childhood best friend. In other words, she wanted to remain as close within the clan as she could. She desired an endogamous marriage and feared marrying someone unknown to her, someone from an even further southern state—Sicily. Louisa's temperament was mild, even, docile. She wanted the same temperament in her husband, the brother figure she knew from childhood. But she was forced out of the clan, into an alien environment, and from that act all of her subsequent miseries derived. We need not look too far to see that this anxiety about exogamous marriage was actually produced by an underlying xenophobia, a fear about boundaries, real or imagined, an apprehension about being invaded. Class anxieties, the sort of class anxieties that Radcliffe and her bourgeois reading audience were experiencing in 1790, are coded and transformed here as anxieties about people from another section of Italy. And the sexual mismatch that Louisa feared with Mazzini did indeed occur. She offered him a sort of northern sexual coolness and three children; he opted for a fiery mistress and a caretaker for the children. One recognizes the origins of Charlotte Brontë's Rochester here.

One can also recognize the origins of Jane Austen's General Tilney in the Marquis de Mazzini, whose only interest is in his son, not because he loves him but because he is his heir and will continue the family name. Mazzini greets his daughters coolly; he is aloof and chilly to all but his evil second wife, of whom he is still passionately fond. It is always a mark of an evil character that he dislikes the good characters. His sensibility, or lack of it, is so stunted that he cannot appreciate good when he is confronted by it; he can only imprison or attempt to destroy it. The villain is always hiding something, has to be hiding something, otherwise he would not act so strangely, so secretively, so guiltily (or so the good characters surmise). When Mazzini tries to explain away the flickering lights and strange sounds emanating from the long-deserted south wing of the estate, he tells his son a series of lies and even conducts an abortive tour of the wing himself. Villains are liars, but in the melodramatic world that is the gothic their lies are always exposed. And villains are always paradoxical and amorphous, as Mazzini is. On the one hand, Mazzini is associated with Louisa's intense class anxieties and the disruption of her aristocratic kinship paradigm, while on the other hand he becomes the father of an oppressed daughter and so is complicit with the corrupt, kinship-based aristocracy. Much like Manfred in Walpole's *Castle of Otranto*, the fissures in his character—as well as his sheer evil—permeate and doom all of his dynastic efforts.

The evil Marquis de Mazzini, who scorns his son for believing anything but reason and the evidence of his senses, is contrasted with Madame de Menon, who represents the moderate middle course that Radcliffe herself espoused. As she speaks to the young women—who now think they must be dealing with ghosts—about the mysterious light and sounds, she observes, "'I will not attempt to persuade you that the existence of such spirits is impossible. Who shall say that any thing is impossible to God? We know that he has made us, who are embodied spirits; he, therefore, can make unembodied spirits'" (36). The Enlightenment sensibility that suffuses these novels centers on this very question, but it is not the tired old query about reason struggling with superstition or fancy. The Enlightenment anxiety in these texts concerns the existence of God and the nature and purpose of human life. Intense anxiety about the existence of an afterlife consumes these characters, although that unease is glossed over in several superficial religious pieties expressed by all the good characters. When a beloved parent dies, the heroine does not accept that death the way a traditional believer would; instead, she seeks to nullify the death and literally bring the dead back to life. All the talk about ghosts merely elides intense fear about the fact that there may be no afterlife at all. This world may be all there is, and that is a prospect that chills gothic heroines to their cores. The desire to find a heaven on earth, a passionless marriage in an enclosed garden, stands as the secularization of Genesis that motivates the female gothic dream. If God does not exist, then fathers and aristocrats and priests have no reason to either.[11]

---

11. The best discussion of the fear of death that looms over Radcliffe's corpus can be found in Terry Castle's "Spectralization of the Other in *The Mysteries of Udolpho*," in *The New Eighteenth Century*, ed. Felicity Nussbaum and Laura Brown (New York: Methuen, 1987), 231–53.

We move next to another related issue—concealed doors, narrow towers, rusty and missing keys, winding hidden stairwells—the standard trappings of any gothic edifice worth its name. We are, in short, inhabiting the corrupted residue that we call history, imagined as if it were a single, gigantic rambling building. The gothic itself—as a period of architectural development—stands as a transitional period between medieval and Renaissance constructions. But the gothic was particularly attractive during the late eighteenth century because it reified a lost world that was somehow not precisely definable. Note that sometimes Radcliffe's heroines are living in 1590, sometimes 1640, sometimes 1740, but all of them are living in a historical world that we would recognize as an elaborately artificial and contrived gothic world. It is almost as if the "gothic" were as nebulous and magical a time and place as Brigadoon, a locus that exists for only one day every century. History is as unreal in this ideology as was Walpole's claptrap estate Strawberry Hill. There is an intense desire in all of these moves to construct history as a fantasy, to pretend that the external world of time and space can be contained and commodified as easily as Walpole added papier-mâché towers to his country barn. The gothic trappings of doors and towers and such reveal to us that the writers and readers of such novels wanted to believe that they could escape from the realities of their present historical circumstances as easily as did the inhabitants of a ruined gothic abbey. A hidden door always exists that will allow the reader to deny the reality of the present and put them instead in an unreal nostalgic past—the "gothic" world where good always triumphs over evil and where right always bests might. The locus of the escape—the gothic castle—becomes the endpoint of the quest. The dream that concludes the gothic is that we can escape into a garden on a gothic estate, shorn of its tyrant and now in the hands of its good, rightful, and magically powerful mistress.[12] What fantasy could be more seductive?

Just one. Radcliffe makes certain that each one of her heroes faces a life-threatening wound before he is ever allowed to be alone with any of the virginal heroines. A hero is not safe or marriageable until he has been made as feminine as possible, and within the gothic corpus that requires a wounding. Furthermore, it is interesting to note how long this emphasis on wounding persists, far beyond the time when it was understood by the heirs of

---

12. Discussions of gothic architecture and its relation to literary conventions can be found in Paul Frankl, *The Gothic: Literary Sources and Interpretations Through Eight Centuries* (Princeton: Princeton University Press, 1960); and Linda Bayer-Berenbaum, *The Gothic Imagination* (London: Associated University Press, 1987).

Radcliffe. For instance, one of the most persistent controversies still plaguing the critical discussions of Charlotte Brontë's *Jane Eyre* concerns the fate
of Rochester, blinded and maimed when he attempts to save his mad wife
Bertha from the fire she has set in his estate. The confusion about this
wound, generally recognized as some sort of symbolic castration, occurs
because Brontë was working in a female gothic tradition that demanded
such a ritualistic wound. But her heavy-handed treatment of the scene
demonstrates what happens to a cultural code that has persisted without
necessarily being understood by its late practitioners. The gothic heroine,
now the proud possessor of a masculine mind, can only be complemented
by the feminized hero, a man who embodies "delicacy and strength" (55), or
so the cultural fantasy dictates.

Just as she bifurcates her presentation of the female characters, Radcliffe
also splits her heroes in this novel, so that we focus on both Ferdinand, the
son and heir of the evil marquis, and Hippolitus, the romantic lead, beloved
of Julia. The sibling as hero will drop out of her gothics after this book, but
the tradition lives on, for instance, in the major Brontë novels—*Wuthering
Heights, Jane Eyre,* and *Villette*—all of which focus on the attraction of the
heroines to sibling figures. The incestuous/narcissistic compulsion at the
core of the female gothic, the persistent attraction to brothers (and one cannot fail to recall the ill-fated Maggie and Tom Tulliver in Eliot's *Mill on the
Floss*), elides the more persistent and even more disastrous desire for the
father. Unfortunately for the gothic heroine, her father is almost always
either evil or dead (only St. Aubert in *Mysteries of Udolpho* was an excellent
father, although his portrait was marred by his tendency to "accidentally"
shoot the hero). Even if St. Aubert liked to shoot his pistols a bit too quickly,
he was no match for the sinister Marquis de Mazzini, who swashbuckled the
sword rather too closely for everyone's comfort. When Hippolitus tries to
save his beloved Julia from her father's evil plan to force her to marry the
Duke de Luovo, he rushes right into the father's omnipresent sword: "'Now,
my love,' said Hippolitus, 'you are safe, and I am happy.' At the same instant
Hippolitus received a sword in his body, and uttering a deep sigh, fell to the
ground. Julia shrieked and fainted; Ferdinand drawing his sword, advanced
towards the assassin, upon whose countenance the light of his lamp then
shone, and discovered to him his father!" (68). Adding insult to injury, the
father has his son and daughter arrested and thrown into the dungeon of
his own castle. One really begins to wonder how many members of his family he can secretly imprison at once—how many he can beat up on at once—
without their bumping into each other eventually. But that, of course, is

exactly what happens. In her continual fleeing, from abbey to convent to ruined corridor, Julia finally manages to stumble upon her long-imprisoned mother. It is no coincidence that the estate of the marquis is connected subterraneously to the abbey of St. Augustin, the corrupt and greedy religious order to which Julia had fled for protection. Religious and political corruption shore each other up throughout the gothic universe. This abbey, built in the twelfth century, stood, we are told, as "a proud monument of monkish superstition and princely magnificence" (116). The implication is clear: monks with their religious prejudices, lack of rationality, and general foolishness provide the trappings and false rationalizations that princes need to justify their greed and abuse of power. When Julia begs the abate for protection, he chastises her for her "heinous crimes" (131): "'You have dared to dispute—nay openly to rebel, against the lawful authority of your father. You have disobeyed the will of him whose prerogative yields only to ours. You have questioned his right upon a point of all others the most decided—the right of a father to dispose of his child in marriage. You have even fled from his protection—and you have dared—insidiously, and meanly have dared, to screen your disobedience beneath this sacred roof'" (131–32). Like other hypocritical clergy, in Lewis's *Monk,* for instance, the good abate was looking for something in all this misfortune for himself. He does refuse to return Julia to her father, not out of concern for her but because he wants to force her to become a nun, live in his convent, and hand over her inheritance to him. In both cases Julia is being forced by an evil father figure into a match with a dead system, either the "prince"—marriage with an odious villain—or the "monk"—marriage to the church, a fate almost worse than death. The promise of fertility becomes sterility in either case. Princes and monks, both are just so much historical residue, the embodiments of an earlier historical moment that the bourgeoisie wants to eradicate so that the world can be made safe for the Protestant, enlightened, and democratic middle class.

The scene in which Julia discovers her mother is one of those great melodramatic moments in gothic fiction, a moment that makes reading the entire text worthwhile. Although the mother goes on to tell her sad tale, it is the moment of discovery that readers remember because it is resonant, almost mythic. After much descent into caverns and then caves, through more trapdoors, bolts, and double locks, Julia finally finds herself in a small room, confronting "the pale and emaciated figure of a woman, seated, with half-closed eyes, in a kind of elbow chair" (174). As Julia approaches, the woman suddenly stands up and screams, "'My daughter!'" and promptly faints. We then enter the realm of pure melodrama as the mother awakes and piteously says, "'Thank heaven!' . . . 'my prayer is granted. I am permitted to embrace one of my children before I die. Tell me what brought you hither. Has the marquis at last relented, and allowed me once more to behold you, or has his death dissolved my wretched bondage?'" (174). The scene suggests that within the gothic universe the mother and father are oppositional powers in the life of a child, and that they cannot both exist as forces in the heroine's life at the same time. Again, if we think about parents and their daughters in the other Radcliffe novels, we realize that the father and mother are present together only once in all four of the works (the brief idyllic interlude that begins *The Mysteries of Udolpho*).

On another level, however, the scene speaks to the gothic child's fantasy that she has the divine power to give birth to her parents. This is a potent moment, the image of a child delivering her mother from the underworld speaks to that child's greatest fear: the loss and abandonment through death of a parent. The fantasy as Radcliffe presents it reverses and denies the fear. In this version the child can repudiate the death of a mother and restore her to life so that the daughter in effect becomes her own mother, the product of generation becomes a generatrix herself, thus denying mortality and the inevitability of the life cycle.

From her mother Julia learns that her father has hidden his wife in this dank underground room for fifteen years, after he staged her burial in great pomp and show. We are told that he buried a wax effigy of her, a device that will recur a few years later when a strange wax figure haunts *The Mysteries of Udolpho*. Although the mother was not literally buried alive, she might as well have been, for she tells Julia that each day is passed "in a dead uniformity, more dreadful than the most acute vicissitudes of misfortune" (177). Sustained by her "firm principles of religious faith," Louisa has experienced gothic marriage with a true gothic antihero. Unable to civilize her husband, Louisa has paid the price. She has been incarcerated as embarrassing and redundant baggage, in much the same way Bertha Mason will later be imprisoned by Rochester.

When Julia understands that her mother now faces execution by her father, who intends to poison the food he brings to her cell, she springs into action, vowing to avenge and free her mother: "'Oh! let me lead you to light and life!' cried Julia with warm enthusiasm. 'Surely heaven can bless me with no greater good than by making me the deliverer of my mother'" (182). With "true piety," they ask God's protection and the melodramatic denouement begins to unfold. In gothic novels the villains always receive the evil that they

have tried to administer to others. There is a simple biblical law of reciprocity operating in gothic morality; one always reaps what one has sown.
Intending to poison his good (nonsexual) wife, Mazzinni is poisoned by his
evil (sexual) wife. His life of crime has brought him to this sorry fate. Trying
to poison his first wife is as low as the marquis stoops in this novel, but it is
low enough to merit his death. And the second wife, caught in an act of flagrant adultery, kills herself after she kills her husband. The symmetry is
perfect.

As is the happy ending. Although Ferdinand rushes to the south wing to
warn his mother about the poisoned food, he fears he is too late. She is missing, vanished into thin air. The hunt is on to find her body and suddenly, as
in a dream, all are reunited in a tower by the sea: "Within appeared a cheer-
ful blazing fire, round which were seated several persons, . . . and in the same
instant he discovered Julia and Hippolitus." Then he sees his mother: "'My
son!' said she, in a languid voice, as she pressed him to her heart. 'Great God,
I am recompensed. Surely this moment may repay a life of misery!'"
(196–97). But surely this moment of joy cannot repay fifteen years of imprisonment. Surely a mother's love for her children, the one supposedly sacred
emotion in the gothic universe, stands here revealed as the source of the
gothic daughter's strength and courage. Maternal love is as sacred as paternal tyranny and abuse are profane. The intense valorization of maternal love,
maternal suffering for the sake of her children, cannot be understood apart
from the intense anxiety that was occurring as middle-class women were
displaced from waged labor and confined to their homes, with no other task
than the bearing and raising of their own children. Intense anxiety over this
role, its importance, and the threats to it from the sexuality of "other
women" occurred because women realized for the first time how completely
dependent they were on the goodwill and munificence of their husbands.

Louisa, the good but buried wife and mother, is supplanted not simply by
Maria, the evil and sexually passionate woman, but by a new cultural ideology that demanded that wives and mothers be both sexually chaste and pure
"virgins" in relation to their children and yet paradoxically emotionally
responsive and sexually voracious "whores" in relation to their husbands. The
dichotomy, played out in various poetical and popular texts of the period,
explains the split women in all of Radcliffe's novels. Her women could not
embody both virgin and whore, and so she presented each stereotype in a
different woman, always poised against each other (Laurentini/Agnes as one
woman is the only strange exception to this rule). Each woman understood
that the other woman was her antithesis and therefore her nemesis.

The punishment that falls on all mothers in Radcliffe's fiction is therefore no coincidence. Mothers are sacred and holy vessels to their children but are defiled and vilified by their husbands and culture for the crime of reifying their sexuality through the production of children. The female gothic heroine is a heroine because she seeks to avoid marriage and children; in fact, one might even say that her role and identity as a heroine are almost completely based on how effectively she manages to avoid marriage throughout the text. The presence of the convent—which on the surface she pretends to loathe and dread—stands as the repressed utopian dream of the Radcliffean heroine. Entombing herself alive with other women is actually a very enticing prospect to all of Radcliffe's pubescent women. In the final analysis, however, Radcliffe's heroines, like Julia, marry only because they have created in their husbands the best and safest possible keeper and protector, much more trustworthy than some power mad monk. The gothic hero stands ultimately as a shadow of a man who bears no resemblance at all to the father, while the gothic heroine exists ultimately as less than a shadow, a woman who will struggle against ever suffering the same fate as her mother.

III

On the night of March 25, 1794, three years after Radcliffe published her third novel, *The Romance of the Forest,* the popular playwright James Boaden produced his dramatic version, *Fountainville Forest.* With his play opening to a large crowd and playing successfully for several weeks, Boaden bragged that he intended to out gothicize the high priestess of the gothic herself. He ensured his success by emphasizing the supernatural elements of the novel and brandished a real ghost in at least four scenes.[13] Whereas Radcliffe took great pains to explain away her supernatural trappings, always relying on rational and commonsensical explanations, Boaden emphasized the dream scenes, the discovery of the missing manuscript fragment, and the eerie ghost sent as a messenger to the dispossessed heroine, this time named Adeline.

---

13. For a discussion of James Boaden's life and work, as well as reprints of all his dramas, see *The Plays of James Boaden,* ed. Steve Cohan (New York: Garland, 1980). All quotations from Radcliffe's *The Romance of the Forest* are from the reprint of the 1829 edition (New York: Arno, 1974), with page numbers in parentheses in the text.

But Adeline is not merely dispossessed like most female gothic heroines; she is literally passed from man to man in this novel as just so much excess and inconvenient baggage. When the novel opens, she is being handed by a hired ruffian into the confused and baffled hands of a fleeing criminal, M. La Motte, who takes her with him and his wife to a deserted abbey in the forest. Later La Motte hands her to the Marquis de Montalt, the owner of the abbey, who also coincidentally happens to be Adeline's uncle, the murderer of her father, and the usurper of the estate she rightfully should possess. Alternately she is protected by one Theodore Peyrou, the romantic love interest and therefore the frequent target of stray swords from various "father" figures throughout the text. The names and identities of all these men, however, are less significant than the fact that Adeline exists in this novel as a fetish of femininity, an exchange commodity passed between powerful men who use her as a pawn in their own vaguely homosocial schemes. These schemes, unfortunately, involve unpleasant activities like fratricide, theft, fraud, blackmail, and the usual unsavory and unsubtle ploys that men use to gain wealth and status in this male-dominated society (this time we are in southern France, circa 1660). We are not at all surprised when all of these dark deeds are exposed by Adeline. The very professionally feminine Adeline does not need to engage in such crude activities to gain her wealth. Instead, her wealth—stolen from her by these unscrupulous villains—is returned ultimately to her by the all-powerful forces of justice, in this novel called "fate." Adeline turns out to be a wealthy heiress, as do all of Radcliffe's heroines. But during her exchanges between men—the beating fantasies she experiences—it is not her wealth that is the issue. She deals in another coin: female beauty.

Like Julia, Adeline is also eighteen as the novel opens, and beautiful even while her "features were bathed in tears, and she seemed to suffer the utmost distress" (1:10). But when Adeline is not crying, she is a striking figure.[14] Radcliffe informs us, however, that Adeline is not simply beautiful but also possesses "good understanding," an "amiable heart," and "genius" (1:64). We might be tempted to say that the only "genius" we regularly see Adeline

---

14. Norbert Elias has shown how in the late seventeenth and early eighteenth centuries the body's secretions and fluids, formerly acceptable even to court elites, became increasingly associated with the "bestial" lower orders and then were gradually expelled from culture altogether. Stephen Greenblatt expands on the idea: "In this separation, the 'lower bodily stratum' steadily loses any connection with anything other than the increasingly disreputable dreams of alchemists and cranks. Eventually, all the body's products, except tears, become simply unmentionable in decent society." (See his article "Filthy Rites," *Daedalus* 3 [1982], 1–16.

demonstrate is a genius for finding herself in perilous situations. She is always fleeing a few steps in front of that ominous "rust-stained" sword or finding messages from the dead in mysterious trunks or having ominous dreams about a dead and bloody cavalier. But finally her "genius" allows her to best all of her enemies and regain her long-lost inheritance. No mean feat, particularly when one considers the number and virulence of those enemies. So how does she do it? In this text, Radcliffe invokes nothing short of God, the divine plan, to help sort out this heroine's familial problems.

The first and most important characteristic of Adeline as gothic heroine, however, is that her parentage is a source of sorrow for her. She believes that her mother died when she was seven years old, leaving her to be raised in a convent. At the age of eighteen her father, a heartless tyrant, demands that she become a nun. When she objects, her father "denounced vengeance on [her] head if [she] persisted in disobedience" (1:80). Once again we are in the terrain of terror at leaving the father, even if, as in this case, it is merely the idea of a bad father she is being forced to renounce. Adeline wants nothing more than to be a dutiful daughter, but she is instead forced reluctantly and unwillingly into the role of female gothic adventurer, and so the novel can begin in earnest: "Since he can forget, said I, the affection of a parent, and condemn his child without remorse to wretchedness and despair—the bond of filial and parental duty no longer subsists between us—he has himself dissolved it, and I will yet struggle for liberty and life" (1:81). Radcliffe had explored this idea before in *A Sicilian Romance*, and this time she revises the scenario ever so slightly. In this second version the evil father is not the heroine's biological father. Whereas the earlier novel had the heroine excavating her mother, this novel drops the mother altogether and has the heroine recover the identity, fate, and real estate of her biological father, murdered by his brother, who later has the audacity to court his own niece Adeline in marriage. Adeline, like Julia before her, plays the part of oedipal detective, decoding the saga of this dysfunctional family romance and once again proving that masculine hubris, greed, and ambition are no match for professionally feminine "genius."

Using Adeline's dreams as clues to the murder mystery she must solve stands as perhaps the most original innovation Radcliffe develops in this work. Dreams have long functioned in literature as privileged sites of meaning, transactions wherein highly charged signifiers intersect with ambiguous signifieds. But dreams also reveal the deepest wounds in the psyche, and remind us of Freud's theories about the work of dreams and of their relation to trauma. In fact, in reading Adeline's four interconnected dreams we cannot help but recall Freud's use of the Tancred and Clorinda narrative in his *Beyond the Pleasure Principle*. Freud relates the story, derived from Tasso, as one example of the peculiar tendency of some people to wound and be wounded over and over again, through a fate that appears to be entirely beyond their own control. Freud writes that Tasso's hero Tancred "unwittingly kills his beloved Clorinda in a duel while she is disguised in the armor of an enemy knight. After her burial he makes his way into a strange magic forest which strikes the Crusaders' army with terror. He slashes with his sword at a tall tree; but blood streams from the cut and the voice of Clorinda, whose soul is imprisoned in the tree, is heard complaining that he has wounded his beloved once again" (*SE* 18:3).

By using this narrative to explicate his theory of trauma, Freud highlights the paradoxical nature of psychic woundings, which the experience of trauma itself repeats through the unconsciously motivated acts of the survivor. In other words, if a psychic trauma is experienced too suddenly and unexpectedly, it cannot be fully known or available to consciousness until it imposes itself yet again—over and over, in fact, in the nightmares and compulsively repetitive actions of the traumatized and traumatizer. Cathy Caruth summarizes Freud on this point, noting that it is the second wounding that finally allows the trauma to be located on the body of the victim: "trauma is not locatable in the simple violent or original event in an individual's past, but rather in the way that its very unassimilated nature—the way it was precisely *not known* in the first instance—returns to haunt the survivor later on."[15] In an uncannily similar manner, Adeline reexperiences the trauma inflicted on her father's body as if that fatal wound were actually being reinflicted on her while she slept. Experiencing the father's trauma allows Adeline to speak and name her father's killer; the wound tells the tale.

But in Freud's *Interpretation of Dreams* he relates yet another powerful narrative of abuse and multiple trauma, this time involving a father's memories of his dead child, an image that stands as the exact opposite of Adeline's dreamlike reconstruction of her dead father:

A father had been watching beside his child's sick-bed for days and nights on end. After the child had died, he went into the next room to lie down, but left the door open so that he could see from his bedroom into the room

---

15. My discussion of the dream motif and the theory of fantasy in *The Romance of the Forest* is indebted to the work of Cathy Caruth, *Unclaimed Experience: Trauma, Narrative, and History* (Baltimore: Johns Hopkins University Press, 1996), 4.

in which his child's body was laid out, with tall candles standing around it. An old man had been engaged to keep watch over it, and sat beside the body murmuring prayers. After a few hours' sleep, the father had a dream that his child was standing beside his bed, caught him by the arm and whispered to him reproachfully: "Father, don't you see I'm burning?" He woke up, noticed a bright glare of light from the next room, hurried into it and found that the old watchman had dropped off to sleep and that the wrappings and one of the arms of his beloved child's dead body had been burned by a lighted candle that had fallen on them. (*SE* 5:509)

Freud relates this dream as yet another instance of trauma, a form of suffering that repeats itself first in the child's death, then in the child's burning through the careless actions of another. The trauma, however, is not the child's but the father's, the survivor's guilt and horror at having outlived his son, while the wish fulfillment of seeing his son speak to him in the dream suggests the father's desperate need to deny the reality of the child's death. In an analogous manner, Adeline hears her father's wounded voice relate his murder through a dream pantomime that denies the reality of his death at the same time it allows her as survivor to assuage her own guilt at having survived to tell the tale he is unable to narrate.

Adeline's dreams are a treasure trove of guilt, anxiety, and wish fulfillment. Consider her narration of the first one:

I thought that I was in a lonely forest with my father; his looks were severe, and his gestures menacing: he upbraided me for leaving the convent, and while he spoke, drew from his pocket a mirror, which he held before my face; I looked in it and saw (my blood thrills as I repeat it), I saw myself wounded and bleeding profusely. Then I thought myself in the house again; and suddenly heard these words, in accents so distinct, that for some time after I awoke I could scarcely believe them ideal,—"Depart this house, destruction hovers here." (1:90)

The images here are classic set pieces: the false father holding up the mirror to his daughter; the daughter wounded, beaten, and bloody. The dream would appear to have rephrased Freud's dream scenario, with Adeline asking, "Father, don't you see that I am bleeding?" Amorphous sexual anxiety and blatant fear of menstruation are imaged here in ways that we cannot fail to recognize. The house that holds "destruction" can be read most obviously as the heroine's own body, changing without her willful consent, a transformation that is instigated in some malicious and threatening manner by the father himself. But the dream can also on some level be read as a seduction fantasy, with the father initiating the daughter into the bloody terrain of her own deflowered body. When Adeline bleeds, she positions herself as the victim of a castration, a mutilation at the false father-seducer's hands. The dream appears to ask, why have I been wounded and why has my father committed this act or allowed another to do it? It appears that we would not be overreading, however, to imagine that Adeline could also be asking herself, how can I cut/castrate my father or his substitute and not be blamed for the act?

Very shortly, however, we are told that the heroine finds herself in her chamber with a "locked door" (1:91). Adeline falls asleep thinking that men are coming in through the locked door. At first we think she's dreaming, then men actually do appear and kidnap her, only to deliver her once again into the hands of M. La Motte. Locked doors on the heroine's bedchamber loom large in female gothic novels, and were it not for their persistent presence, we might be tempted to merely dismiss the locked doors as blatant and too crude symbols for a dread of genital sexuality. But throughout these novels the daughter locks the door not simply on her own sexuality but also on her parents'. The gothic heroine seeks not simply to reject motherhood herself but to obliterate all mothers, all fathers, all families. The locked bedroom door denies generation in ways that reveal the real anxiety motivating the ideology. The body that defines the gothic woman's essential nature—that ties her to the emotions, sentimentality, blood, childbirth, milk, nature— that body has to be not only denied but also destroyed by the conclusion of the text. The mirror the father holds up to his daughter bespeaks her worst fears: she is flesh and therefore mortal; he is reason and spirit and therefore immortal. She desires nothing less than to become a man or at the very least a manly woman.

When Adeline is placed once again in the protective custody of M. La Motte, she realizes that she feels toward him "the affection of a daughter" (1:98). And no sooner do we hear this confession than we are informed that Madame La Motte is seized by "pangs of jealousy" toward Adeline. She can only understand Adeline's devotion to her husband in sexual terms, and so we are presented with another family romance gone awry. The husband and wife can view a child only as an interloper, an unwanted third party in the eternal dyad that we know as marriage in the patriarchy. Because her financial and social existence depends completely on her husband, Madame La Motte is not in the mood to brook competition, especially from such a young and beautiful woman. We know that Adeline's days in this particular surrogate family can only be numbered.

But if the first dream served as a précis for the first section of the novel, Adeline's second dream introduces us to the next portion of the text's action. In this second dream she sees herself in a large old chamber of the abbey, long deserted and mysterious. Suddenly she hears a low voice calling her. When she attempts to find the source of the voice she sees a dying man stretched on a bed, his face possessing "an expression of mildness and dignity." Suddenly his features convulse, and he grabs her hand:

> [S]he struggled in terror to disengage herself, and again looking on his face, saw a man, who appeared to be about thirty, with the same features, but in full health, and of a most benign countenance. He smiled tenderly upon her, and moved his lips, as if to speak, when the floor of the chamber suddenly opened, and he sunk from her view. The effort she made to save herself from following, awoke her. (1:239).

In this dream we can see charted the psychic movement away from the false father and to the true, lost, and dead father. His youth and attractive appearance are ambivalently undercut by his sinking from view just when he attempts to speak to his daughter. His fate draws the daughter to him; it is the pull of the death instinct, the thanatotic impulse that lures her to his side, a side that must be rejected if the daughter is to survive where the father did not. But what is also evidenced here is the guilt of the survivor. As Freud has noted, "Dreams occurring in traumatic neuroses have the characteristic of repeatedly bringing the patient back into the situation of his accident, a situation from which he wakes up in another fright" (*SE* 18:13). What is suggested in this phenomenon, according to Caruth, is "that the trauma consists not only in having confronted death but in having survived, precisely, without knowing it. What one returns to in the flashback is not the incomprehensibility of one's near death, but the very incomprehensibility of one's own survival. Repetition is not simply the attempt to grasp that one has almost died but, more fundamentally and enigmatically, the very attempt to claim one's own survival" (64).

Before Radcliffe gives us the time to fully interpret this dream, however, we are presented with the third one. In this dream Adeline finds herself in winding passages of the abbey at dusk, unable to find a door. She hears a bell toll, and then the confusion of distant voices. Lost and trapped, she suddenly sees a light and tries to follow it. She is led to a man who looks as if he is trying to take her to a funeral; she is afraid to follow him, but then he suddenly turns and begins to chase her. Her terror awakens her. This dream appears to present us with a rather crude version of the query, "Daughter, don't you see that I have been murdered by my brother?"

As if three dreams were not sufficient textual overload, Radcliffe quickly gives us a fourth. Adeline returns to sleep as if to solve the mystery. In this final dream she follows the same mysterious man into a room hung with black wall hangings, prepared for a funeral. At the center of the room stands a coffin, and while she gazes at it she hears "a voice speak as if from within":

> The man she had before seen, soon after stood by the coffin, and lifting the pall, she saw beneath it a dead person, whom she thought to be the dying chevalier she had seen in her former dream: his features were sunk in death, but they were yet serene. While she looked at him a stream of blood gushed from his side, and descending to the floor, the whole chamber was over-flowed; at the same time some words were uttered in the voice she heard before; but the horror of the scene so entirely overcame her, that she started and awoke. (1:242)

These four dreams, strung together as a sort of crude nocturnal melodrama, reveal the history and fate of Adeline's father, imprisoned in the abbey by his avaricious brother, the evil Marquis de Montalt, and then murdered by him and left to molder in a trunk. But there is also in this final dream an element of sadistic voyeurism evidenced in the need of the daughter to see the father's body bloody and wounded in her stead. If the first dream positioned the daughter as the bloody victim, the fourth dream neatly reverses the power equation between the two. And once again castration imagery intersects with a quasi-seduction scene, so that in some sense the daughter seems to be asking another version of the question she began to formulate, albeit in muted form, in the first dream: How has my father's death made my life possible? How have I fed on and consumed my father's life force and energy? And note how very strange it is that the mother and the maternal body as the true source of origins is never mentioned by this very paternally identified daughter.

Sent by fate to uncover and punish this horrible fratricide, Adeline has been taken to the one spot in the world where she can solve the crime. And not only does she have the moral force of justice and the inexorable laws of fate on her side, but she has the residue of her psychic wounds—her repetitious and traumatic dreams—to lead her to the murderer. She may sleep no more that night, but do not think the female gothic heroine is not up to the task of decoding her dreams and solving the mystery of her own father's murder and her own disinheritance. Notice, however, how the stock beating fantasy—I am being beaten by my father—is transformed here in a most peculiar manner: my father is being beaten by my uncle.

The four dreams in this novel—as well as the female gothic genre itself—finally can be read as a series of hysterical fantasies in the sense that Freud defined hysteria: first, the hysteric suffers from a psychic trauma, the origin of which she does not know or has repressed yet which has remained as a memory trace in her psyche. Freud labels these memories "pathogenic," and he notes that hysterical patients suffer from incompletely abreacted psychical traumas. Adeline suffers, however, not from her own memories of past trauma, but from her father's unresolved legacy of betrayal and murder. She in a sense stands in the stead of her dead father and relives his trauma in order to release him and herself from the ghostly presence he has assumed in her fractured psyche. In other words, the patriarchy as a corrupt system of barter and exchange is the very nightmare from which the female gothic heroine seeks to awaken.

Second, the gap in conscious knowledge between the trauma and the partial memory of it causes what Freud calls the "hysterical conversion," that is, the somatization of conflictual unconscious representations. According to Freud, "hysterical symptoms are nothing other than unconscious fantasies brought into view through 'conversion.'" All of which is another way of saying that the body is compelled to act out its psychical overload either through excitation (tears, fits, hallucinations) or various forms of inhibitions (melancholy, paralysis, catatonic senselessness). The gap, then, between knowledge about the trauma and the ability to process it consciously constitutes the origin of hysteria. We can conclude that in some way the four dreams related in this novel embody the conflation of that very gap between the trauma committed on the father's body and the consciousness or processing of the memory on the daughter's substituted psyche and its representation, the female gothic text.

In his *Interpretation of Dreams*, Freud claims that a dream is not a phantasmagoria but a text to be deciphered, and he further claims that it is in the very nature of sexuality to have a traumatic effect on the ego; therefore, he justifies the connection among sexuality, trauma, and defense. For Freud, fantasies are the conscious articulations of a lack, a loss of the psychic plenitude we experienced in childhood, while in both fantasies and dreams the Ego dominates and determines all the actions and consequences so that the lack is denied. Most fantasies, therefore, center on scenarios of self-aggran-dizement and are structured around a narrative in which the ego regains a protective home, loving parents, and autoerotic objects suitable for affec-tion. Freud would later resort to an explanation that he called "primal fan-tasies of phylogenetic endowment," claiming that all fantasies are not individual but traces of a racial or primeval experience (similar to Jung's notion of the collective unconscious). For Freud the primal fantasies that recur in all individuals—and by extension, the human race—are all narra-tives of origin: the primal scene, fantasies of seduction and the upsurge of sexuality, and the source of the difference between the sexes with its mani-festation in the fantasy of castration.

If we apply these theories to Adeline's dream scenario, we can recognize that she is fingering an archaic trauma, the need to solve the riddle of her own existence, to explore the issue of origins by asking who she is in rela-tion to the identity and history of her father and her mother. The female gothic novel tradition would appear to be constructed over the body of the bloody father and the absent mother but only because the mediating con-sciousness is that of the alternately melancholic and hysterical daughter. In articulating her fantasies, the female gothic heroine dreams textuality and textualizes her dreams.[16] And in doing so she reshapes her personal and his-torical trauma into a triumphant literary saga that asserts the woman's fic-tive power to seize and control her origins, or rather, her fantasies of her origins. Adeline has no choice but to slip ever deeper into a kind of para-lyzing melancholy or act out the mystery of her origins and solve the crime. Because she is a gothic heroine, she acts and in the process she eroticizes her melancholy.

Adeline's dying father, his side pierced and bleeding, functions here as a Christ-like figure who leads her on to uncover the truth and unmask and punish evil. The dying father as Christ figure, weak, wounded, ritualistically sacrificed so that his true heir—the meek gothic daughter—can inherit the earth, this cultural construct is a potent one because it speaks to the female reader's sense of self-importance, her self-divinization. If Christianity were to survive as a cultural force into the modern era, it would do so because it was feminized, the Christian Everyman now a young woman, a daughter

---

16. See Laplanche and Pontalis, "Fantasy and the Origins of Sexuality," in *Formations in Fantasy;* Elizabeth Bronfen, "Hysteria, Phantasy, and the Family Romance: Ann Radcliffe's *Romance of the Forest,*" in *WW* 1 (1994), 171–79; and Alison Milbank, "Milton, Melancholy, and the Sublime," in *WW* 1 (1994), 143–60.

seeking her identity in an increasingly godless universe. Christian melo-drama intersects here with gothic trappings; the result is intended to be irre-sistibly attractive to its targeted female reading audience.[17]

If the four interlocking dreams are the dramatic high point of the first volume of the novel, the discovery of the rust-stained dagger and the "oblit-erated" manuscript form the crux of the mystery in the second volume. With the dreams we are in the rudimentary realm of the unconscious mind; we are, in short, within the psyche and soul of the female gothic heroine. But as she is a heroine, her internal world is an exact replica of her external sit-uation. Inner reality mirrors outer reality in a reciprocity that we know is only characteristic of the universe of moral allegory. With the dagger and the tattered manuscript we move to the level of proof, the material clues that allow Adeline to close in on her suspect, the marquis. The dreams, however, have already provided her with the bare outlines of the murder: the who, what, when, where, and how of the crime. All she needs to discover is the motive, and that is provided when she reads the manuscript, the written record of her father, kept in his own hand as he faced murder by his brother. This device, the partial, fragmented manuscript, became after Radcliffe a stock gothic topos. In fact, the unearthed manuscript was such a tired con-vention that it was both ridiculed and valorized in several later gothic (or antigothic) novels. We can recall, for instance, the crumbled laundry list in Austen's *Northanger Abbey* or the Catherine I's fitful writings used at the beginning of *Wuthering Heights* to introduce us and Lockwood to the mys-tery of her amorphous identity. Writing is a powerful sign in texts that were themselves written in spite of considerable odds and with more than a fair amount of struggle by women. The power of the word, the sacred status of the Logos, is not easily seized by women, and yet in the fragmented manu-script we get a clear indication of the word's power to survive death and the forces of time and decay.

Adeline is not able to spend much time with the manuscript because right outside her bedroom door the marquis and La Motte can be overheard plotting as to how she will be handed over to the marquis, who confesses that he "adores" Adeline and hints that her father is in the vicinity, ready to hand her over to him if La Motte fails to cooperate in his lustful schemes (2:14–15). At the mention of her father's name, Adeline "shudders" and sinks

---

17. Ann Douglas's *Feminization of American Culture* (New York: Knopf, 1977) makes this same argument in relation to the cult of a feminized Jesus in nineteenth-century American sentimental literature.

into "a new terror" (2:15). Like Julia before her, this female gothic heroine believes her father to be her mortal enemy. In fact, what hurts Adeline even more is the realization that her beloved parent substitutes, the La Mottes, are in league with her evil false father and the marquis to betray her: "To discover depravity in those whom we have loved, is one of the most exquisite tortures to a virtuous mind. . . . 'Is this human nature?' cried she. 'Am I doomed to find every body deceitful?'" (2:16–17). She believes herself to be in a desperate situation with her father, "whose cruelty had already been too plainly manifested," on one side of her and the marquis on the other, "pursuing her with insult and vicious passion" (2:28). This is the dark night of the soul for the female gothic heroine, the anxiety that the adult world is as dark and lustful and avaricious as her worst fears have suggested to her. Or put another way, we might say that the gothic heroine is beginning to discover dark desires and evil intentions within herself, and when she sees those emotions in others, when she sees that society at large embodies and then institutionalizes those flaws, she recoils from the realization that evil is the way of the world. The campaign, the war she conducts against her parents, concerns just this issue. If experience and adulthood are inherently soiling, then she will reject her parents and remain perpetually poised on the brink of full adulthood, always just ready to assume her inheritance but never quite in possession of the money and property that will implicate her in the entire cycle of getting and grasping and spending and lusting that appear to constitute "life."

When Adeline finally does manage to find a moment of privacy, she repairs to her locked chamber and spends the dark and dreary nights there reading the mysterious manuscript. After one particularly ominous section of text, Adeline chances to glance up and see a mirror, but "she feared to raise her looks towards it, lest some other face than her own should meet her eyes; other dreadful ideas and strange images of fantastic thought now crossed her mind. A hollow sigh seemed to pass near her. 'Holy Virgin, protect me!' cried she" (2:52–53). Reading her father's manuscript has produced just this dislocation of identity; the face she fears to see in the glass is, we suspect, the face of her father, the murder victim. Later female gothic heroines will see their faces in the faces of others, and this mirroring is not for them a pleasant phenomenon (for instance, Emily St. Aubert thinks she resembles the mysterious Sister Agnes; Catherine II's resemblance to her mother is considered uncanny and unnatural by Heathcliff in *Wuthering Heights*). Again, we can see here the daughter's fear of the generational cycle—the anxiety about being displaced by a younger version of the self—as well as the more obvious dislocation between body and mind that is evidenced. Rabid fear of childbirth and the rejection of motherhood—seen on some deep level as the loss of the pristine self in another—are evidenced here all too clearly. Fear of motherhood as a manifestation of the instability of identity and an assault on the boundaries of the self, however, is elided by Radcliffe when she has her heroine invoke the "Holy Virgin," the mother of Jesus. When the matriarch appears in female gothic texts, she frequently surfaces in just such a contradictory manner: a mother who is paradoxically a virgin or a buried mother as we saw in *A Sicilian Romance* or the mother as a nun living safely in a convent as we will see in *The Italian*. Good mothers cannot be actively sexual in the female gothic universe; only bad mothers (like the stepmother in *A Sicilian Romance* or the marchesa in *The Italian*) exude sexuality, and they suffer horrible deaths as a result of such unnatural desires.

Adeline does not spend all her time reading musty manuscripts by candlelight. She has attracted a good and virtuous man, this time named Theodore, and he has been rewarded for his troubles by being wounded in his attempt to help her escape the clutches of the marquis. Adeline realizes that she loves Theodore as she is waiting for his wound to be dressed: "Upon the whole, Theodore's present danger, together with the attendant circumstances, awakened all her tenderness, and discovered to her the true state of her affections" (2:150). When the doctor treating Theodore asks Adeline if she is his sister, he is not too far off the mark. Adeline longs to nurse Theodore, but her actual psychic relationship toward him is more like a mother to a son. This strategy enables the Radcliffean heroine to gain a son without sullying her body with blood and milk: she marries him.

But before the way is cleared for Adeline and Theodore to marry and live happily ever after, Adeline must once again fall into the clutches of the evil marquis, who has finally solved his own mystery and realized the true identity of Adeline. He sees a mailing seal given to Adeline by her dead mother, and used by Adeline to send a letter to Theodore. The family crest—functioning with the later-discovered miniature portrait as the only residual traces of the mother in this text—precipitates the denouement at the same time it reveals to the uncle the basis of his attraction to Adeline. He has, he belatedly realizes, been pursuing his own niece, daughter of the brother he had murdered years ago in the deserted abbey in the forest. Murder as well as sex are, it seems, family secrets that one inflicts only on one's nearest and dearest. The marquis now avidly pursues Adeline, not to marry but to murder her, for he realizes that her continued existence threatens his hold on the estates.

This time Adeline stumbles into another surrogate family—the La Lucs—and finds another sibling figure in their daughter Clara and another substitute father in M. La Luc, who is also recovering from a wound in his arm. But as luck would have it, M. La Luc just happens to be Theodore's father (oddly, they have different surnames), and the "daughter" can now become officially accepted into the family through marriage to Theodore. When Theodore does arrive at his home and learns that Adeline is living with his ailing father, he leaves; however, he presents Adeline to his father: "'Receive her,' added he, 'as the most precious legacy I can bequeath: consider her as your child'" (3:219). Exactly how Adeline has become the "legacy" of Theodore to possess and distribute is not exactly clear. What is clear is that she has passed from man to man to man throughout this text, so that by this time Theodore concludes he has ownership rights to her. Even more interesting, however, is the image of the suitor handing off his future bride as a "child" to his own father. The patriarchal implications of marriage as a barter system could not be clearer than they are in this interlude.

The novel concludes, like the majority of melodramas of the time, with a courtroom scene and a trial that exposes evil and dispenses justice, the deus ex machina represented by the dagger and manuscript that provide the crucial material evidence against the present marquis. At the trial of her uncle, Adeline learns the secret of her lost parentage, and receives a miniature portrait of her mother from a distant relative to complement that potent and powerful familial stamp. The moment is crucial, for the mother is now definitively dead and buried, existing only as a talismanic presence in a vague portrait and a disembodied family crest. The father is instead the source of all anxiety in this novel. Identifying him, exposing his cruel murder and punishing the murderers, enshrining his manuscript as a "relic," and finding his bones and interring them in the family vault—these are the tasks that consume the female gothic heroine who "was suffered to live as an instrument to punish the murderer of her parent. . . . Justice, however long delayed, will overtake the guilty" (3:257).

But justice is not simply meted out, for Adeline recognizes that there has been a "divine pattern" to all these events; life for the female gothic heroine is not subject to the whims of fate but is the province of divine intervention and protection. As the date for the verdict nears, the evil marquis poisons himself, as evil people are wont to do. The way is now clear for Adeline and Theodore to marry and live happily ever after in M. La Luc's parish, where he presides as a good father over the entire community. With his wife's remains buried close by, La Luc is the perfect nonphallic father: the "venerable La

Luc sat among the elder peasants, and as he surveyed the scene—his children and people thus assembled round him in one grand compact of harmony and joy—the frequent tear bedewed his cheek, and he seemed to taste the fulness of an exalted delight" (3:296). Treading "the flowery scenes of life" (3:293), Adeline and Theodore live surrounded by their friends and family, affording to all observers "an example of trials well endured . . . virtues greatly rewarded" (3:299). The trials of simply escaping adolescence, however, have been so great that we can expect to hear little more about the newlyweds. They never speak in the novel again, and we never hear of children or their adult lives. But that is the very meaning and substance of life for the female gothic heroine: she lives suspended in the realm of experience deferred, poised between childhood and adulthood, forever in the act of becoming someone. The goal for a heroine can only be to remain a young woman, free from the ravages of time and the decay of the body. Each one ends where she begins. The circle is as complete as it is fictitious and self-deceptive.

THREE

~

Gendering
Vindication

Radcliffe's Major Gothics

These women [hysterics], to escape the misfortune
of their economic and familial exploitation, chose to
suffer spectacularly before an audience of men; it is
an attack of spectacle, a crisis of suffering.
—CATHERINE CLÉMENT

I

It is no coincidence that Radcliffe's *Mysteries of Udolpho*, her next novel after
The Romance of the Forest, was adapted for the stage not once but three times
by 1808, and that two of these adaptations identified themselves as "operas."[1]
Female gothic novels themselves appear to be set to music; they are in fact
orchestrated by an acoustics of pain, toxic nostalgia, and desire. But when
the female gothic heroine listens to music or produces it, she is not merely
passively absorbing the strains. First of all, in valuing music the gothic heroine is displaying her professional femininity, as well as demonstrating her
allegiance to an earlier mode of communication, a different language, the
voice of the mother. And in validating that other tongue, the female gothic
novelist asserts her sensibility, her cultured and trained appreciation of "art."
But most important, the female gothic heroine listening to music endorses
a female tradition of communication, an oral, elliptical mode that precedes
the written system of discourse practiced by her society.

---

1. See Evans, *Gothic Drama from Walpole to Shelley*, 91.

A female-marked communication system—the gossip of servants, the tales and legends that have their own oral histories, the painted miniatures and portraits, as well as visual theatrics—struggles continually in these novels with a male-marked system—wills, letters, and legal documents. And as we might guess, the female system, based on the sensual eye and ear, is ultimately privileged and provides the heroine with her best and most complete access to truth and power in the nebulous gothic landscape in which she is forced to negotiate. Music, a strange, haunting, and yet vaguely familiar song, pervades Radcliffe's *Mysteries of Udolpho* (1794), while the singing voice of Ellena Rosalbo first attracts her noble lover in *The Italian* (1797). Female gothic novels, particularly those by Radcliffe, are filled with sounds; they have been compared to operettas, interspersed as they are with poetry and songs. Whereas the novels of Radcliffe were particularly prized for their visual power—their stunning evocation of an ersatz Middle Ages, complete with ornate tapestries, stained glass windows, and picturesque landscapes and costumes—they were also filled with music in a way that novels had not been before.

Quite clearly, the music that fills *The Mysteries of Udolpho* can be understood as the voice of the female gothic struggling to emerge from the prior and enabling discourse system—the domestic and sentimental novel tradition. If the first part of *Udolpho*, the description of Emily's life with her parents in La Vallée, is a sentimental idyll, so is the last section of the text. Here Emily reconstructs her childhood memories courtesy of the Villefort family and the suddenly purified Valancourt. But the middle section of *Udolpho*, Emily's surreal escapades in Montoni's Appenine castle, stands as the buried gothic text struggling to extricate itself from the conventions of the more prosaic sentimental novel. The "haunting" quality of the music, the vaguely familiar voice and song that recur throughout the novel, represents the female gothic tradition attempting to carve itself out of the stone that was the sentimental and male-originated novel genre. As the first widely successful female gothic novelist, Radcliffe sought to write in a new style but in a manner that was also familiar to her readers. What was that voice they all thought they were hearing? What was the voice they all dimly remembered? Was it a public voice of female subversion or, more likely, a private voice that they had heard only within themselves and finally dared to speak? The whisper that is the female gothic in this novel, the middle section of the text, finally drowns out the sentimental overtures at the beginning and the end of the work. Radcliffe found her true voice in *The Mysteries of Udolpho*; she found the female gothic when she freed herself from the conventions of the *music — transcendental language —*

sentimental novel and listened to the self-haunting and haunted cries of the gothic. She heard Emily.

Like all of Radcliffe's heroines, Emily St. Aubert plays a musical instru- *(music)* ment and is particularly sensitive to music. She *feels* music and understands that the ability both to produce and to appreciate music indicates a sympathetic and sensitive soul. But in the final analysis, Emily learns that music provides the key to understanding her identity; music is the epistemology that unravels and reveals the characters and identities of Valancourt and Signora Laurentini (aka the mad nun Sister Agnes). For the female gothic heroine, music is the subjective and feminine equivalent of reason and objective data; music does not lie. When we first enter the world of *The Mysteries of Udolpho,* we are introduced to our characters through a poetic passage from James Thomson, and the very first word of this passage is "Home." In many ways this novel, like the majority of female gothics, is concerned with the struggles attendant on finding a home, that "resort / Of love, of joy, of peace and plenty." The idyllic home of the female gothic novel is inhabited by "polish'd friends / And dear relations," just like the childhood home of Emily St. Aubert, in many ways the most definitive female gothic heroine.[2] The novel begins like a fairy tale with Emily and her perfect mother and father living an only child's ultimate fantasy life along the banks of a river, deep in a luxuriant forest in the immensely picturesque province of Gascony, France, circa 1584.

Many sounds fill Emily's childhood days, including festivals and carnivals of the local peasants, who throughout Radcliffe's novels stand as the traces, the historical residue of an earlier rural existence. Rousseau's "noble savage" shares much in common with Radcliffe's noble and good-hearted peasants, but most important for the female gothic novel, the peasant and his community figure the ideological impetus of much of the work. The novels of Radcliffe project a deep disdain for the growing urban world; they embody a fear of industrialization and the rise and spread of the a new commercial culture that increasingly characterized Radcliffe's own decade—the 1790s. Radcliffe's novels present an ideology that appears to fear the growth of cities and the proliferation of an industrial economy largely for reasons of class.

But there is also in her works an anxiety about the displaced female. In a rural economy based largely on products generated within the home,

---

2. Ann Radcliffe, *The Mysteries of Udolpho,* 1. All quotations from *The Mysteries of Udolpho* are from the Everyman edition (London: Dent, 1973), with page numbers in parentheses in the text.

women had a certain status and worth that would not be theirs in an urban, industrialized society filled with a working-class labor force. Although I would not claim that Radcliffe was a self-conscious feminist or a particularly profound social critic, she did recognize the tremendous social, cultural, and economic upheaval that her country was experiencing, and she projected that upheaval into the past, safely away from her. Such a desperately nostalgic gesture, of course, was futile, but it did serve to highlight not the conditions of the sixteenth century but instead the anxieties of a middle-class British woman writing during the 1790s. As Mary Poovey has observed about the bifurcated presentation of the sentimental ideology in *Udolpho*, there is a peculiar condemnation of the gendering of sensibility in both the novel's heroine and the villain in that the principles of sensibility encouraged "imaginative and libidinal excesses in both Emily and Montoni. But sensibility's more telling liability resides in its inability to resist the masculine version of desire—the lust of [Montoni's] unregulated avarice." As Poovey notes, the novel presents sensibility as a flawed feminine code of conduct that was not an effective antidote to "unregulated, individualistic, avaricious desire.... Yet even as [Radcliffe] unmasks the hideous incarnation of capitalistic energy she returns to the very values she has just proved inadequate. For Radcliffe can imagine no force apart from sensibility's feminine principles to control this masculine force.... And once such feminine, sentimental principles as sensitivity, responsiveness, decorum, and generosity are no longer considered 'manly,' there will be no governing code to socialize aggressive energy."[3] It would appear that Radcliffe was trying to present herself as something of a social critic, gently pointing out the dangers of a lost rural tradition but without fully understanding that this bucolic tradition was wrapped up and complicit with a flawed and already-outmoded gendered code of behavior that went under the name of Sensibility.

If we know that the truest content of a literary work can always be found in that which it tries most to bury and elide, then we know that in addition to celebrating the lost rural traditions of England and the flawed heritage of sensibility as a civilizing principle, Radcliffe was also trying to condemn the growing legalization of family and property relations. The complicated property arrangements of M. St. Aubert were based on the goodwill of his brother-in-law, M. Quesnel, and his sister, Madame Cheron, later Madame Montoni. But both used the law—papers, documents, signatures—to effectively disinherit and to tyrannize over Emily, and Radcliffe suggests that in

---

3. See Poovey, "Ideology and *The Mysteries of Udolpho*," 322–23.

an earlier, more matriarchal-rural culture, such behavior would not have occurred.

The novel, split as it is between sentimental and gothic conventions, makes extensive use of stock character types: the idealized father, the persecuted heroine, the feminized hero, the gothic villain, and examples of what I have come to consider "gothic antiheroines," Signora Laurentini and Madame Montoni. In examining each of these character types, I want to make a few key observations: each character originates in the prior sentimental discourse system but is given what we might recognize as a "gothic spin." Each is, to be more precise, a caricature of a caricature, a character seen through the eyes of a child, a character writ large, almost cartoonish, in an attempt to mime the mime, we might say. Good characters are all good; evil characters are irredeemably evil. We are inhabiting the landscape of dreams and nightmares, fairy tales and wish fulfillment, Barthes's neither-norism and Hertz's double surrogation. In short, we are examining a genre (and a class) that is struggling to bring itself into existence.

But to begin with the idealized father, St. Aubert is the first truly feminized man we meet in female gothic novels. He is the ideal husband and father, shunning society for the pleasure of tending to his wife and children. He communes with nature, strolls among his favorite trees (indeed he is almost pathological in his devotion to trees), dispenses money to his pensioners, listens for snatches of music in the wind, and lives in total contentment, a man of "refined senses" (1:4). We are given no extended description of Madame St. Aubert; in fact, the only time she speaks in the novel is to prepare her family to accept the inevitability of her death (1:18). The training and education of Emily, the only surviving child of this estimable couple, are left solely to the father (much against traditional norms of the supposed and actual historical periods, the sixteenth and late eighteenth centuries, respectively).

St. Aubert undertakes to create a daughter very much in his own image. One is tempted to conclude that somehow he had read Wollstonecraft's *Vindication*. Emily's "feminine" traits—"delicacy of mind, warm affections, and ready benevolence," her "susceptibility," pensiveness, and softness—all are characteristics that St. Aubert realizes are "dangerous." Instead, he superintends an instructional regime that sought to "strengthen her mind," give her "habits of self-command," so that she might be able to "resist the first impressions, [in order] to acquire that steady dignity of mind that can alone counterbalance the passions" (1:5). In short, St. Aubert sought to create in his daughter his opposite—a manly woman. If he is the ideal feminized and sensitive man, she must be the perfectly masculinized and sensible woman. We are witnessing here a prose version of the androgynous compulsion, which I have argued elsewhere permeated the poetic consciousness of the male canonical Romantic poets. The impulse to transmute rigid gender stereotypes was endemic throughout the late eighteenth and early nineteenth centuries. The cultural attempt to create a new type of gendered being, a person who embodied the best stereotyped qualities of both sexes, recurs obsessively in the literature written by both men and women throughout this era.

Emily receives instruction from her father in the classics of Latin and English literature (she is, you must remember, French) and in science. She also is quite the botanist, a respectable artist, and of course a musician. We are told that she has been instructed by her father to play several "musical instruments" (1:97), while her musical sensitivity is intended to indicate her superior intelligence and character. In her free time Emily is allowed to ramble over the natural scene, exhorted always to remember that the natural world is but an emblem and manifestation of a beneficent God (1:6). Emily's religious beliefs are first tested when her mother dies after the sudden onset of a fever. Although plagued with despair, St. Aubert and his daughter grieve moderately, for, as he warns Emily, "All excess is vicious" (1:20). Reason and self-command are the orders of the day; however, the death of her mother allows the life of Emily the female gothic heroine to begin.

We are introduced now to the characters who will provide the central testing (read: gothic) episode in Emily's life—Madame Cheron and her darkly Italian and highly suspicious fiancé Montoni (who is distantly related to the wife of St. Aubert's brother-in-law). Later we learn that Madame Bonnac is also related to Montoni, as is Signora Laurentini. All Italians, it seems, are coded as "other" to the normative "French" (read: English) characters. The xenophobia that pervades these novels can be understood on a purely social level, but finally the Catholic Church, with its almost incestuous connection to Italian politics and intrigue, seems to be the actual target.

The "mysteries" that Emily must solve throughout the text are largely epistemological issues, and the first one is presented by her father. As a sort of paternal legacy, he hands her the key to a long buried family secret—the history of her aunt the Marchioness de Villeroi. The introduction of this sad woman's fate is bound up with the destruction of some papers buried in her father's study and a miniature portrait that Emily decides to keep and wear because of its vague resemblance to someone she thinks she recognizes as related to her. While we might be tempted to conclude that the face in the portrait resembles her father, we learn later that the miniature actually resembles Emily. The portrait, in short, functions as a mirror. Emily learns to "read," that is, understand the portrait when she learns to accurately determine her own identity and destiny.

The last task imposed by the father on Emily (according to fairy-tale formula) prohibits her from reading the papers in his study; she is simply to locate and then destroy them without perusing their contents. This proves impossible, for try as she might she cannot avoid letting her eyes fall on a few lines that cause her such apprehension and anxiety that she never tells us exactly what they said. We learn later and periodically throughout the text that these few lines are not an accurate indicator of the relationship of brother and sister; they suggest instead that the woman in the miniature is actually Emily's biological mother. The enigma facing Emily is a sexual and familial one: Who is her mother? (Her father's identity is never in doubt.) The very odd mystery facing the gothic heroine can be understood as both genealogical and epistemological, that is, what is her maternal legacy? How is she to understand herself in a maternally defined line?[4]

But Emily does not solve this mystery in order to assert a rival matriarchal claim or some sort of allegiance to a maternal realm. She instead dissociates herself from every woman in the text; she repulses or is repulsed by virtually every female character so that she can shape herself more fully in the image of the father. Every woman in the text fails Emily's high standards because each and every one of them is too unprofessionally feminine, that is, too emotional, too sexually passionate, too vulnerable to the wiles and snares of her own feelings. Emily seeks to make herself a "manly woman," much as her father and Valancourt make themselves "womanly men." We

---

4. By far the most discussed of Radcliffe's works, *The Mysteries of Udolpho* has received several useful and provocative analyses. Claire Kahane's reading has been most influential among feminist critics for its discussion of the psychic boundaries female characters explore within the gothic castle: "If nonseparation from the castle as mother—mother as nurture, as sexual being, as body, as harboring a secret—is a primary Gothic fear, women whose boundaries are at the very least ambiguous because of their own femaleness, must find that fear dramatically rendered in the secret center of the Gothic structure, where boundaries break down, where life and death become confused, where images of birth and sexuality proliferate in complex displacements" (see her "Gothic Mirrors," *CR* 24 [1980], 43–64.) Other provocative approaches can be found in Patricia M. Spacks, "Fathers and Daughters: Ann Radcliffe," in *Desire and Truth* (Chicago: University of Chicago Press, 1990), 147–76; Jacqueline Howard, "Gothic Sublimity: Ann Radcliffe's *The Mysteries of Udolpho*," in *Reading Gothic Fiction: A Bakhtinian Approach* (Oxford: Clarendon, 1994), 106–44; Adela Pinch, "Phantom Feelings: Emotional Occupation in *The Mysteries of Udolpho*," in *Strange Fits of Passion* (Stanford: Stanford University Press, 1996), 111–36; and E. J. Clery, "Like a Heroine," in *The Rise of Supernatural Fiction*, 115–30.

appear to be inhabiting the realm of sense and sensibility as it was understood in prose. If the androgynous ideology pervaded poetry, so did a similar androgynous compulsion characterize both sentimental and gothic fiction. Gender was fled even as it was being rewritten.

Consider the characters of both Madame Cheron-Montoni, the foolish aunt, and Signora Laurentini, also known as the mad nun Agnes. Both are positioned in the text as substitute mothers to Emily. Both have been involved with Montoni, the evil father figure, and both figure in a quasi-incestuous triangulation of mommy, daddy, and me in Emily's rather vague consciousness. Finally, both caution Emily against the same thing: sexual passion. While Madame Montoni on her deathbed directs Emily to some papers that Emily never quite gets around to finding, Laurentini delivers the text's crucial speech. Many critics have cited Laurentini's dramatic deathbed warning, a set piece of indoctrination into the central tenets of professional femininity:

> "Sister! beware of the first indulgence of the passions; beware of the first! Their course, if not checked then, is rapid—their force is uncontrollable.... Such may be the force of even a single passion, that it overcomes every other, and sears up every other approach to the heart. Possessing us like a fiend, it leads us on to the acts of a fiend, making us insensible to pity and to conscience." (2:318)

Laurentini, whose sexual history is erroneously related later by Sister Frances, further confuses Emily by informing her—on the basis of Emily's resemblance to the woman in the miniature—that she, Emily, is the daughter of the Marchioness de Villeroi. Emily has puzzled over portraits, *tableaux vivants* behind veils, and miniatures throughout the text. What the author implies is that visual ways of knowing, like verbal and written codes, all have to be informed by the heart and head simultaneously. One cannot navigate the gothic cosmos we call life without all of one's senses functioning in harmony with one's reason and one's emotions. We can recall here the vogue for a brand of faculty psychology that Blake transformed into the four Zoas. For the gothic heroine at sea in epistemological confusion, the struggle to harmonize the faculties becomes one of her best means of survival.

The sad fact is that Emily St. Aubert cannot recognize the face in the miniature as her own because she cannot accept the fate of woman as her own. She cannot admit that she too could be coerced by a father who might want to sell her into a financially advantageous marriage; she cannot admit that she too could passionately pursue a man, only to be deceived and betrayed by him. The fates of Signora Laurentini (Sister Agnes) and the marchioness, St. Aubert's sister, entwine in a sad saga of lateral violence, gender treachery, two women turned on each other as adversaries, whereas their most effective opponent could more accurately be found in the patriarchal system that held both in thrall. When Emily learns that the music that haunted her at the chateau of Villeroi was played by Sister Agnes, she learns that her family—by extension, that she—is complicit with and connected to her violent tale of thwarted love, jealousy, adulterous passion, and murder by poison.

Emily rejects the women in this novel not simply because they are victims of themselves and their own excessive passions but because they are victims of a system that uses them as objects of exchange and barter between powerful men. Marriage as a business proposition is a dominant leitmotif throughout the text. Women do not marry for love; they marry because they are forced to do so by the men who "own" them. Thus Montoni breaks off Emily's engagement to Valancourt and takes her to Venice with him, to be used in a series of aborted exchanges with a number of men to whom he owes gambling debts. At one particularly nightmarish moment in Udolpho, Emily is pursued by two thugs, both intent on raping her. She has been promised to both men by Montoni, who owes each of them money. The "double chamber" that she is forced to sleep in at the castle of Udolpho images just this sort of sexual vulnerability, this nightmare fantasy of double rape, a doubled beating fantasy.

One might conclude that Emily rejects sexual women in the text because she fears her own deviant and uncontrollable sexual passions. She is even vaguely aware of this fact—as are we. But even more appalling is her uncomfortable awareness that she is attracted to and desires Montoni.[5] And that would appear to be the fear haunting the gothic heroine—that she desires sex with the dark "other" man, that she is capable of unspeakable crimes motivated by perverse and perverting sexual mania. In short, she fears that she is just like Signora Laurentini, that, in fact, all women (even perhaps her

---

5. Consider an analogous observation: "the more Emily investigates her origins, the more such mementi she comes upon in the form of progressive, replicated corpses. . . . behind the veil is an image of the generating marriage bed of her parents, of the violence and 'death' of the sexual act." (See Mary Laughlin Fawcett, "*Udolpho*'s Primal Mystery," *SEL* 23 [1983], 487–88.) Leona Sherman has made a similar claim: "[t]he 'family curse' convention of the Gothic fits in as another element of desexualization in this child's world. . . . The death of the villain, the demise of a family, and the symbolic castration of the hero all connote the end of generation—the denial of parental sexual relations and birth, and the falsity of heterosexuality" (169).

sainted mother) are prone to becoming violently passionate criminals and murderesses. The only cure for such a fate is to reject/abject as much "femininity" as possible, to make oneself as much of a manly woman (read: controlled, reasonable) as possible. Emily, in short, appears to have been reading Wollstonecraft's *Vindication* just as thoroughly as did her father.

Immediately after the death of Madame St. Aubert, Emily and her father decide to assuage their grief by setting off on a journey through the French countryside. This excursion allows Emily to meet her love interest, Valancourt, who proves his worth by handing out his last penny to the poor and taking a gunshot wound in the arm from the father of his beloved. In fact, Valancourt will be wounded twice by gunshots in the novel, in what reads very much as a sort of ritual punishment or taming of the male flesh. On the second occasion, after his disastrous foray in Paris, the wounding clearly suggests that he is being punished for his follies, but the first wounding by the father suggests something else—a ritualized passing on of weakness ("castration") from one generation to the next. The legacy that St. Aubert passes to Valancourt in that shot is the legacy of emasculation. Before Valancourt can be acceptable to Emily or her father he must be feminized, made as sensitive and delicate as St. Aubert himself is. The masculine flesh that led Valancourt to the gaming tables, to a courtesan's house, and ultimately to prison, is ritualistically excised in those two woundings. The Valancourt who emerges from both shots will be a tamed man; he will stand as a sibling figure who has survived the beatings handed out by the father. In short, he will not wander far from the innocent pleasures of the country life and rural values again.

The most interesting aspect of the journey—apart from the once highly regarded (and extended) descriptions of the natural scenery—is that St. Aubert travels exactly to his sister's grave. He concludes his life's journey by being buried next to her in the Villeroi family tomb (1:90). What is particularly intriguing about this fact is that the tight bond of kinship, the relation of a brother and sister, is privileged in this text over the relation of marriage. St. Aubert does not insist that his body be taken home to La Vallée to be buried next to his beloved wife. In fact, when he learns his location it is almost as if he wills himself to die at precisely that spot. His sighing over his sister's miniature, his rereading of her letters, all testify to the continuing strength of the bond. He chooses to be buried not with his wife of many years but with his long-dead sister. Foucault has reminded us that the dominant struggle during this period—the late eighteenth century—was the establishment of the modern exogamous family, with the concomitant breakdown of kinship ties and the notion of the family as a clan or tribe. The upper classes, further, based their status and social claims on the notion of their "blood," while the middle class based its claims for status on its "sex," the attractiveness of its bodies as objects of exchange on the marriage market. In choosing "blood" over "sex," St. Aubert in death reasserts his upper-class privileges and effectively traces his middle-class wife out of existence. She truly never existed in his world except as the vehicle for the bearing of his children (who then effectively disown her by forgetting her and asserting their allegiance to their father only).

Manfred

But of what value is St. Aubert's class to Emily? Madame Cheron, as his only surviving relation, is a sorry excuse for a woman. Vain, snobbish, pretentious, and crude, she behaves so horribly that when she meets her terrible fate (death by starvation in a ruined tower while she is tyrannized over by her vicious husband Montoni), we have a very difficult time feeling sympathy for her. If Madame Cheron is supposed to represent the upper-class woman, then we can only conclude that Radcliffe intended us to condemn the moral corruption, sexual depravity, and petty vileness of such people. Madame Cheron brags to Emily that she never judges people by their "countenances" but by their "actions" (1:124). And yet this elderly woman marries a handsome Italian adventurer, gambler, and murderer and expects to live the life of a "princess" in Venice. When Montoni learns that Madame does not have the cash to sustain his gambling habits, he leads her on a chase around a ruined castle in the Italian Appenines. Rather than living as a princess, she lives as what I will call a species of the gothic antiheroine. She, like Signora Laurentini, another antiheroine, is victimized by her oppressor. She does not triumph over evil but is actually brought down by its power because she is complicit with it. The true female gothic heroine always triumphs over evil because she is totally good; her motives are always utterly pure; her conduct and speech always above reproach. No spot of corruption touches her, and thus she always fends off and destroys her oppressors because good always triumphs over evil. This very powerful ideology—that professional femininity or goodness always wins out—exists at the core of the gothic feminist mythology, assuring women that their carefully cultivated facade, their masquerade of patience and long-suffering will be rewarded. Again, we appear to be in the terrain of "wise passiveness," of waiting for the tyrant to self-destruct through the consequences of his own misguided evil deeds.

But how does Emily win her victory over such a powerful and diabolical villain as Montoni? One could claim, rather cynically, that the secret to her success is luck. Never in the annals of literature has a heroine traveled so extensively and managed to meet everyone connected to two families. Emily would appear to deserve her heroic status because she learns to control her emotions; she learns to stop seeing people running around the trees; she learns to stop hearing haunting music. Instead, she names her feelings; she finds out who is stalking her estate, and she investigates until she finds the source of the music. She learns, that is, to privilege reason over fancy, but she does not do this merely by becoming a sleuth, a sort of feminized Sherlock Holmes. She learns to gather whatever information she can from the servant Annette; that is, she taps into the folk sources of wisdom and gossip that the patriarchy has suppressed or marginalized.

Next she learns to control her emotions and draw conclusions from incomplete data. The painting covered with the black veil is a prime example—like the partial words in her father's destroyed papers—of an incomplete sensory message. Emily reads the veiled portrait as the mutilated corpse of Signora Laurentini, largely because she is piecing together partial bits of information that do not cohere around any other reading. But in fact by the end of the book, we learn that another quite different reading is the "correct" one for this wax figure: it is a religious icon, meant to be a meditation on the inevitability of death and constructed by the monks of the abbey for what they considered to be the best of purposes. This patriarchal construction of the ultimate beating fantasy, spiritually sadistic and voyeuristic, is read by a woman as an emblem of another passionate woman's fate. And who is to say that Emily's first instincts were not, in fact, correct, at least as far as Laurentini is concerned. She did, after all, spend the rest of her days entombed in a convent, a living reminder of the wages of her sin.

The sexual pursuit of Emily, first by the chubby Count Morano, then by the assassins Verezzi and Orsino, and finally by Valancourt's double, DuPont, all indicate the dominant struggle for the female gothic heroine: to find a man worthy enough to replace her perfect father. In many ways *The Mysteries of Udolpho* is a melodramatic romance, characterized by its heavy use of doubles and foils, all of whom throw into relief the crucial goodness of the major hero and heroine. Thus Morano and Montoni double each other, the assassins are doubles, while DuPont and Valancourt replace each other throughout the text. Emily is doubled by Lady Blanche, and the fates of the Marchioness de Villeroi and Laurentini mirror each other in that neither was allowed to marry the man of her own choosing. This sort of excessive doubling of characters suggests that history is indeed the real subject of the novel. The interchangeableness of the women, the identical passions and

follies of the men, all point to the pervasiveness and universality of the novelist's vision. Radcliffe is not trying to depict realistically the fate of one or
even two characters; she is trying to paint a large social and historical can-
vas: "The Way of the World, Europe, circa 1790." And Emily St. Aubert, the
first modern individual in Nancy Armstrong's terms, is trying to oppose the
inherited prejudices and corruptions that have brought such misery for
many centuries under the names "religion" and "family."

The Mysteries of Udolpho attacks, in the final analysis, the corruption of
the propertied, aristocratic, and privileged family, buttressed as it had been
by the power of the Catholic Church. When Emily senses that her "destiny"
lies in understanding Udolpho, she is correct. The corrupt, ruined, isolated
castle in the inaccessible mountains represents the corrupt and inbred aristocratic European family. The fact that Montoni repairs the battlements and
walls of Udolpho only so that he can more safely hide there and rob travel-
ers and neighboring villages is revealing. E. P. Thompson has noted that it
was commonplace among Jacobins of the 1790s to assert that there was no
such thing as the English Constitution, because the country had been taken
by force at the time of the Norman invasion. In the writings of Tom Paine,
a persistent attack was made of the hereditary principle of government as
inherently corrupt: "A banditti of ruffians overrun a country, and lay it
under contributions. Their power being established, the chief of the band
contrived to love the name of Robber in that of Monarch; and hence the origin of Monarchy and Kings." Although I would not attempt to claim that
Radcliffe was even vaguely Jacobin in her political sympathies, I find her
explicit description of Montoni as a banditti significant in its implications.
She seems to be suggesting that the aristocratic family lives like a cancer, a
parasite on the growing mercantile and middle class. Feeding on the innocent and unsuspecting, it produces nothing but exists by endlessly consuming the blood and sexual energy of those unfortunate enough to come
within its domain. When Emily enters Montoni's force field, she must use
all her resources to escape unscathed (read: not raped or forcibly married
to an aging lecher or a youthful assassin).

Emily St. Aubert, held as a prisoner in a ruined and remote castle in the
Italian Appenines by her aunt's diabolically evil husband, about to be sold
to the highest bidder to pay off this uncle's gambling debts, compelled to
watch her aunt starved and tortured by her husband for her properties, in
the grip of the most blatant beating fantasy meted out to a female gothic
heroine, suddenly hears "notes of sweet music" (1:335). This strange music
calms her in such a way that it "now seemed to her as if her dead father had

spoken to her in that strain, to inspire her with comfort and confidence" (1:336). Music suffuses *The Mysteries of Udolpho,* and although we learn eventually that all of these mysterious ditties have natural origins, Radcliffe goes to some lengths to suggest that the acoustics that reverberate throughout this text originate in a long-buried memory or fantasy of parental and specifically paternal protection. But it is most revealing that Emily consistently reads the music that floats through her bizarre imprisonments as sent from her father, not her mother.

At Udolpho after a particularly trying day attempting to find her dying aunt, Emily gazes out the turret window and recalls that her own father was comforted by music after his wife's death, and that he came to believe that the music had been sent by God. Hearing similar music she muses, "Perhaps my father watches over me at this moment!" (2:10). The psychic equation Emily makes here between God and her earthly father is revealing, particularly in light of Radcliffe's own devout form of Anglicanism. This is a woman who would reject the "supernaturalism" of Catholicism in favor of the more sensible anthropological basis of Protestantism. Heaven must be understood as analogous to what we know of this world, God must be like good fathers, while the devil must be like Montoni. Further, the passage reveals that this is a woman who has so thoroughly internalized her father's values that all beauty, all art are filtered through his eyes. Although women are most consistently seen singing or playing musical instruments, it is the men who make and appreciate music and who have the qualities that allow them to love and value Emily (M. St. Aubert, DuPont, Valancourt). But then all three of these men are coded as "good," that is, womanly men, who possess "feminine" qualities, who are sensitive, long-suffering, patient, and who appreciate art, literature, and music.[7]

Valancourt's intrusion into the family journey of Emily and her father allows him to display his character to St. Aubert, presumably for approval

---

7. On sensibility and the triumph of tasteful nuance over plot in literature, see Leo Braudy, "The Form of the Sentimental Novel," *Novel* 7 (1973), 5–13. Braudy observes that, "In general, the sentimental novel opposes intuition to rationality; disjuncture, episode, and effusion to continuity and plot; artlessness and sincerity to art and literary calculation; and emotional to verbal communication. . . . [T]he self conditions the form of the fiction rather than the other way around" (12). On the same subject, see Patricia M. Spacks, "Female Orders of Narrative," in *Rhetorics of Order, Ordering Rhetorics,* ed. J. Douglas Canfield and J. Paul Hunter (Newark: University of Delaware Press, 1988): "[T]he change in the narrative function of religion between Richardson and Radcliffe suggests also a more general shift in narrative, from plots whose action derives from movements of power to those incorporating sensibility, too, as a principle for generating happening. If the cost of such incorporation includes breakdowns of narrative order, Radcliffean fiction also in some respects radically challenges the hegemony of order itself" (171).

as a future husband (father substitute) for Emily. Thus his books—volumes of Homer, Horace, and Petrarch (1:35)—pass scrutiny, as does his good humor at taking a bullet in the arm from St. Aubert's pistol. But his attitude toward the natural landscape, his appreciation of the "grandeur" and "sublimity" of the Pyrenees, proves his worth. Valancourt confirms his good sense and sensibility by lecturing St. Aubert and Emily: "'These scenes soften the heart like the notes of sweet music, and inspire that delicious melancholy which no person, who had felt it once, would resign for the gayest pleasures. They waken our best and purest feelings; disposing us to benevolence, pity and friendship" (1:46). According to the sentimental code operating here, viewing the external landscape in awe parallels feeling the internal landscape of the heart through the power of music (or aesthetic pleasure is intrinsically bound up with moral goodness).

But in the final analysis it is Valancourt's tears that win Emily's love and confidence. When, we might ask, did a hero ever spend so much time crying and haunting the home of his absent beloved? In his letter to Emily (1:196) he presents himself as a lovesick girl, bereft of all comfort after her departure for Italy (1:196). He cries easily, rather too easily (1:159, 164). Radcliffe's purpose is to create a man who has imbibed the civilizing and civilized qualities of a woman, and one major characteristic of such a man is the ability to reveal his emotions, to advertise his sensitivities, to assert the primacy of his internal world—thoughts, feelings, speculations. The sensitive Valancourt, however, is considered nothing but a "boy" or a "puppet" by Montoni (1:204), who subscribes to the earlier masculine code of the corrupt ancien régime.

Montoni, in contrast, is a "man," with no feminine qualities at all tempering his innate fierceness. He thrives on risk and challenge (1:185), standing as a sort of secularized Miltonic Satan figure. His energy, greed, gambling, treachery, and false accusations against Morano, his smuggling and his successful life of crime—all these are depicted by Radcliffe as the logical outcomes of subscribing to a completely masculinized and anachronistic aristocratic code of values. Radcliffe suggests further that in addition to his greed, Montoni's greatest crime is his adultery; his sexual appetites are depicted as limitless when we are introduced to his mistress. This is a man, we are told, who is so corrupt that he married not simply for money but to protect the good name of his mistress.

And just as Valancourt deserves his heroic status because of his feminized behavior, so does Emily earn her right to be a heroine by aping traditional masculine qualities. Throughout the text she is motivated by "duty" and "good sense" (1:159); she is praised by Montoni for being different from others of her sex (1:234, 247, 275). Unlike other women, Emily, he claims, understands that "strength of mind," willpower, is the only quality worth having. Later the Count de Villefort, Emily's convenient substitute father figure, also praises her tendency to resist emotion and stifle her tears when he attempts to convince her to marry DuPont rather than the fallen and soiled Valancourt (2:235). "Tears" are "another language" that men do not want to hear, and so Emily and the count stop speaking with them.

Much has been made of the "double chamber" in which Emily lives at Udolpho. With two doors, only one of which can be fastened from inside the room, the heroine is in a continually besieged condition—open to all comers. And when she is chased down a dark hallway by not one but two men intent on raping her, we know that the fate Emily must face within the castle is her own deeply repressed attraction to illicit and promiscuous sexuality. At many points *Udolpho* reads like sanitized pornography, as if Radcliffe had traced over all the monotonous sex in the Marquis de Sade and substituted extended descriptions of the landscape or the chase around the castle as more exciting. Again, when Emily is forced into the Venetian gondola and sits between Morano and Montoni, she is not simply reduced to an object of exchange between two men who are themselves in a homosocial scenario.[8] The quasi-pornographic threat in this and the rape chase scene concerns the fear that a woman's fate in this society is to be sexually used by numerous men in a polygamous fashion. If "civilization" as we know it is predicated on monogamy, then polygamy is a distinctly recurrent male fantasy, one that will not die a quiet or easy death just because women find it offensive and dehumanizing. The female gothic ideology of the daughter poises itself against the polygamous desire of the sons, who attempt to seize all the women for themselves after they have killed the father. The female gothic heroine stands behind the father, knowing that he is the best defense against the mob of men who would usurp women as spoils of war, as so much booty.

But just as music functions throughout the text as a leitmotif, so does "the track of blood on the floor" (1:276, 328). When Morano is almost mortally wounded by Montoni, he leaves a track of blood that later leads Emily to her dying aunt. Later a "track of blood" leads to the wounded Valancourt, shot by Emily's servant on suspicion of being a thief (2:260). Blood, which con-

---

8. For the fullest discussion of homosocial desire and its development in the gothic novel, see Eve Kosofsky Sedgwick, *Between Men: English Literature and Male Homosocial Desire* (New York: Columbia University Press, 1985).

nects Morano to the imprisoned aunt and the servant to the master, functions as a symbol of lack; it leads Emily to the wound that we recognize as history. Morano and Madame Cheron/Montoni both embody the weak and corrupt aristocratic tradition that finds itself incapable of being sustained or even surviving in a changing, increasingly mercantile society. The second wound inflicted on Valancourt by the servant Jean, a stand-in for Emily, effectively punishes him for his sins, his dallying and attractions to the fallen urban world of Paris.

The track of blood, the music, the buried family secrets, the mysterious portraits, the whispered gossip and oral traditions—all of the conventional trappings and paraphernalia of the gothic—stand as the residue of an earlier, woman-marked culture, an oral and maternal legacy that the female gothic attempts to resurrect and validate. The voice of Annette earlier in the text is replaced later by the voice of Dorothée, both servants who gossip with their mistress in an attempt to inform her of her potential fate. Whereas each one is frequently mistaken, often erring on the side of dramatic romance, both help Emily construct herself as a gothic heroine. Both, that is, help Emily hear the voice of an absent woman-marked culture. When Annette warns Emily about the veiled portrait and Dorothée tells Emily the sad story of her poisoned aunt, both are connecting her to the world she would like to forget, reject, or repress. Both are informing her that the destiny of women who allow their passions to dominate them is to suffer at the hands of more powerful men who embody the world of the patriarchal tyrant. But both are also offering her a means of escape and sabotage through the masquerade of professional femininity—controlling one's passions and seizing the verbal, storytelling, narrative power of the voice of the mother.

Power, both women suggest, resides ultimately in the ability to tell one's own narrative, and by doing so to shape one's own destiny. One can tell one's story in such a way that the victim triumphs over the victimizer, the weak overcome the strong. Both women tell false stories, but their narratives empower them because they expose men to public humiliation and censure. This is precisely the subversive power that Emily gains from these two servants, and it is the core fantasy of the female gothic novel. If power in late eighteenth-century England is no longer simply a matter of class, then one can negotiate individually and privately for one's status and claims. The female gothic heroine is she who learns to tell the tale and thereby seize the more dominant power of narrative and discourse as it circulates freely in a rapidly changing and unstable social system.

But before the body and voice of the mother can be heard, the power of the father (the written, logocentric tradition of wills, letters, patrimony) must be confronted and either overthrown or co-opted. When the gothic antiheroine attempts to overthrow the father directly, she fails. The gothic feminist heroine, in contrast, co-opts the father; she survives and creates a new androgynous culture, a world in which men exist as chastened versions of themselves and women retreat into a visionary form of utopian marriage. All we ever see of Emily or the later Ellena after marriage is hazily clouded in moral hyperbole. Sitting around a table, amid a carnival atmosphere, eating and drinking and making merry, the moral of *Udolpho* bears repeating: "though the vicious can sometimes pour affliction upon the good, their power is transient and their punishment certain; innocence, though oppressed by injustice, shall, supported by patience, finally triumph over misfortune!" (2:344). These, gentle readers, are words to remember.

In this novel, however, we also recognize a powerful ideology designed to appeal to middle-class women, buffeted as they were by displacement both from below (by lower-class workers) and from above (by aristocrats). With enemies, real or imagined, on all sides, middle-class women were able to construct a potent species of ideology. They learned to take their worst nightmares of abuse, their real and imagined scenes of persecution and objectification, and shape them instead into sagas of revenge and triumph. They learned, in short, to use a new discourse system to empower themselves. They spoke a new language, and it was not a language marked by anything other than crocodile tears.

II

On August 15, 1797, James Boaden opened his dramatic adaptation of Radcliffe's final gothic novel, *The Italian Monk,* to a rapturous audience. In Boaden's version of the story, the villain Schedoni reforms his evil ways by the conclusion of the play and is rewarded with a reunion with his long-suffering wife, who has been hiding in a convent, and his daughter Ellena. Boaden's version, or what we might recognize as bowdlerized Radcliffe, actually makes explicit Radcliffe's connection to her source, Shakespeare's *Winter's Tale,* while it sentimentalizes the gothic elements that Radcliffe perfects in this, her final and what is generally considered her best work.[9]

---

9. See *The Plays of James Boaden,* xxv–xxvi. All quotations from *The Italian* are from the Oxford University Press edition, ed. Frederick Garber (London, 1970), with page numbers in parentheses in the text.

But exactly how do the sentimental and gothic codes intersect in Radcliffe's text? And finally, how does that intersection create the gendered subject we recognize as the gothic feminist? The gothic heroine as social construct has learned that she should not openly express her emotions, let alone her sexual passion, to her beloved. But if she is not allowed to speak, how can she make her desires known? In true melodramatic fashion, the female gothic novel confronts the problem by posing the heroine in what I would call a form of masquerade, the "theater of the voyeur." It places the gothic heroine in a very revealing *tableau vivant* that enacts her feelings while she is being observed, seemingly all unaware of the fact that she is the spectacle of the text. We witness one of these stagings in *The Italian* when Ellena grasps her lute (witness to her musical sensitivities and *"virtu"*) and flings herself on her windowsill to moan aloud her thwarted love for Vivaldi, with him, of course, just outside the window. When she concludes her declaration of love and begins strumming a few mournful notes on her lute, he joins in and she learns—horror of horrors—that he has overheard everything: "'Forget that you ever heard it; I know not what I said,'" she pleads with him. The gothic heroine is forced to deny her own words because she is not allowed to speak. Speaking is not decorous, and so she "smiles" an "involuntary smile [which] seemed to contradict the meaning" of her words (27). The female gothic heroine is forever confined to communicating through body language because the verbal is not permitted in her element. Like a child, she is truly expected to be seen and not heard.

Radcliffe's final novel succeeds because it reworks melodramatic conventions to a veritable fever pitch. The orphaned beauty, persecuted by her lover's evil mother, sentenced to die in a convent dungeon, almost murdered by her own uncle, miraculously saved by the triumph of virtue and the powers of recognition at just the last moment—such is the stuff of its melodramatic acoustics. The operatic motifs—the lute, the singing voice that draws Ellena to her own long-lost mother, the pantomime of the murder of Virginia by her father, the chambers of the Inquisition—all function in this final novel as signs, significations of meaning that the adolescent heroine must interpret correctly in order to be ushered safely into adulthood. What is at stake in this work is the nature of that rite of passage, that ritual movement from pubescent sexuality to full status as an adult woman. The journey is fraught with perils, and many women are not able to make the adjustment—just witness Ellena's own mother or her maiden aunt or all the bleeding nuns that Ellena encounters scattered across the landscape of Italy. But Ellena is a true heterosexual heroine. She will by the end of the text be able to divest herself of her emotional ties to her parents and swear allegiance to her husband as her rightful protector and guardian. She will, that is, become a gothic feminist heroine.

The Italian has often been ridiculed for its blatant historical anachronisms: its pretense to being set very specifically in the Naples of 1764 while it presents a thriving Inquisition that had not existed in Italy for over a hundred years. The psychological action of *The Italian* occurs in the same time and place as do all of Radcliffe's novels—England, 1790–97. And once again we have a melodrama of gender and ideology played out on a supposedly safely distanced historical field. The historical parallels are significant, however, for what they reveal about the author's cultural anxieties. This is a gothic world in which the inquisitional tribunal—or the traditional hierarchical authority that had so recently been destroyed by the forces of the French Revolution—actually does discover the truth about Ansaldo, Schedoni, Vivaldi, Spalatro, and Zampari. From a veritable *A* to *Z*, the Inquisition ferrets out the truth and punishes villainy, although these crimes occurred almost twenty years earlier. Radcliffe it would seem is conservative to the very end.

The Italian is presided over by the confessional, and one need not read much Foucault to understand that the confessional is not a uniquely medieval invention but a strikingly modern one. What better way to control and discipline the populace than to invite them into an enclosed, womb-like embrace in order to have them tell you all their most secret thoughts and actions.[10] *The Italian* begins at the scene of the crime—the confession that Schedoni gave almost twenty years earlier to Ansaldo—and it concludes some four hundred pages later with that same fully articulated confession. Radcliffe, however, has not made the crime the center of her text but the telling of the crime. It is narration that is the sustaining interest in her work; narrations that are cut off, twisted, partially told, exaggerated, and finally enacted form the central impetus of her novel. The text, so to speak, is reified

---

10. Judith Wilt has observed that Radcliffe "is distinguished in the history of the Gothic for the invisibility of her God, the inaudibility of heaven's vengeful, signalizing thunder." Further, she notes that the Protestant compulsion to distinguish between God and the church finds its clearest manifestation in *The Italian*: "Here the old institution, its ministers and appurtenances, are voluptuously painted, seen, abhorred, even strengthened. And the great God rules, even as His Church is purged of its villain, its evil fathers. Yet the reader will find it difficult to distinguish the evil father from the good, since they are both—Gothic antihero and Enlightenment God—distinguished primarily for an obsessive, hidden, tyrannous, ambiguous will" (*Ghosts of the Gothic* [Princeton: Princeton University Press, 1980], 32). On a similar note, Victor Sage, in *Horror Fiction and the Protestant Tradition* (London: Macmillan, 1988), points out that for Radcliffe "the habit of the monk is a symbol of deviousness and secrecy, which has a directly theological meaning," that is, it imagistically participates in her culture's evolving discourse of rabid anti-Catholicism (34).

in the very bodies of the characters, such that their identities (shifting, partial, changing) encode the nature of narrative itself. Schedoni is actually Ferando Count di Bruno, deliberately confused with another evil madman the Baróne di Cambrusca, his daughter may or may not be Ellena, and his wife is supposedly dead (because he stabbed her), but she is really living safely as a nun who is recognizable only through her voice. This is a deeply encrypted world, where the mother is reduced to a series of signs—her nun's veil, her voice—and the father/uncle is often nothing more than a cowl and a scowl. Identities are impossible to distinguish from the disguises that are adopted, put on and off at will, like clothing.

Radcliffe begins this novel with a brief quotation from Walpole's *Mysterious Mother,* that strange drama about incest that haunted literary imaginations throughout the nineteenth century. Incest is the "secret sin" that no "art" or "penance" can cleanse, and it is the "secret sin" that all melodrama conceals only to teasingly reveal. The "incest" that lies hidden in *The Italian* is the rape of Olivia by her dead husband's brother—who later pretends to be the pious monk Schedoni. It would seem that Radcliffe begins her novel where Monk Lewis concluded his own. Radcliffe begins with the originating crime: parental sex as violent and taboo, that is, parental sex as it is imagined by the adolescent female imagination. It is the mother Olivia who undergoes the first beating fantasy in this text, and the script reads, my mother is being beaten (raped and stabbed) by my father. We are in this novel in the realm of the female adolescent mind as it struggles toward some sort of accommodation with the realities of sexuality and the act of birth. The sexual act that engendered Ellena can only be imagined by her as either asexual (her dead father) or violently and perversely lascivious (her mother and Schedoni, which equals "rape"). The need to place the "parents" in religious orders after such an act serves as an expression of the child's fantasized power to punish the parents for their passion. The continual positionings of Schedoni whipping himself, violently punishing himself at his confessional—all of these are the child's attempts to extract vengeance on the father for the crime of his passion, his "rape" of her mother.

It is surely significant that the hero Vincentio di Vivaldi first sees Ellena Rosalba in a church and that it is her voice that attracts his attention. He follows this veiled icon and her chaperon home, and manages to get a glimpse of her face: "more touchingly beautiful than he had dared to image" (6). The stage is now set for the triangulations of desire that proliferate throughout this text. Ellena and Vivaldi are alone together only once; consistently throughout the work they are positioned in a variety of oedipal postures either with Ellena's aunt, mother, and father or with Vivaldi's parents or finally with Vivaldi's doglike servant Paulo. The nature of adolescent sexuality as presented in gothic texts makes it so fearful that one seeks as much company as possible in order to mitigate the intimacy. There would appear to be safety in numbers, or a recognition of the communal aspect of sexuality—both impulses seem to be operative in this compulsion.

But no sooner are we introduced to Ellena, the epitome of beauty, sweetness, and docility, than we are given our first description of Vivaldi's mother, the Marchesa di Vivaldi, "vain, proud, violently passionate, haughty, vindictive, yet crafty and deceitful; patient in stratagem, and indefatigable in pursuit of vengeance" (7). It is a fearful thing to be loved by such a mother, as Vivaldi learns throughout the novel.[11] Dare we say the obvious? He chooses to love a woman he knows will bring him into a deadly struggle with his mother. He desires, that is, to kill his mother and free himself from the stranglehold that he experiences as her love. He becomes a gothic hero because he finds the strength to persist in this struggle against the mother, even when his own life is at stake. He succeeds in ridding himself of his mother and replacing her with a much more docile and obedient version of her, his girl-bride. He assumes the status of culture hero because he has absorbed and introjected his own origins: he has become self-sufficient and able to originate a new community. He has earned the right to marry and, by extension, to become a father. But it is important to notice that the struggle for Vivaldi mirrors the struggle of Ellena to achieve adulthood. The stakes for a male in this culture are just as high as they are for a woman. Vivaldi must destroy his mother and supplant his father before he can marry Ellena. She, on the other hand, must kill her father (both versions of him) and rediscover her mother, bring her out of Hades so to speak, before she can marry happily. The two lovers, like inverse images of Greek fertility deities, must each survive this fearful rite if they are to achieve the Utopia that is the transformed aristocratic (read: companionate) marriage that concludes this novel.[12]

Although Ellena proves in the end to be of noble blood and therefore worthy of marriage to Vivaldi, we are introduced to her first as a sort of

---

11. On Vivaldi's mother and Ellena's father as theatrical embodiments of sheer "villainy," see the discussion in Elizabeth Napier, *The Failure of the Gothic: Problems of Disjunction in an Eighteenth-Century Literary Form*, 133–46. On the same subject, see Susan Greenfield, "Veiled Desires: Mother-Daughter Love and Sexual Imagery in Ann Radcliffe's *The Italian*," *EC* 33 (1992), 73–89; and Elizabeth Broadwell, "The Veil Image in Ann Radcliffe's *The Italian*," *SAB* 40 (1975), 76–87.

12. On the valorization of marriage and the development of the companionate family as a bourgeois ideal, see Lawrence Stone, *Family, Sex, and Marriage in England, 1500–1800*.

semiproletarian seamstress who supports herself and her aunt with her needlework and artistic copies of flowers and fruit on pseudoantique furniture. The class issue enters the world of *The Italian* only to be elided by Ellena's later abrupt elevation to the aristocracy. Again, the operative compulsion here is "magical thinking": I am what I want to believe I am. I create my own reality. I am the daughter of noble aristocrats, not struggling peasants, and therefore my desires will become reality. Gothic adolescence is consistently characterized by just this sort of magical thinking. And as long as it is confined to matters of class, it is fairly harmless. It is not so harmless, however, when it confronts the sexual.

Volume 1 of *The Italian* concerns the quite literal haunting of Vivaldi by the mysterious monk who accosts him under the arch of the Paluzzi castle. In the continual proliferation of arches throughout this text, we cannot fail to be reminded of Victor Turner's theory of the "threshold" or liminal antistructures in rites of passage. If all ritual processes have three stages: separation, threshold (limen), and aggregation, then it would seem that Vivaldi spends an inordinate amount of time trying to get out from under arches. Turner tells us that all threshold entries *entrance* the initiate thus; when he finds himself under the arch of the Paluzzi and for the first time confronts the mysterious messenger monk, Vivaldi does become entranced. But ultimately he is entranced by his own self-dramatizing construction of a rival. When the monk warns Vivaldi away from Ellena, it is because he is in the hire of Schedoni and Vivaldi's mother; but instead Vivaldi immediately thinks that the monk is his rival for Ellena's love. He has again placed himself in an oedipal position in regard to Ellena, and the irony, of course, is that he *is* in a triangular relation with Ellena, but it is not the triangle that he thinks it is. It is instead a much more heavily loaded triangle with his mother and her "father." The identity of the monk—later identified as Zampari, former accomplice of Schedoni—serves as perhaps the most creaking aspect of the gothic. His heavy-handed villainy, at least in all of the initial encounters with him, reeks of melodramatic staging in a way that Schedoni's more subtly ambiguous evil does not. He personifies that element in Vivaldi's consciousness that would seek to keep him in thrall to his mother and her class prejudices. Zampari is murdered in the end by Schedoni, an example of evil turning on evil and consuming itself, which, as we all know from the structure of melodrama, has to occur if a new and reformed community is to come into being.

But what has Zampari really done to deserve death? He has slandered the good name of Ellena to her future father-in-law. The standard melodramatic device of the false charge (adultery, illegitimacy, or poverty) is a stock convention and the one reliable obstacle that the gothic heroine always has to overcome.[13] In Ellena's case the charge is left rather vague, but the implication is that Ellena is widely known to be a wanton seductress, with Vivaldi simply her latest victim. Like Vivaldi, we also know that a woman who wears a veil, poses at her altar, and expresses her passions only to her lute is pure. Such are the signs of purity and professional femininity, and we do not question their veracity. But the young lovers are in a quagmire, and that locale is peopled by ferocious, engulfing, and suffocating parental love. Adolescents in the gothic novel cannot simply separate from their parents and childhood home. The separation instead is charged with all the trauma, all the turmoil that traditionally is associated with life or death situations.

In the adolescent imagination, adults are either all good or all evil, and thus we are presented with Ellena's aunt, Signora Bianchi, a good woman who presides over a sort of mock marriage between the two lovers early in the novel (39). Their problems begin in earnest almost immediately, however, as Bianchi is soon after poisoned and Ellena kidnapped by ruffians hired by the marchesa. Bad mothers/good mothers fluctuate throughout this text, with Olivia later replacing Bianchi, her sister, just as Bianchi had earlier replaced Olivia as mother so that she, Olivia, could flee from Schedoni. The splitting of parental figures is a standard characteristic in fairy tales, and it is surely no coincidence that we never see Vivaldi's parents together. He speaks to his father in his chamber and then he speaks to his mother in her chamber. Do these parents ever talk to each other? Not likely. And what does such a strange situation reveal about the adolescent imagination? Once again we are in the realm of magical thinking. The adolescent wants to imagine that her parents have no relationship separate from her; her existence must be the center of each of their lives.

After Ellena is kidnapped, she finds herself in the isolated convent of San Stefano at the mercy of a snobbish and vindictive abbess. In this anti-utopian female community the holy sisters amuse themselves with gossip—"busy whispers"—and practice the "malignant envy that taught them to exalt themselves upon the humiliation of others" (68). Women, like other

---

13. Brooks in his *Melodramatic Imagination* discusses the motif of the slandered melodramatic heroine, the embodiment of victimized innocence under persecution. According to Brooks, her dilemma "dramatizes a nightmare struggle for recognition of the sign of innocence, which is also the struggle for the assertion of selfhood" (52). Apropos of Olivia's voice, he also discusses the "*voix du sang*—the secret impulse by which parents and children and siblings are irresistibly drawn to one another despite mistaken and lost identities" (45).

Agnes

"minority" groups, have been a traditionally scapegoated population, and like these other groups they have been encouraged to scapegoat certain of their own members in order to fictitiously shore up the larger membership. Ellena's status as "seductress" and "fallen woman" would make her a particularly attractive target to a group of women who imagine for themselves some sort of special status based on their celibacy. But their humiliation of Ellena is not confined solely to their ability to gossip about her; the abbess is able to exert real power over the very life of Ellena when she presents her with a nonnegotiable ultimatum: accept the veil or marry a man of the marchesa's choice. In such a doubly negative situation, Ellena's only recourse is one of passive-aggression; she is silent. When pressed by the determined abbess, Ellena responds in the manner of a true melodramatic heroine: "'I am prepared to meet whatever suffering you shall inflict upon me; but be assured, that my own voice never shall sanction the evils to which I may be subjected, and that the immortal love of justice, which fills all my heart, will sustain my courage no less powerfully than the sense of what is due to my own character.'" When the abbess responds, it is to remark that Ellena is "rash" and to wonder where she could have learned "these heroics" (84). Indeed, the female gothic heroine has learned her heroics from the constructions of femininity that were prevalent throughout the eighteenth century. If Pamela can resist the advances of Mr. B until safely married and Clarissa can triumph over Lovelace only in her willed death, then the convention of virtue besieged and ultimately triumphant was an established one, at least in sentimental literature, by the time Radcliffe was writing.

But lest we should falsely conclude that the convent is inhabited only by petty and spiteful women, we are soon acquainted with that paragon of real maternity, Olivia, Ellena's biological mother who has been forced to live for the past eighteen years as a nun. In a repetition compulsion Ellena is drawn to Olivia by her singing voice at mass, just as Vivaldi had been drawn initially to Ellena through her voice. The voice as maternal envelope makes us aware that the quest to immerse oneself in the sound of the mother's tongue is a powerful one in the melodramatic novel. But it is not simply the voice that draws Ellena to Olivia; it is also Olivia's face—"touched with a melancholy kind of resignation," a "paleness, and the air of languor"—that reminds Ellena of a "head of Guido" (86). Guido's most famous painting, a virtual cultural icon during this period, was the head of Beatrice Cenci, victim of rape by her father and later with her brother an accomplice in parricide. The association of Ellena with Beatrice Cenci makes clear the "secret sin" that pervades gothic fiction—not simply incest or aberrant sexuality, but parricide, the overthrow of a corrupt hierarchical system by the sons and daughters of an emerging middle class.[14]

But before Ellena can fully understand her situation in the convent, she hears the "cry of the mother," a stock melodramatic device that figures the mother's recognition, however unconscious, of her child. The voice of the mother attracts Ellena, just as the mother's face—"so supplicating and expressive . . . frank, noble, full of sensibility, [with] a gentle melancholy in her eye"—draws her (87). It is as if the two had always known each other. On the following day Ellena finds the courage to approach her mother: "it seemed as if the soul, which beamed forth in that smile, had long been acquainted with hers" (88). Ellena knows that she cannot live without "the regard of this nun, [it] seemed necessary to her heart." When they finally do meet privately, Ellena's first words to her mother are, "'I understand you'" (88). It is significant that Olivia cannot recognize her own daughter, although she does notice that her features "have some resemblance to those of a friend I once had" (93). We can only conclude that the "friend" is Ellena's father, the "good husband," the elder brother of Schedoni. Ellena would appear to be marked by her father's face and her mother's veil. She is a sort of composite of parental inheritance—the unfortunate recipient of her parents' dual legacy of betrayal, murder, and passion. Her life until this point has been shrouded in lack of knowledge about the true nature of her parents, or we could claim, she has been uncertain about the true nature of adult sexuality. In finding her mother and later in naming her mother's rapist, Schedoni, she fingers the pain that is one form of adult passion. She recognizes the wounding power of passion and she—like her mother—flees from it. The convent, with its dream of escape from the female body, stands as one polar possibility in the adolescent psyche. One can choose marriage—with its risks—or one can choose the nunnery. But the sheer profusion of bleeding nuns who inhabit these convents, the unfortunate Agnes as well as Olivia, suggests that there is no final haven, no escape from the realities of the physical female body. Women will always bleed; they will always be unclean in the eyes of the patriarchy and finally in their own eyes.

Later when Ellena is dragged into the church to accept the nun's veil in a very hurried ceremony, she protests and is miraculously saved at the last

---

14. I have discussed the figure of Beatrice Cenci as a historical icon in "La Cenci: Incest in Hawthorne and Melville," *ATQ* 44 (1979), 247–59. The painting of Beatrice by Guido Reni was a particularly potent representation during the nineteenth century and has also been discussed by Stephen Behrendt, "Beatrice Cenci and the Tragic Myth of History," in *History and Myth* (Detroit: Wayne State University Press, 1990).

moment by both her voice and the simultaneous appearance of Vivaldi. When she raises her voice it is to assert, "'I protest. . . . I protest'" (119). Vivaldi, just arrived at this church of all others in the country, takes it from there. He manages to orchestrate their escape from the convent, although his incompetence is revealed when he hires a monk who betrays them just as they reach the final door. Once again it is Ellena whose voice stirs the pity of the old monk, and they manage to escape at the last minute. Vivaldi loves to pose; he loves to swashbuckle around displaying his "enthusiasms," his causes. As the abate says to him on very short acquaintance indeed, "'Would that the whole world were wrong that you might have the glory of setting it right!'" (121).

But before Vivaldi can manage to do anything right, Olivia has arranged for Ellena to escape in her nun's veil. The conversation that occurs between mother and daughter before this escape is significant because of what we would now recognize as its cultural codings. When Ellena observes that she will fight evil with courage, Olivia cautions restraint, dissembling, passive-aggression. She tells Ellena, "'It is sufficient that you understand the consequence of open resistance to be terrible, and that you consent to avoid it.'" She warns Ellena to "'abandon at least the appearance of resistance,'" in favor of "deceit" practiced "in self-defence," hoping that in the meantime "something may occur to rescue you from your present situation" (97). We recognize this strategy now as playing for time, passive-aggression, a long-practiced and well-established strategy in the arsenal of female survival. This device, not revealing your true feelings or intentions, is so well known to women that it comes as somewhat of a shock to see it being openly taught here to a daughter by her mother. And yet that is the cultural condition of professional femininity. It consists of a learned strategy of deception and dissimulation, and it stands as the inheritance that mothers pass on to their daughters in the melodramatic world of the female gothic novel.

Putting this advice into a cultural context, however, is particularly revealing given the discourse system that had arisen around just this topic. Wollstonecraft had earlier condemned the official mistress system in her *Vindication* by denouncing it as a corrupt residue of the aristocracy, a form of covert influence, manipulation, and cunning that women could only practice behind the scenes, never openly in their own names or within their own rights: "Women . . . sometimes boast of their weakness, cunningly obtaining power by playing on the weakness of men; and they may well glory in their illicit sway, like Turkish bashaws, they have more real power than their master" (*Vindication* 40). Similarly, Mary Hays condemned an

educational system that encouraged women to please their husbands as if
such behavior were based on some recognized form of morality rather than
expediency. Such a notion, Hays observes, "is perhaps as unfortunate a system of politics in morals, as ever was introduced for degrading the human
species" (*Appeal to the Men of Great Britain in Behalf of Women* 56): "And if
indeed, women do avail themselves of the only weapons they are permitted
to wield, can they be blamed? Undoubtedly not; since they are compelled to
it by the injustice and impolicy of men. Petty treacheries—mean subterfuge—whining and flattery—feigned submission—and all the dirty little attendants, which compose the endless train of low cunning; if not
commendable, cannot with justice be very severely censured, when practiced by women. Since alas!—Necessity acknowledges no law, but her own!"
(91). Hays would encourage Ellena to "feign submission" just like Ralph
Ellison years later would encourage his compatriots to "grin em to death."
Clara Reeve and Hannah More, generally considered to be conservative during the feminist debates of the 1790s, also condemned the "veil" of ignorance
and prejudice that kept women from seeing clearly the conditions of their
lives.[15]

But when Olivia succeeds in passing on this "professionally feminine"
wisdom to her daughter, the mother-daughter cultural dyad is complete,
and from this point until the conclusion of the novel, Ellena is never without the nun's veil that her mother bequeaths to her. This ambivalent physical marking of femininity—a veil that not only conceals the female body
and face but also marks the body as asexual and antimaternal—serves as a
protective device, a camouflage, a coloration that belies the actual sexuality of both women. It is no coincidence that the veil serves not only to aid
Ellena's escape but later is used against her and Vivaldi when they are
arrested by the officers of the Inquisition on the trumped up charge that
Vivaldi has kidnapped a nun and forced her into marriage. The religious
habit, put on and off as a sort of disguise by both Ellena and Schedoni, figures one aspect of adolescent sexuality. In both characters there is an
attempt to conceal and bury the recognition of adult sexuality, the mature
sexual body. Whereas Schedoni as a monk seeks to assuage his guilt by
whipping himself, Ellena analogously whips herself into a similar asex-
ual/sexual ambivalent frenzy: she will marry Vivaldi; she won't marry

---

15. Mary Wollstonecraft, *A Vindication of the Rights of Woman*, 2nd ed., ed. Carol H. Poston (New
York: Norton, 1988); Mary Hays, *Appeal to the Men of Great Britain in Behalf of Women* (1798; reprinted
New York: Garland, 1974).

Vivaldi. She will be a bride; she will be a nun. In either case, of course, she knows she will bleed.

If the duality between the benevolent mother and the corrupt abbess forms the inner core of the narrative in volume 1, then the confessional where Schedoni and the marchesa plot Ellena's murder embodies the core of volume 2. The confessional, as many critics have noted, stands at the beginning of this text and at the end, framing it as it were with gigantic ears.[16] Paranoia runs rampant in this text; there is no such thing as a secret sin, in fact, because the sinner is always compelled to confess and the confessor is always compelled to repeat at least part of the tale of sin. As with the peasants who know bits and pieces of the Schedoni saga, the saga of sin is related by the narrator to random passersby, every pair of eyes and ears at every keyhole. Partial narratives of Schedoni's sin run like a leitmotif through this book. The tale is not told completely until the Inquisition very kindly invites Schedoni to tell all.

But the set piece of *The Italian* resides in the verbal dueling between the marchesa and Schedoni in her closet and then in the confessional (his closet so to speak). In a section of the text filled with references to the fall of the Roman Empire, the corruption of history, and the role that spying clergy have played in all historical crises, we see a mother so evil, so perverse, that she brags about her ability to "lose the mother in the strict severity of the judge" (111). In these two extended scenes, Schedoni and the marchesa decide that the only solution to the Ellena problem is murder. But neither one wants to actually say the words, so they verbally dance around the marchesa's desire not only to have Ellena, her rival for her son, killed but to have Schedoni do the deed himself. So much cleaner that way because Schedoni, the marchesa suggests, has ecclesiastical protection in being a monk, is above the civil law. What is encrypted here is the woman as deviously, murderously manipulative of the weaker, passive male. Such is the stuff of melodrama even if it is not particularly historically accurate. This scene encodes anxiety about the powerful, encroaching female, out of control, operating within the network of a corrupt counterpublic institution, the church. Women and priests, both

---

16. Daniel Cottom comes closest to my argument when he observes that "the heroine must be victimized but made transcendent through this victimization. . . . In such a character, Radcliffe's heroines *are* the landscape of her art, as their bodies as well as their perceptions are designed to deny conflict by making a virtue of suffering" (see his *Civilized Imagination* [Cambridge: Cambridge University Press, 1985], 50). For other discussions of sensibility and the language of the confessional and the body in pain, see Louis Bredvold, "The Exaltation of Unhappiness," chap. 3, *The Natural History of Sensibility* (Detroit: Wayne State University Press, 1962); and John Mullan, *Sentiment and Sociability: The Language of Feeling in the Eighteenth Century* (Oxford: Clarendon, 1988).

supposedly outside the mainstream and both marked as other by the dominant political power structure, have served as natural allies to each other for centuries. Here the alliance is perverse.

The phallic mother—the "masculine feminine" woman—haunts gothic fiction, just as the castrated father appears with unpleasant regularity. And the dueling between Schedoni and the marchesa is posited on the gender stereotypes that they both impose on themselves and each other. When the marchesa wants to brag, she presents herself as a man, unsexed, a Lady Macbeth of Naples. And when she wants to motivate Schedoni, she employs Lady Macbeth's rather crude arsenal of stereotypes: Are you a man or not? The gendered constructions that they both employ are frightening in their simplicity. First the marchesa claims to possess "a man's courage" (168), and then she worries that "some woman's weakness still lingers at [her] heart" (169). Finally, she allows herself to cry when she hears music in the church, fittingly a requiem for the dead. Schedoni by this time has nothing but contempt for the woman, "the slave of her passions, the dupe of her senses . . . the victim of a sound! O, weak and contemptible being!" (178). Women are marked and marginalized by their susceptibility to emotion, the passions, and their senses, the qualities they were trying so diligently to abject, commodify, and control.

The word "judge"—used first as a noun, then a verb—functions throughout these scenes as a talismanic lure. Both the marchesa and Schedoni fancy that they are in privileged positions that allow them to "judge" Ellena's character, motives, status, and fate. They pronounce that she deserves death. In fact, Ellena had been earlier warned by Olivia that the abbess had condemned other wayward nuns to death and that she feared the same fate was in store for Ellena. The fantasy that the phallic mother and the castrated father are plotting your death—such is the central core fear of *The Italian.* When the marchesa finally obtains Schedoni's assent that he will kill Ellena in that mysterious house along the shores of the Adriatic, she proffers a stunning piece of advice: "'Avoid violence, if that be possible, but let her die quickly! The punishment is due to the crime'" (176). It is, as we all know, impossible to kill someone without using violence, unless of course one employs poison, the passive-aggressive method of lethal choice used by other gothic antiheroines in Radcliffe's books. But the two have conducted in these two scenes a sort of mock trial, in which they have presented evidence, passed sentence, and determined punishment, all out of sight of the intended victim. They have, in short, formed their own little private Inquisition, all neatly kept in the family so to speak. Now they only need the victim's presence—her physical reality—to accomplish their "justice."

But if Schedoni and the marchesa convince themselves that they have fairly tried the Ellena whom they have constructed, they are both continually confronted with vestiges of their senses that warn them they are committing an evil deed. For instance, the marquesa hears the requiem mass and gives way to tears, or she sees the words "God hears thee!" emblazoned over the confessional and quakes. She is, in short, continually assaulted by the reality of the body through her own senses of hearing and sight. In this way she is strikingly different from Schedoni, who closes himself off from his senses and lives almost totally in the universe he has constructed in his head. If woman valorizes the senses in this ideology, man reifies his reason, what we euphemistically call "the life of the mind." Neither reason nor the emotions in isolation from one another are sufficient, as both the marchesa and Schedoni learn in the end.

The melodramatic set pieces continue in the aborted wedding scene that follows, in which Ellena and Vivaldi approach the altar only to be stopped in their vows by command "of the most holy Inquisition!" (186). The power of the patriarchy to prevent the younger generation's happiness, indeed their survival, is nowhere more in evidence than in the use Radcliffe makes of the Inquisition as a symbol of authoritarian power. Although we know that the driving will behind the murder plot against Ellena is the marchesa, the avenging phallic mother out of control, we also know what the marchesa does not: namely, that Schedoni also plans to have her son arrested by the Inquisition for the unpardonable sin of recognizing his hypocrisy. The neat reversals are significant, for Schedoni has been put in the position of killing his own daughter (or so he later thinks) unbeknownst to him, and the marchesa has unleashed a plan to kill her own son, also unbeknownst to her. Radcliffe suggests through these convolutions that the gendered warfare that each character is carrying on causes both the male and female to consume, cannibalistically, the next generation. Indeed, the gendered caricatures that we know as Schedoni and the marchesa are so extreme that neither can brook competition, even from their own offspring. We have seen the same sort of compulsion in Walpole's *Castle of Otranto* and in Radcliffe's own earlier gothics. The *senex* figures in the gothic, unlike the worlds of comedy and romance, are not simply laughed off the stage. In this universe the younger generation has no choice but to kill them.

And in the struggle that ensues over possession of Ellena, Vivaldi—like Valancourt in *The Mysteries of Udolpho*—is wounded in a ritualistic manner. The male hero always has his blood shed in order to earn the right to the heroine. The bleeding nun stands in some ways as his mirror image, although in the woman's case the blood signifies that she is shorn of her sexuality rather than empowered by it, but both the male and the female experience versions of the beating fantasy with what we can only recognize as a compulsive regularity. Vivaldi in the vaults of the Inquisition, "thrilled with horror" (196), and is a voyeuristic participant in the tortures of others (not, significantly, his own). His presence here reifies the Protestant/English consciousness confronting its own buried and repressed primitive/Catholic past. Wandering through the underground tunnels and prison cells, Vivaldi is very much the Enlightenment man excavating an unpleasant historical era, characterized not simply by superstition but inhuman cruelty and degradation: "'Brutes do not deliberately slaughter their species; it remains for man only, man, proud of his prerogative of reason, and boasting of his sense of justice, to unite the most terrible extremes of folly and wickedness!'" (198). Of course, Vivaldi fails to reckon with the fact that his own mother's boasted "sense of justice" as well as Schedoni's "reason" have placed him squarely in this hell.

But if Vivaldi wanders belowground searching for his missing Eurydice, Ellena is pursued aboveground by her would-be father and murderer. In a bedroom with no lock in a mysterious house on the beach, a house that evokes the decay and murderous corruption of Udolpho, Ellena first fends off the passive attack on her by Spalatro. No female gothic heroine would eat or drink the food offered by such a man. Such an attempt was not even worth the effort. The second attempt on her life, this time by Schedoni, is more interesting because it presents the female gothic heroine with the perfect opportunity for posturing and self-dramatization. In another great set piece, a beating fantasy, Schedoni approaches Ellena on a desolate beach along the coast of southern Italy. For the eighteenth-century English imagination, one could hardly imagine a more threatening location in which to place Innocent Young Female Beauty. And in the midst of a violent approaching storm the gothic heroine, taught from infancy to rely on the kindness of strangers, approaches the very man who has been sent there to kill her. Her first words to this man, who she thinks later is her father, are overdetermined with a significance that can only be appreciated within the melodramatic tradition: "'Alas!' said she, 'I have no longer a home, a circle to smile welcomes upon me! I have no longer even one friend to support, to rescue me! I—a miserable wanderer on a distant shore! tracked, perhaps, by the footsteps of the assassin, who at this instant eyes his victim with silent watchfulness, and awaits the moment of opportunity to sacrifice her!'" (220). Perhaps indeed. Calling him "Father," we are given the first instance of Radcliffe's curious use of the word "consciously," as in Ellena "had never consciously seen Schedoni" (221). Although she wears a portrait of him around her neck and although she has no memory of her own father, the implication is that she has seen Schedoni "unconsciously," that is, in her dreams. The dream of the bad father—punishing and murderous—is about to awaken into the conscious mind of Ellena. She is about to become the complete gothic heroine, engaged in a life or death struggle, not with banditti or common ruffians, but with her real enemy—the father and the entire patriarchal inheritance that would seek not only to disinherit her but to destroy her.

The male hysteria, the grappling for the dagger between Schedoni and Spalatro, the niceties about who will kill Ellena, all these dissolve as Schedoni enters her room as she sleeps, defenseless and unprotected, in that ominous unlocked bedroom. Once again he has trouble finding his dagger, but as he closes in on his target about to strike, he suddenly stands "aghast and motionless like a statue" (234). The cause of his "horror" is the miniature Ellena wears like a talisman around her neck, the portrait of the man she has been told was her father—Marinella, the man Schedoni once was before he forfeited the right to that name by committing fratricide and rape, and attemptingto murder his wife. Although he reveals himself to be that very father, come to protect his long-lost daughter, there is the unpleasant detail of the dagger, which he keeps tripping over and which presence speaks of phallic mania, mayhem, and murder. The irony in this section, perhaps the most famous scene in all of Radcliffe's works, reeks with melodramatic overload: I am being beaten and there is no doubt that it is my father who is wielding the knife. Trying to hide the dagger, Schedoni remarks to Ellena that it is indeed "'too true, you never have known a father's tenderness till now!'" (237). But as readers we know that this "tenderness" has been wrapped in a dagger; Ellena's survival depends on a misunderstanding and misrecognition of the father. The tenderness offered to women by the patriarchy depends on the daughter's ignorance about her father's true identity and character. It would appear that the tenderness offered to women by the patriarchy depends on the daughter's continued ability to ignore the dagger lying at her feet. Finally, the tenderness offered to women by the patriarchy is eminently embarrassing to the father. The word "embarrassing" becomes from this point on in the novel almost a refrain. Schedoni finds Ellena's existence an embarrassment to his identity (one might be tempted to say disguise) as a monk, but more than that he is embarrassed by the revelations he knows he will have to make about his personal history. It would seem that killing one's brother and wife are the sorts of embarrassing details that just keep coming back to haunt one.

The third volume of the novel, often criticized as the weakest section, presents us with the working out of the complications that have been carefully developed throughout the first two sections. We witness with Schedoni and Ellena the peasants' staging of a carnivalesque and ritualistic enactment of the murder of Virginia by her father the judge. We also witness further refinements on the oedipal triangle that is the relationship between Schedoni, the marchesa, and Ellena. Or we realize that in the marchesa's mind the oedipal triangle consists of herself, Ellena, and Vivaldi. In all the various configurations, and as with any dreamwork there are multiple possibilities, the parental figures exist as blocking, intrusive, encroaching figures who would seek to cannibalize their young before they would willingly give them up to another.

The theme of the interrupted and partial narrative is once again played out, this time in relation to someone named the Baróne di Cambrusca. Like a sort of Vathek figure, the baróne had supposedly died in an earthquake while conducting various and sundry experiments in a tower and while sullying his own daughter. This gothic tableau, the incestuous father/brother committing evil deeds within the cover of the isolated phallic tower, recurs most obsessively throughout male gothics (recall Byron's *Manfred*), but here it functions to confuse us about the identity and crimes of Schedoni. It suggests that Schedoni may be more than simply two people; he may actually be three. In fact, the most fearful aspect of the baróne narrative is the amorphousness it suggests about human identity. People, like animals, can change their skins, adoopt new coloration, and become something quite different from who we think they are. The anxiety about the lack of a stable subjectivity haunts the gothic, as it was to haunt the nineteenth century in its persistent attraction to a number of different Jekyll and Hyde incarnations.[17]

The amorphousness of identity is played out further in regard to Father Ansaldo and the mysterious monk Zampari. Forming a veritable human

---

17. See Mark M. Hennelley, Jr., "'The Slow Torture of Delay': Reading *The Italian*," *SH* 14 (1987) 1–17, for a discussion of the "chiasmic association between Baróne de Cambrusca and Count di Bruno" (13). Critics do not agree on these figures; Hennelley concludes that the two men are different (14), while Napier concludes that they are the same (143). And for a related discussion of resolving multiple claims on property among competing parties, a crucial issue to the female gothic tradition and as persistent as confusions about identity throughout Radcliffe's fiction, see David Punter, "Fictional Representation of the Law in the Eighteenth Century," *ECS* 16 (1982), 47–74.

chain from *A* to *Z*, human nature is multiple and a man who is one day the suspected adulterous lover of your wife can the next day be the priest sitting and hearing your confession. Or consider Zampari, one day your accomplice and the next day your betrayer. The depths of treachery that pervade all these characters are less about male personality than they are about encoding the fluidity of identity. Identity in the female gothic novel seems to be an elaborate masquerade, a series of poses, costumes, gestures that one adapts to accommodate one's most immediate audience. When Schedoni poisons Zampari and kills himself, he simultaneously destroys the false burden of history that he had made of himself. He is not Ellena's father, which had been the fear that most haunted both her and Vivaldi in this final section of the text. One can accept an orphan more easily than one can accept someone descended from a man like Schedoni.

But killing himself is not sufficient to remove Schedoni from the historical record. For that we need the testimony of Olivia, Ellena's mother, who is the only one in possession of the biological facts. And how does Ellena find her mother again? That should be obvious by this time—Ellena hears her mother's voice once again in the "good" convent—Our Lady of Sorrows. But the identification is not complete until the old servant Beatrice appears and recognizes Olivia, also through her voice. Faces may change, veils can go on or off, but voices are the only stable imprint of identity in a world where people are continually hiding from one another. After a remarkably civilized reunion, Olivia tells Ellena the facts of her life. Olivia, once the blushing bride, became a widow, then the victim of incestuous rape by her brother-in-law, and then his wife in fairly short order. Olivia's maternity produced two daughters—one the daughter of the "good husband" and one the product of rape by his brother. Olivia is able to assure Ellena that the daughter of the "cruel husband" died before she was a year old (380, 382). A sort of Darwinian survival of the fittest, that is of the good, seems to be operative here. Evil always self-destructs in the gothic universe, as both Schedoni and the marchesa learn in their dying moments.

But if Ellena never "consciously" knew Schedoni, why do we see the same word used in relation to Olivia's dealings with Ellena? We are told that while she was in the convent of San Stefano, Olivia had "unconsciously" saved her daughter (384) when she led her to safety and loaned her the disguising veil. The implication in both cases seems to be that goodness operates at a level of conscience that is simply not operative in evil characters. In contrast, we hear repeatedly that Schedoni's only emotion throughout the last section of the text is "embarrassment" (259, 269, 272, 293). He appears to be capable of shame and seems to feel guilt, but he is unable to go beyond either of those self-involved emotions and experience an "unconscious" giving of himself to others.

The various trials that run through this final, most melodramatic section of the text suggest at last a gothic compulsion to public forms of confession. Vivaldi is tried on the false charges that Schedoni has trumped up against him. Then Schedoni is tried for his very real but very old crimes. Then Ellena faces the slanderer who has poisoned her good name and reputation. Of interest, the worst charge that can be brought against a woman in this world is the accusation or indeed even the insinuation of sexual promiscuity. Zampari is revealed to be the slanderer of Ellena, and this crime alone seems to make him deserve the murder that Schedoni so quickly delivers to him. To use a cliché well known to Radcliffe, a devoted reader of Shakespeare, evil characters are forever hoisting themselves on their own petards. The outcomes they so cleverly plan for others invariably end up as their own fates. Planning the death of Ellena, the marchesa ends up dead herself. Planning to slander the good name of Ellena, Schedoni succeeds only in revealing his own evil deeds and character.

Evil has a strangely projective quality in the gothic novel. Evil characters do unto others what will end up being done to them. And strangely we find ourselves drawn to this powerful ideology because it is one we want very much to believe. We know we live in a world peopled by oddly evil characters, and sometimes they are even our parents. The adolescent need to break free of the parental bond, to establish a new identity and a new family, is sometimes so fraught with anxiety that the break becomes possible only if one imagines that one's life is at stake.[18] It is surely somewhat peculiar that Radcliffe wrote her four major novels all within the first ten years of her marriage, and then never wrote anything for publication again. The novels all concern one topic—the anxieties that a young woman faces in deciding to marry and leave her parental home. We know so little about Radcliffe that it is virtually impossible to conclude that the novels are autobiographical in any way. But there is a clinging adolescent quality to all of Radcliffe's work in that her heroines are finally unable to embrace the genitality that motherhood entails. These are wom+en who put up a life or death struggle just

---

18. David Punter in *The Literature of Terror* has discussed the "adolescent" quality of the gothic in terms of "disgust with the body" and "the liminal position of the adolescent, between a past which is to an extent remembered but, at least in part, as a site of embarrassment and injustice (the conflicted norms of Gothic and of our reaction to it), and a future which may be perceived as desirable but, for the present, *belongs to someone else* (a part not yet restored from the grave)" (2:209).

to get to the altar. They would appear to be incapable of becoming mothers themselves. Frozen like perpetual adolescents on the frieze of the gothic urn, they can only attend the marriage feasts that end these novels like *tableaux vivants.* Anything more than that is beyond them. Once again the servant functions as the voice of the redeemed community as he provides the heavy-handed moral of the novel: "'You see how people get through their misfortunes, if they have but a heart to bear up against them, and do nothing that can lie on their conscience afterwards: and how suddenly one comes to be happy, just when one is beginning to think one never is to be happy again!'" (414). In the gothic universe one simply and suddenly finds that everything is set right because nothing was ever permanently wrong. Evil, that is, is as ephemeral as good is potent and everlasting. Never mind that Olivia was almost stabbed to death by her violently jealous husband Schedoni. Never mind that Ellena was almost stabbed through the heart by that same Schedoni, who spared her life only because of a misunderstanding. Never mind that women prey on one another in a continual feeding frenzy of jealousy and misplaced pride. In the female gothic novel justice is finally triumphant—not the perverted justice of the marchesa but the real justice that is done when the truth is heard and acted upon.

The phallic mother's "justice" is finally a sort of perverted and inverted sexual illogic that would castrate women and men alike. It would cause them to reject their children as sexual competitors rather than see them as the beneficiaries of their sexual bounty and generosity. If a mother can turn on her son and if a father can turn on his daughter, then we are indeed living in a world of perverse and perverted sexual maniacs. These passions are finally repudiated in *The Italian,* and the marriage that concludes the novel—the stylized utopian union of Ellena and Vivaldi—is a moderate, temperate match. As the blushing bride Ellena and the bleeding nun Olivia sit down at the wedding banquet, we do not see the happy ending that James Boaden scripted for his audience. We see instead that sexual violence and jealousy will never be fully eradicated but only staved off momentarily by acts of courage and daring goodness. The fact that Olivia sits at the table as a nun with her daughter, the young bride, suggests the continued polarization of those two options for women. Ellena has narrowly escaped her mother's fate, but she stands only one generation removed from the perils and continued threat of rape and incest, unbridled and uncivilized aristocratic masculinity in its most perverse forms. The specter of history as a ravening and brute force that feeds on and fattens by consuming women is present in muted form at the table. They eat in silence.

FOUR

~

Hyperbolic
Femininity

Jane Austen, "Rosa Matilda," and Mary Shelley

Where is the ebullient, infinite woman who,
immersed as she was in her naïveté, kept in the
dark about herself, led into self-disdain by the
great arm of parental-conjugal phallocentrism, has
not been ashamed of her strength? Who, surprised
and horrified by the tumult of her drives (for she
was made to believe that a well-adjusted normal
woman has a divine composure), hasn't accused
herself of being a monster?

—HÉLÈNE CIXOUS

I

Twelve years after the stage performance of Henry Siddons's adaptation of Radcliffe's *Sicilian Romance* was all the rage in London, Charlotte Dacre Byrne, who published under the dramatic pen name "Rosa Matilda," would present another chained gothic victim heroine in her hyperbolically gothic novel, *Zofloya, or the Moor* (1806). In Dacre's version, however, it is Satan disguised as a black servant who suggests to the gothic antiheroine Victoria that they dispose of Victoria's inconvenient rival by chaining her to a damp stone cave, where later she is murdered in a perverse sexual frenzy, a very real beating delivered by the demonic and sexually voracious Victoria. But early in the female gothic tradition, one might be tempted to observe that even from its beginnings, there was a self-conscious deflating of the gothic, a parodying of the outrageously extravagant, hyperbolic, and unrealistic situations that recur in all of these works.[1] By presenting a parodic victim of the patriarchy the heroine of her *Northanger Abbey,* Austen, for instance, was attempting to rewrite the extravagant and hyperbolic claims made by her more popular sentimental precursor Charlotte Smith.

Austen, Dacre, and Mary Shelley all found themselves responding to the sentimental codes of conduct advocated by female writers like Smith, and Austen at least felt the comparison strongly. In one of her pieces of juvenilia, Austen has her heroine Kitty ask a new acquaintance, Miss Stanley, about her taste in books. Kitty admits that she likes "books of a lighter kind, books universally read and admired." She then launches into her rhapsody about Charlotte Smith:

> "You have read Mrs. Smith's Novels, I suppose?"said she to her Companion—. "Oh! Yes, replied the other, and I am quite delighted with them—They are the sweetest things in the world—." "And which do you prefer of them?" "Oh! dear, I think there is no comparison between them— Emmeline is *so much* better than any of the others—" "Many people think so, I know; but there does not appear so great a disproportion in their Merits to *me;* do you think it is better written?" "Oh! I do not know anything about *that*—but it is better in *everything*— Besides, Ethelinde is so long—"

Whether this is an early example of the satiric voice Austen was to perfect in her later works or a serious early assessment of Austen's own attitudes toward Smith, there is no doubt that Austen knew Smith's works well. And surely there is some basis for the claim made by Mary Lascelles that Catherine Morland's behavior in *Northanger Abbey* is a deliberate inversion of the career of Smith's *Emmeline*.[2] But what exactly is it that female gothic

---

1. Jacqueline Howard's chapter, "Gothic Parody: Jane Austen's *Northanger Abbey* and Eaton Stannard Barrett's *The Heroine,*" in *Reading Gothic Fiction,* 145–82, analyzes female-authored parody as an attempt to "expose the ruses of patriarchal power and recontextualize common 'official' languages which represent women as naturally weak in constitution and understanding" (181). Gothic parody has been most extensively analyzed by Leland Chandler May, *Parodies of the Gothic Novel* (New York: Arno, 1980), while the genre is analyzed most fully by Linda Hutcheon in *A Theory of Parody: The Teaching of Twentieth-Century Art Forms* (New York: Methuen, 1985).

2. See Jane Austen, "Catherine or the Bower," in *The Novels of Jane Austen,* ed. R. W. Chapman, vol. 6 (Oxford: Clarendon, 1954), 199; and Mary Lascelles, *Jane Austen and Her Art* (London:

writers are parodying when they poke at, mock, and gently deride the excessive and hyperbolic behaviors of their extravagant heroines? I would claim that what is at stake in the parodies of gothics, excluding works like Eaton Stannard Barrett's *Heroine* (1813), a later, male-authored work, is an attempt to inflate the importance of the issues explored in women's literature under the cover of deflating the excesses of such literature. Bakhtin has called this device "stylization," and has claimed that it is a "double-voiced" discourse that involves the appropriation of the utterances of others for the purposes of allowing a new meaning to reside alongside the original viewpoint.[3]

Austen, Dacre, and Shelley were also all writing out of the impetus that Norbert Elias has called the "civilizing process," and as we have seen, this project was serious business, for defining appropriate behavior for women and understanding woman-marked codes was crucial if the middle class was to supplant the aristocracy, co-opt the lower classes, and "professionalize" England in its own image. Women writers were attempting to codify in their works appropriately gendered behavior for each of the sexes. Tears were acceptable for women when issues of love or honor were at stake; wild excessive displays of emotion—either of a sexual or a physically violent nature—were not acceptable for men, ever. The bourgeois code was, of course, considerably more complex than this, but the important issue for sentimental writers was control over one's emotions and by extension, one's body.[4]

Clarendon, 1939), 60. Deborah Kaplan sees the influence of *Emmeline* on Austen's early "Love and Freindship" [sic] (see her *Jane Austen Among Women* [Baltimore: Johns Hopkins University Press, 1992], 145), while Frank W. Bradbrook claims that "Charlotte Smith's fiction was only of negative use to Jane Austen in providing burlesque material for *Northanger Abbey*" (see his *Jane Austen and Her Predecessors* [Cambridge: Cambridge University Press, 1971], 105). For the opposing position, that Smith was the single greatest influence on Austen's work, see William H. Magee, "The Happy Marriage: The Influence of Charlotte Smith on Jane Austen," *SNNTS* 7 (1975), 120–32; and Eleanor Ty, "Ridding Unwanted Suitors: Jane Austen's *Mansfield Park* and Charlotte Smith's *Emmeline*," *TSWL* 5 (1986), 327–28.

3. Michel Bakhtin, *Problems of Dostoyevsky's Poetics,* quoted in Gary Saul Morson, "Parody, History, and Metaparody," in *Rethinking Bakhtin: Extensions and Challenges,* ed. Gary Saul Morson and Caryl Emerson (Evanston: Northwestern University Press, 1989), 65.

4. For an overview of the "cultural revolution" of the bourgeoisie, see Gary Kelly, *Women, Writing, and Revolution: 1790–1827:* "The first [objective] was to consolidate the middle class under the leadership of the professionals, detach them from ideological and cultural dependence on the dominant classes of court, aristocracy, and gentry, and secure them from cultural and ideological contamination by the lower classes. Secondly, and somewhat later, the cultural revolution aimed to professionalize the dominant classes and form a coalition with them while detaching the lower classes from their historic subordination to the upper classes and conferring on them a diminutive version of middle-class culture and consciousness" (3). Kelly's work places Elias's insights, which are primarily based on French paradigms, in their British context.

Although Austen and Dacre both satirized the sanitized gothic/sentimental heroine, they differed radically on the ideological implications to be found in women's fiction. Whereas Austen, like Wollstonecraft, valorized education for women and the gradual reform of women's living conditions through companionate marriages, Dacre presented the radically simplified version of Wollstonecraft for simpleminded public consumption. Throughout Dacre's novel we hear only one litany: if only mother had not become an adulteress and deserted her husband and children to live illicitly with a licentious rake, none of this would have happened. Female gothic writers focus on women making moral choices in what they perceive to be an institutionally immoral society. They differ, however, on the role of individual responsibility and the importance of a strong and educated mother in leading her daughters to a future of not merely survival but success. "Gothic feminism" takes on a new ideological face in these works because each author was working within a different literary tradition that shaped and to a large extent controlled her vision. Smith and Radcliffe clung to the earlier sentimental postures of victimization for women; Austen struggled to satirize an essentially unsatirizable subject; Dacre hyperbolized the conventions; and Shelley melodramatized the gothic heritage she found in the novels of her mother, father, and husband.

All of these female gothic writers, however, sought to authenticate narratives of female complaint, and, as Helen Small has observed about Dacre, they were forced to use hyperbole because male rhetoricians like Hugh Blair claimed that female passion "naturalized" hyperbolic expression, "making it the rhetoric not only of opera and oratorio, but of less heroic genres, including the novel." Thus it was that the traditional "woman's lament is typically overheard and ventriloquized by a male voyeur. It produces intricate, arguably inextricable interdependencies between male and female voices, between a femininity predicated on passive suffering, and a masculinity which defines itself only tacitly in contradistinction to this damaged version of the feminine. Perhaps most fundamentally, it operates in the treacherous gap between testimony and description." Women obsessed by love, in other words, are like monsters of nature and simply cannot be believed because their narratives of pain are simply too hyperbolic and extravagant to read, and so we are generally presented with another narrative voice to filter out the hurt, to water down the blood. But the hyperbolic female gothic novel refuses to defuse the monstrous wound that lies at the core of the genre. Each of these texts is written from the point of view of a severely hurt child confronting the crimes of a treacherous parental figure.

The hyperbole, the hysteria that suffuses these texts can only remind us of the persistent problem that had always bedeviled the female gothic and sentimental fiction. As Small has queried, can female sexual desire be rendered significant other than through the hyperbolic distortion that causes that desire to be a synonym for madness?[5]

II

When Jane Austen sat down to write the novel that was published posthumously as *Northanger Abbey,* the year was 1798.[6] More topical than any of her other works, *Northanger Abbey* reads as a critique of both the gothic and the sentimental sensibilities that were being foisted on women at the time. If Catherine Morland, coded as "gothic," is foolish, then so is Isabella Thorpe, coded as "sentimental." In many ways, *Northanger Abbey* fictionalizes the major points in Wollstonecraft's *Vindication of the Rights of Woman,* showing that women who are given inadequate educations will be victims of their own follies, in addition to masculine hubris, lust, and greed. Taught from birth to fetishize their physical appearance as their only means of survival, women will become as comical as Mrs. Allen or as cunningly seductive as Isabella. Like lapdogs, coddled and petted, such women are physically weak and mentally vacuous, living only for the attentions occasionally doled out to them by their reluctant masters.

Into such a world of slaves steps the gothic tyrant, the ultimate male master with a whip. But in true Hegelian fashion, the master is as obsessed with the slave as the slave is with the master. If the slave were to write a novel, it would be about the master, and thus we have the Radcliffe oeuvre. If masters were to write novels, they would be about slaves, and thus we have the Rousseau and Richardson corpus. In *Northanger Abbey,* Austen attempts to

---

5. Linda Hutcheon modifies Bakhtin's definition of parody by observing, "Parody . . . is a form of imitation, but imitation characterized by ironic inversion, not always at the expense of the parodied text. . . . Parody is, in another formulation, repetition with a critical distance, which marks difference rather than similarity." See her *Theory of Parody,* 6, 104. See also Helen Small, *Love's Madness: Medicine, the Novel, and Female Insanity: 1800–1865* (Oxford: Clarendon, 1996), 77–80, 87.

6. The contested composition history of *Northanger Abbey* is reviewed in several sources. Cassandra Austen's memorandum dates the novel at "about 98 & 99," while C. S. Emden claims that it was written as early as 1794 (see his "*Northanger Abbey* Re-Dated?" *N&Q* 105 (1950), 407–10. On the same subject, see B. C. Southam, *Jane Austen's Literary Manuscripts* (London: Oxford University Press, 1964), 60–62; and A. W. Litz, *Jane Austen: A Study of Her Artistic Development* (New York: Oxford University Press, 1965), 175–76.

rise above both postures and see both master and slave simultaneously. Her Catherine Morland is as sympathetic (or unsympathetic) as her Henry Tilney. But her Mrs. Tilney is dead and the patriarchal general, her tyrannical husband, is still very much alive, still haunting the dreams of young women who would like to live in the sentimental landscapes constructed from their readings. Wollstonecraft hovers over *Northanger Abbey* as blatantly as Radcliffe, Burney, and Rousseau do. In writing this most literarily dense work, Austen sought to reshape and redefine the central historical, social, and intellectual debates of her era. She sought finally to suggest that masquerade or playing at the role of professional victim were as close as many women would ever get to being "feminists" in a society that polarized the genders as thoroughly as hers did.

By 1803, the year Austen sold the manuscript of *Northanger Abbey*, the gothic heroine was a highly codified ideological figure, complete with stock physical traits, predictable parentage, and reliable class indicators. Clearly, this heroine was ripe as a subject for parody, and such, presumably, was Austen's motive when she created her gothic heroine-in-training, Catherine Morland. Trying to determine exactly what *Northanger Abbey* is or is not as a work of fiction and who Catherine Morland is or is not as a heroine have occupied Austen critics since the book was published in 1817.[7] But there is no clear consensus on the novel nor on Catherine nor on Austen's motives in writing a novel seemingly so dissimilar from her first two works, *Pride and Prejudice* and *Sense and Sensibility*.

Austen appears to be dealing in all her novels with structured moral dichotomies, while the binary permeating the world of Catherine appears to be place as made manifest in moral and gendered values: Bath or the abbey. But there is no real juxtaposition here. The "feminine" world of Bath—social artifice, hypocrisy, surface show contradicting reality, a species of "imprisonment" (16)—does not actually contrast with the "masculine" world of Northanger Abbey—psychic artifice, self-haunting and haunted, concealment through deception of the mercenary motives for marriage in a vacu-

---

7. The critical commentary on *Northanger Abbey* is, like much of the work on Austen, contradictory and highly speculative. Among the hundreds of secondary studies that exist on this novel, I have found the following most suggestive: Coral Howells, *Love, Mystery, and Misery*, 114–30; Judith Wilt, *Ghosts of the Gothic*, 121–72; Eric Rothstein, "The Lessons of *Northanger Abbey*," *UTQ* 43 (1974), 16–30; George Levine, "*Northanger Abbey*: From Parody to Novel and the Translated Monster," in his *Realistic Imagination: English Fiction from Frankenstein to Lady Chatterley* (Chicago: University of Chicago Press, 1985), 22–67; and Marilyn Butler, *Jane Austen and the War of Ideas* (Oxford: Clarendon, 1989), 172–81.

ous society. Both worlds are equally unreal, rejected by and rejecting of the heroine. Both worlds are essentially the same, with Bath being only what we might recognize as the tamer, "cooked" daytime version of the "raw" Northanger, while the abbey at night, as constructed by Catherine's gothic imaginings, is the nightmare version of Bath. The parody or lack of parody in Austen's work stems from the ambiguity or confusion about this notion of gendered place: either the entire external network that we know as society for women is a gothic monstrosity or there is no gothic realm at all—only faulty education and the overactive imaginations of female gothic novelists feeding false fantasies to young women. We are reminded here of Berkeley, Locke, and other empiricist philosophers who would tell their readers that all epistemological reality is ultimately a mental construct subject to one's own psychic control and manipulation. If one can conceive of Catherine Morland as a tabula rasa, then one can begin to appreciate what Austen was trying to accomplish with this most misunderstood of her novels.

Individual women in Austen's novels are the raw material on which Wollstonecraft's theories about female education and socialization can be tested and proved. *Northanger Abbey,* like Radcliffe's novels, reads as a sort of fictionalized *Vindication,* personifying in its various female characters the living results of stunted and pernicious educations. All of the female characters in the novel are pawns, powerless before or fearful of male prerogatives. All, that is, except Catherine. She is the heroine of the novel because she is too dense to understand at any time what is going on around her. She bungles her way to a good marriage, not through any merits of her own but through the author's conscious manipulations of our (and Henry's) sympathies. When Catherine is victimized by General Tilney and shown the door in very uncivil terms, she earns her status as a "victim" of oppression, malice, and fraud. And once she has earned such status, the heroine is worthy of her man. A victim is always rewarded because such is the case in the melodramatic scheme of things. Her suffering is reified as value and stands as lucre to be exchanged for a husband.

But all this is to get ahead of ourselves. Let us begin at the beginning and examine exactly how Austen constructed and at the same time deconstructed "femininity" as "feminism." We could begin by examining Catherine's surname, suggesting that like all gothic heroines she exists to accrue "more land." Her social and financial status are the crucial issues throughout the text, as, indeed, they are throughout all sentimental and gothic texts. But Austen passes lightly over this point and begins her novel with the self-consciously literary statement: "No one who had ever seen

Catherine Morland in her infancy would have supposed her born to be an heroine."[8] Such is the first sentence of the book, and such is the first instance of Austen's self-conscious deflation of her heroine. But if we read this line and conclude only that Catherine does not fulfill the physical characteristics of a heroine, as she clearly does not, we miss the larger allegorical implication that Austen intends here. All women, she hints, are born the heroines of their own rather inconspicuous lives, whether they look the part or not. All women, whether they live in the south of Italy or in France or in the middle of England, have the desire for exciting, fulfilling, meaningful lives, and all are engaged in quests for such lives whether the conditions are propitious or not. Catherine is Austen's Everywoman heroine—plain, ordinary, insufficiently educated, nothing special—but she still manages to become a heroine by following her instincts, waiting passively, and learning to keep her mouth shut.

In addition to her physical plainness—her "thin awkward figure, a sallow skin without colour, dark lank hair, and strong feature"—Catherine has quite ordinary and shockingly healthy parents (13). Her father, a clergyman named Richard, has no taste whatever for "locking up his daughters" (11), and this very untypical mother of a gothic heroine manages to produce ten children and remain in the best of health. No hidden vaults here, no foundlings in the neighborhood, but never fear; in short, "something must and will happen to throw a hero in her way" (12). The implication is clear: a young woman needs only one thing to be a heroine, a hero. Appearance, parentage, social trappings, and complications, all of these are mere excess baggage. A woman needs a man to test her spirit and define her character, and Catherine is introduced to two: the false suitor John Thorpe and the true suitor Henry Tilney. The double-suitor convention with its attendant double-plot structure, typical of allegorical poems like *The Faerie Queene* and sentimental novels like *Emmeline*, reminds us once again that Austen is manipulating the fairy-tale associations of the double-suitor plot to suggest the entire artifice of the mating customs that prevail in a supposedly enlightened society. Substitute parents are quickly provided for in the guise of Mr. and Mrs. Allen, who actually take on the qualities of fairy godfather and godmother in that their supposed dowry for Catherine propels all of the subsequent complications in her identity. By innocently presenting herself

---

8. All quotations from the text of *Northanger Abbey* are from *The Novels of Jane Austen: Northanger Abbey and Persuasion*, vol. 5, 3rd ed., ed. R. W. Chapman (Oxford: Oxford University Press, 1966–69; reprinted 1982), with page numbers in parentheses in the text.

as the ward or heir of the Allens, Catherine participates rather unwittingly in the Bath game of social deception. Her first catch is John Thorpe, but ironically Thorpe snares bigger prey for her by spreading the unfounded rumor of Catherine's wealth to General Tilney, who bites.

So Catherine sets off for "all the difficulties and dangers of a six weeks' residence in Bath," "her mind about as ignorant and uninformed as the female mind at seventeen usually is" (13). We chuckle at the uneventfulness of Catherine's separation from her mother. With so many children at home she is, one can only surmise, grateful to have one taken off her hands. But the contrast to the gothic world is made explicit when Mrs. Morland cautions Catherine about the dangers she may face in the outside world. Does she warn her daughter against "the violence of such noblemen and baronets as delight in forcing young ladies away to some remote farmhouse"? No, her concerns are more prosaic: "'I beg, Catherine, you will always wrap yourself up very warm about the throat, when you come from the rooms at night; and I wish you would try to keep some account of the money you spend; I will give you this little book on purpose'" (13–14). This is the first time we have seen a gothic heroine handle the books, so to speak. In all of Radcliffe's novels the heroine never handles her own money. In fact, money appears in Radcliffe's works only as a landed estate or as an inheritance, not as something that can be freely spent and accounted for by the heroine. The change is significant, for with Catherine, whose pseudoinheritance is central to the plot, we have the figure of a woman who represents empty cash value and yet who spends her own money. The opposite had been true with Radcliffe's heroines. The change represents a subtle shift in how the middle class represented and thought about itself. Once mere potentiality, they have become embodied. They can spend, whereas before they merely had the potential to spend.

But if Catherine is not the typical gothic heroine, neither is Mrs. Allen the typical antigothic duenna figure. Austen alludes to the older woman who conspires against the innocent young heroine and contrasts this figure to the slow-witted Mrs. Allen. The narrator asks us to wonder whether this woman will "by her imprudence, vulgarity, or jealousy—whether by intercepting her letters, ruining her character, or turning her out of doors"—victimize the gothic heroine (14–15). In fact, it is not fashion-crazed Mrs. Allen who will commit any of these untoward deeds on poor Catherine; she will be too busy trying on dresses to pay much attention to her young ward. But these outrages will occur and they will be committed by Catherine's "dear friends," the Thorpes and General Tilney. This instance of foreshadowing, used throughout the text, suggests the ironic distance, the narrative control Austen employs over both her authorial sympathies and her readers'. By laughing at the stock gothic tortures that assail the typical gothic heroine before they occur, Austen preemptively defuses their power when they actually do happen in the text.

No, the greatest tragedy to confront Catherine is not being asked to dance her first night out in Bath. Totally ignored, Catherine spends her first night as an empty signifier: "Not one, however, started with rapturous wonder on beholding her, no whisper of eager inquiry ran round the room, nor was she once called a divinity by anybody" (18). The gothic novel, in elevating to a ridiculous level a young woman's sense of herself as the object of the obsessive male gaze, masculine scrutiny and praise, can only fail to set up a frustrating disappointment for Everywoman. Not to be noticed and praised by a room full of strange men—not to be the object of the controlling and validating male gaze—is for Catherine almost as ignominious a fate as an attempted kidnapping and rape in the gothic arsenal of shock and abuse techniques. In fact, later in the week, when the same sad situation occurs again and Catherine finds herself without a dancing partner, she muses that her lot is identical to the fate of a besieged and harassed gothic heroine: "To be disgraced in the eye of the world, to wear the appearance of infamy while her heart is all purity, her actions all innocence, and the misconduct of another the true source of her debasement, is one of those circumstances which peculiarly belong to the heroine's life, and her fortitude under it what particularly dignifies her character" (43). A more succinct and self-conscious description of the female gothic heroine could hardly be found. But there is also a deconstruction here of the female gothic heroine. Austen has trivialized not simply Catherine but Adeline and Ellena and Emily and all the other gothic heroines whose "disgraces" perhaps were not so immense after all.

It is not long, however, before the hero is introduced and the real education of Catherine begins. The first conversation between the two lovers is instructive, for it reveals the artificial playacting that passes for polite discourse between the sexes. Although Henry Tilney is aware that they are acting, Catherine is not, and the humor in the situation arises from her complete naïveté about social conventions. When Henry presses her on the contents of her journal, she is flustered because she does not keep a journal. A journal, after all, would suggest a level of self-consciousness that Catherine at this stage of her life simply does not possess. But it is significant that for the first time in the novel the act of writing appears as a metaphor for defining and inscribing one's femininity. Indeed, Henry goes so far as to state the following, "'My dear madam, I am not so ignorant of young ladies' ways as you wish to believe me; it is this delightful habit of journalizing which largely contributes to form the easy style of writing for which ladies are so generally celebrated. Everybody allows that the talent of writing agreeable letters is peculiarly female. Nature may have done something, but I am sure it must be essentially assisted by the practice of keeping a journal'" (21) . But if keeping a journal is supposed to hone a woman's skill for letter writing, then some sort of not very veiled panegyric on the epistolary sentimental novel tradition appears to be the real subject of discussion here. Consider that it was not women who wrote the letters that formed *Clarissa* and *Pamela* but a man ventriloquizing a woman's sensibility and subjectivity. Austen ventriloquizing here as Henry seems to suggest that both sexes have come to a new level of understanding and rapprochement through the acts of writing and reading each others' literary works. If Richardson can depict a woman's situation as sensitively as he does in *Clarissa*, then a female author should be able to understand a man's mind as thoroughly and present that vision to the world through her writing. Needless to say, all this passes right by Catherine.

Henry in fact continues to act out this female ventriloquizing when he next engages in a conversation with Mrs. Allen about the price of muslin. If she can haggle over muslin by the yard, so can he. Henry wins Mrs. Allen's total devotion by confessing that he managed to buy "a true Indian muslin" for just five shillings a yard. He impresses her even further by worrying aloud about how Catherine's muslin will hold up to washing. By this time, even Catherine begins to suspect that the two of them have been the objects of his ever-so-solicitous mockery: "Catherine feared, as she listened to their discourse, that he indulged himself a little too much with the foibles of others" (22). Austen is making a point here about education and about who is best qualified to instruct young women in the arts of "femininity." That is, Henry implies to Mrs. Allen that she has failed miserably in her duties to Catherine and that he, a mere man, has been forced to step in and complete her educational process. As a credential he brandishes his superior knowledge of bargaining and caring for fabric. But the more serious intent is to suggest that women's education is too serious a subject to be left to female amateurs. Only men have the sufficient backgrounds and knowledge to educate women, and until they do so women will continue to suffer in their ignorance.

Henry also parodies in these exchanges the "man of feeling," the effeminate man who is acceptable to women because he has been effectively feminized by the social conventions of sensibility and civility. Catherine finds him "strange" (22), suggesting that his female ventriloquism is not to her more primitive tastes. She is going to insist on playing the gothic game, and as such she needs a strong abusive father figure before she can appreciate and accept the castrated son figure. Enter Henry's father General Tilney, benighted enough to put credence in the self-inflating rumors spread by the oafish John Thorpe. The general's villainy, as several critics have noted, is not particularly on the grand gothic scale but merely a matter of simple mercenary greed and insensitivity to Catherine once he learns that she is not the heiress he had assumed she was. Although compared several times to Radcliffe's "Montoni," the general is only a common garden-variety father: boorish, self-important, overbearing.

But the issue that has gone largely unnoticed in this confusion about Catherine's supposed inheritance is the importance of the role rumor and gossip play in shaping people's perceptions. Both forms of unofficial and unsanctioned "feminine" discourse constitute the crux of a suppressed female oral tradition that preserves the stories that male tyrants want long forgotten. Largely employed by female servants, the rumors and gossip that circulate about the Marquis de Villeroi's role in the murder of his wife (in *The Mysteries of Udolpho*) and Schedoni's murder of his brother (in *The Italian*) take the entire text to be spelled out. But the power of accumulated rumor finally forces the truth out into the open, thereby saving the heroines from the mystifications that occur when one is dealing only with false surmises and conjectures based on partial narratives. Power structures exist by mystifying their own edifices and methods. Rumor and gossip force those methods out into the light of day for examination. It is no coincidence that gossip as a negative term is generally associated with women, servants, and other marginalized and easily scapegoated groups. They have, after all, nothing to lose and everything to gain by circulating stories about tyrants and the abuse of power.

What does it mean that John Thorpe is the source for most of the gossip and rumor throughout this text? Does dealing in rumor and gossip "feminize" him? In fact, quite the contrary. The anthropological studies we have on gossip show that the right to gossip is generally viewed as the province of those who have earned their membership in the inner circle of the tribe or clan. Gossip is only condemned when it is engaged in by those who do not have full membership status in this inner circle (i.e., women and servants are condemned for dealing in gossip because they are not accepted as full members of the power community). But anthropological research consistently demonstrates that the more powerful a man is, the more he deals in gossip as a source for information about the community—all of its dealings and events.[9] It makes perfect sense that John Thorpe and General Tilney would be gossiping about Catherine Morland, a new source of income on their market. Discussing her supposed financial status would be little different in their minds from discussing the value of stocks and bonds and any other projected or potential investment. The fact that neither has the slightest idea of her real worth forms the core of the humorous irony. When John Thorpe thinks he has a chance to acquire Catherine, then she is immensely rich and desirable. When he learns that she has decisively rejected him, then he constructs her as a pauper. Neither version is an accurate depiction of her financial standing. And yet both versions of Catherine reveal the woman as blank slate. For the Thorpes and generals of this world, woman is only what the more powerful man says she is; she has no ontological reality in herself but only as much or as little as he assigns to her.

The stage is further set for the pedagogical project when Catherine meets her false female mentor, Isabella Thorpe, John's hopelessly mercenary and manipulative sister. Isabella shrewdly decides that novel reading will be the basis of their alliance, and once again the subject of writing emerges in the text as an indicator of gender acculturation. The discussion about novels, particularly women's novels, reveals a defensiveness that is both amusing and painful to read. Catherine loves to read novels because, as the narrator shrewdly observes, she is in a novel herself: "Alas! If the heroine of one novel be not patronized by the heroine of another, from whom can she expect protection and regard?" (29). The narrator's self-conscious fictitiousness here is strikingly original, as is the narrator's dismay that women are embarrassed to be seen reading the novels of, say, Fanny Burney, when they would be praised instead for reading some dull volume of the *Spectator*. But why does Isabella want Catherine to read gothic novels with her? The answer appears to lie in Isabella's desire to find someone who will share her novelistically induced fantasies about life. In Isabella's mind she is a penniless but deserving

---

9. Some of the most influential anthropological studies done on gossip were conducted by Max Gluckman (in "Gossip and Scandal," *CA* 4 [1963], 307–16) and Robert Paine (in "What is Gossip About? An Alternative Hypothesis," in *Man*, n.s., 2 [1967], 278–85). Paine concludes that "a man gossips to control others and accordingly fears gossip as it threatens to control him. Hence, a man tries to manage the information that exists about others and himself by gossiping about others (and drawing others into gossip-laden conversations), on the one hand, and by trying to limit gossip about himself" (283). For a more literary treatment of much of the same material, see Patricia M. Spacks, *Gossip* (Chicago: University of Chicago Press, 1986).

and beautiful heroine, the object of love and adoration from countless men who will be only too willing to lavish riches for the privilege of purchasing her. She also has read too many novels and imbibed from them the false belief that women can manipulate and control men in life as easily as can cunning novelistic heroines.

Isabella as false confidante is doubled by Henry's sister Eleanor, the true confidante who is shown at the end of the novel to have more power over her father than anyone. Eleanor's power stems from her rather sudden marriage to a titled aristocrat, giving her both social and economic leverage over the general. But throughout the text Eleanor acts as a foil to the showy, empty Isabella, who is supposedly engaged twice and comes up finally with nothing. The subplot we would rather see would concern the courtship of Eleanor and Lord Longtown, the adventures of the lord's maid and her laundry list, and the identity of "Alice." When Eleanor asks Catherine to write to her at Lord Longtown's residence "under cover to Alice" (191), we sense that the real gothic plot has been occurring elsewhere.

But when Catherine picks up *The Mysteries of Udolpho*, she knows she is reading a book that, as she admits, she could spend her whole life reading with pleasure. The conspiracies that Catherine is compelled to spin out about the general murdering his wife—or perhaps just burying her alive in a deserted wing of the abbey—these imaginings are more obviously cribbed from *A Sicilian Romance*. Later *The Monk* is named as his favorite novel by John Thorpe, who is perhaps unaware that its tale of matricide and incestuous rape of a sister reveals more than he might like about his own suppressed interests. We understand the character of these fictitious beings by being familiar with the moral visions of the novels they prefer. This is a world of mirrors where blatantly self-consciously fictional characters define themselves by their allegiance to other blatantly self-conscious fictional creations. In this hall of mirrors, there is no reality, only constructions and constructions of constructions. One senses Catherine's challenge as a literary character is to emerge from the gothic universe of Radcliffe and situate herself instead as a character in a Burney novel. It is a particularly propitious sign that John Thorpe does not like Burney's work, "such unnatural stuff" (39), for his lack of understanding suggests that it must possess merit beyond his limited abilities of appreciation.

With the major characters and conflict established, let us examine the three major gothic incidents in the text as keys to understanding Austen's construction of "femininity" as "feminism." The first episode concerns the general's character and the abbey as a pseudoruin, the second, Catherine's discovery of ordinary domesticities in the dead mother's cabinets and bed-room, and the final, Catherine's expulsion and flight from the abbey. These are familiar scenes and have been discussed at length, but I suggest that there is a certain ambivalence about Austen's attitude toward gothic feminism and that this ambivalence causes the alternate hyperbole and deflation in these episodes. Almost as though they were melodramatic set pieces in a period drama, Austen inserts the gothic incidents as virtual *tableaux vivants* designed on the surface to garner our amusement and cause us to chuckle. But the net effect of mingling the gothic with the domestic and sentimen-tal romance produces instead a strange hybrid—the awareness that the domestic is gothic or that we cannot think anymore about the domestic without at the same time recognizing its gothic underpinnings, its propen-sities for playing with the topoi of violence, abuse, and exploitation of women.

The first time Catherine sees the general, she is struck by his physical attractiveness. Later when she visits the Tilney residence, she finds the gen-eral infinitely more attractive than Henry. In fact, she muses to herself that the general was "perfectly agreeable and good-natured, and altogether a very charming man, . . . for he was tall and handsome, and Henry's father" (107). That last phrase, tacked on as if as a reminder to herself, suggests that Catherine's initial attraction is less to the son than to the father. All this changes, however, almost as soon as she sets off for Northanger Abbey. Catherine is convinced that it is the general who changes once he is within his own castle. But clearly his character—imperious, demanding, manipu-lative, and dominating—is simply revealed more starkly in his own domi-cile. Suddenly Catherine sees that the general "seemed always a check upon his children's spirits, and scarcely anything was said but by himself" (129). He is a veritable master of the dining room, pacing up and down with a watch in his hand, pulling the dinner bell "with violence," and ordering everyone to the table immediately (137). Only in his presence does Catherine feel fatigue. The strain from answering his boorishly probing questions about the size of Mr. Allen's estate has begun to wear on her.

The general, living in his abbey, is a patriarch and usurper, very similar to the patriarch and usurper inhabiting Walpole's *Castle of Otranto* or Smith's *Emmeline*. Northanger Abbey, we are told, was "a richly endowed convent at the time of the Reformation" (117), but it fell, as did all property belonging to the Roman Catholic Church, like spoils into the hands of Protestant war-lords. General Tilney, whose military mien is no accident, continues the war on convents, so to speak, by preying on the prospects both of his daughter and of Catherine and her supposed inheritance. The female gothic, suggests Austen, concerns itself with just this sort of tale of female disinheritance and suppression. Catherine thinks that in living in an abbey she will wander around "long, damp passages," explore "its narrow cells and ruined chapel," and thrill to "some traditional legends, some awful memorials of an injured and ill-fated nun" (117). It is the buried nun, the recovery of the sacred rights of women, who is the rightful owner of the usurped abbey and who haunts the female gothic universe. But within the domesticated landscape that Austen and her heroine inhabit, the nun becomes first the murdered wife and then the murdered wife becomes simply an ordinary woman beaten down and defeated by the demands of life with three children and an ill-tempered husband. The idea of the abbey as a female community of nuns—living in seclusion from men and escaping the demands of marriage and childbirth—this is what the general and his ancestors have usurped. There is no longer in England any form of communal escape for women. There is only the reality of women as property, sources of income, breeders of heirs—the sad and oft-told tale of female disinheritance, "buried nuns."

Northanger Abbey as an edifice has managed to elide its gothic past almost totally. The general, we learn, is an energetic remodeler, even transforming the ruined section of the abbey into a suite of offices for himself. Instead of dark and dank, Catherine finds light and airy. Instead of old and moldering, she finds new and absolutely up-to-date furnishings. She does succeed, however, in locating two old chests, and we know ourselves suddenly to be in *The Romance of the Forest*. As we know, one chest in that text contained the father's skeleton and the other the manuscript he left behind recounting his final hours awaiting murder. Catherine has been primed by Henry to play the gothic game with the chests, and she is only too willing. Both, however, disappoint. The first contains only linen and the second the famous laundry list left by Lord Longstown's maid. To the overly imaginative Catherine hoping to find a broken lute, perhaps a dagger (preferably blood-stained), instruments of torture, a hoard of diamonds, or the "memoirs of the wretched Matilda" (131–33), the domesticities can only be a bitter disappointment: "She felt humbled to the dust. Could not the adventure of the chest have taught her wisdom? A corner of it, catching her eye as she lay, seemed to rise up in judgment against her. Nothing could now be clearer than the absurdity of her recent fancies. To suppose that a manuscript of many generations back could have remained undiscovered in a room such as that, so modern, so habitable!—or that she should be the first to possess the skill of unlocking a cabinet, the key of which was open to all!" (144). The self-chastisement that occurs here is predicated on the belief that other women have gone before Catherine and that they have had the same compulsions to ferret out the truth that lies buried within the patriarchal family. The large and imposing cabinet with the visible key figures the family's apparently transparent status as an institution that is open to complete scrutiny and understanding by all. A deeper examination of this episode suggests that in fact women have not opened up and analyzed the family or its source of power. They have accepted its bulk and its power to contain and define them. They have, in very real senses, allowed themselves to be buried alive within all of the separate cabinets that dot the landscape of England. The linen and the laundry list are the visible residue of women's lost and unpaid labor for the family.

We are next presented with Catherine's growing obsession with the dead Mrs. Tilney. She is figured first through her daughter's memories of her mother's favorite walk, a path that the general now studiously avoids. Next we learn that the general is so insensitive as not to want to hang his dead wife's portrait in a prominent place in the abbey. From these two facts Catherine spins out her murder plot, and finally admits to herself that she truly hates the general: "His cruelty to such a charming woman made him odious to her. She had often read of such characters, characters which Mr. Allen had been used to call unnatural and overdrawn; but here was proof positive of the contrary" (151). But why does Catherine make such an investment of emotion in the general? Why does he elicit such strong feelings in her? Protesting too much, she can only hope to conceal her attraction to him from herself, an attraction that she can repress and deny by inventing such a horrible crime that he would have to be truly unworthy of her regard and admiration. Yes, the general must have killed his wife; therefore, I cannot be drawn more to him than to his son.

Further playing the oedipal detective, Catherine decides to snoop next into the circumstances of Mrs. Tilney's death, learning that it was caused by a fever that came on suddenly when her daughter was not at home. Catherine leaps to the conclusion that Mrs. Tilney, like the Marchioness de Villeroi in *Udolpho*, has been poisoned by her husband and that the general has been suffering from guilt ever since. No wonder he stays up late at night: "There must be some deeper cause: something was to be done which could be done only while the household slept; and the probability that Mrs. Tilney yet lived, shut up for causes unknown, and receiving from the pitiless hands of her husband a nightly supply of coarse food, was the conclusion which necessarily followed. . . . [A]ll favoured the supposition of her imprisonment. Its origin—jealousy perhaps, or wanton cruelty—was yet to be unravelled" (157). Can the search for Siddons's stone cave be far behind? The psychic transition here from imagining murder to revising it to imprisonment — all this suggests childhood and adolescent anxieties about adult sexuality. The fixation on "something" that is "done which could be done only while the household slept"—all this is too familiar. We are dealing here with a child's imaginings about what her parents do at night when they are no longer under her watchful gaze. The notion that the mother is secretly imprisoned, "shut up for causes unknown," and fed only at night by the father, this is a crude version of a child's sense of sex as a violation and a physical assault. We need not ponder too long to realize that Catherine fears marriage as much as she claims to desire it.

Catherine has no knowledge of life except as it has been presented to her in novels, mostly female gothic novels. She chooses to read the general as a character in a novel, mixing Montoni and Mazzini with a dash of Montalt and Schedoni. Yes, she muses, she knows his type all too well. She has, after all, read dozens of novels: "She could remember dozens who had persevered in every possible vice, going on from crime to crime, murdering whomsoever they chose, without any feeling of humanity or remorse; till a violent death or a religious retirement closed their black career" (159). But whether the general literally murdered his wife or merely made her life so miserable that she found her own way to the grave is really irrelevant. The result in either case is the same: the mother is dead and the general is alive.

Let the scene shift to Catherine's greatest gothic adventure: the perilous journey down galleries and deserted wings of the abbey to the dead mother's bedroom. The room itself is bright and ordinary and empty; there is absolutely no mystery or intrigue or wax figure or prisoner at all. Death is as real as the female gothic tries to make it unreal. The empty room stands as a simple reminder that in real life death cannot be wished away, cannot be denied, cannot be covered over with fantasies of a mother who comes back as if from the dead. The female gothic, in dealing with the territory of wish fulfillment, attempts to convince its readers that evil and mortality can be denied by the resourceful female gothic heroine. Catherine receives here instead the slap of life across her face. And Henry's rebuke does not make the realization any easier to accept:

"If I understand you rightly, you had formed a surmise of such horror as I have hardly words to—Dear Miss Morland, consider the dreadful nature of the suspicions you have entertained. What have you been judging from?

Remember the country and the age in which we live. Remember that we
are English, that we are Christians. Consult your own understanding, you
own sense of the probable, your own observation of what is passing around
you. Does our education prepare us for such atrocities? Do our laws con-
nive at them? Could they be perpetuated without being known, in a country like this, where social and literary intercourse is on such a footing, where
every man is surrounded by a neighbourhood of voluntary spies, and where
roads and newspapers lay everything open?" (165)

This statement is generally considered to be the high point of antigothic sensibility in the text, and it has been exhaustively analyzed by a number of critics, most of whom read it straight.[10] But it is a highly coded ideological
statement that positions masculine "newspapers" as discourse systems
against female gothic novels as more reliable sources for the ascertainment
of truth. It suggests that in the perfect state that is England, "education" has
eradicated evil, and yet there is no educational system for women or the
lower classes. It smugly asserts that "neighbourhood spies" will report all
wrongdoing, as if such a system of veritable espionage were a selling point
for the area. And what about "our laws"? Surely they do not protect the lives
or estates of married women and children. In short, Henry seeks to persuade
Catherine that she has all the advantages that he as an upper-class, educated,
and employed male possesses. The logic here seems to run something like
this: as a male I consider the visions proffered by female gothic novels to be
foolish and untenable, and if you were as wise and privileged as I am you
would agree with me. In reifying Henry's speech, it would appear that
Austen is either sharing Henry's outlook or she is undercutting it; it would
appear that either Austen wants to believe that women can share in the
advantages of the patriarchy or she is suggesting that such a position—honorary membership in the "club"—is a futile dead end for women.

The final gothic episode is almost anticlimactic. Catherine is expelled
from the abbey at seven o'clock in the morning with no escort and even less
money. This incident is frightening and embarrassing for Catherine, largely
because it is so inexplicable. But Catherine has been unable to understand

10. For an interesting Foucauldian reading of the culminating antigothic set piece, see Paul
Morrison's "Enclosed in Openness: *Northanger Abbey* and the Domestic Carceral," *TSLL* 33 (1991),
1–23. Morrison concludes, "And therein lies the principle of her claustration: not in an economy of
gothic scenery, but in a domestic sphere, at once social and psychological, in which there are no secret
spaces, in which there is no escape from an openness that encloses.... As text, *Northanger Abbey* the-
matizes the reinscription of the gothic carceral in the mode of panoptic discipline" (12, 13).

the general's motivations throughout the novel, and this final episode merely reverses his behavior. Whereas before he had been laboring under the mistaken notion that she was a wealthy heiress, now he is laboring under the mistaken notion that she is a pauper. The general as evil gothic villain is just perpetually and perceptually confused and mistaken, and such, apparently, is the nature of evil in Austen's novelistic universe. The rejection Catherine suffers, however, is smoothed over as effortlessly and hastily as an antigothic novelist can manage. Eleanor appears as deus ex machina, Henry proposes offstage, and the newlyweds begin their life together surrounded by "smiles."

The gothic as historical residue, it would appear, has finally been buried, and all's right with the world. But the gothic has functioned throughout this text as a continually disruptive and undercutting presence, and the conventions of romance cannot bury the atavistic presence of Radcliffe and her imitators. The dead mother, the usurped convent, the incestuous and adulterous impulses that seethe just beneath the surface of this highly polished veneer of a novel, all suggest that Austen was as attracted to the potential for evil in life as she was compelled finally to deny its power and allure. Voicing Henry's Enlightenment pieties gives Austen as author a certain amount of safety and power, an immunity to the decay and death inherent in marriage and childbearing, realities that affect other women, not her heroines. Her Catherine will find out what's behind the black veil only on her wedding night, and by then the novel will be safely concluded.

Once again the female gothic text circles anxiously around the issue of female sexuality. Once more we see an author ambivalently trace the transformation of the female body into a medium of exchange culminating in a brokered but unconsummated (at least at the conclusion of the novel) marriage with a feminized man. *Northanger Abbey* can be read, however, as an attempt to parody the cunning machinations of the typical gothic heroine. Catherine is not cunning or clever. She is not well educated, neither is she canny nor sophisticated in the ways of the world. By presenting a naive heroine Austen suggests that the female gothic project is hopelessly out of touch with the social, cultural, and educational realities for most women. Or Austen is suggesting that women do not need even a modicum of intelligence or education to triumph in the marriage market. She parodies the extravagant adventures of a Radcliffe heroine; she undercuts the challenges posed to Smith's Emmeline by presenting a young woman who bests the patriarchy by doing nothing much at all.

Austen may mock *Udolpho* and the other gothic texts rewritten as parody throughout this novel, but we can only conclude that *Northanger Abbey* was written in large part to exorcise the gothic compulsion from the late eighteenth-century literary landscape. In unearthing the gothic tradition, not simply of Radcliffe but of the entire popular gothic repertoire *(Castle of Wolfenbach, Clermont, Mysterious Warnings, Necromancer of the Black Forest, Midnight Bell, Orphan of the Rhine,* and *Horrid Mysteries),* Austen intended to expose the false premises and inadequate stereotypes upon which the genre was based.[11] By revealing to the light of common day the implausibilities of gothic conventions, Austen thought she would free herself and her fellow female novelists from the artificialities and limitations that the genre inflicted on them. Instead of debunking the gothic, however, she reified it. What she discovered was that there was no escape from the gothic morass once you allowed yourself ever so slightly into its territory.

III

Victoria, the Venetian in "Rosa Matilda's" (Charlotte Dacre Byrne's) sensational gothic romance *Zofloya, or the Moor* (1806), stands as a grandiose, hyperbolically feminine, gendered, and ethnic stereotype, a passionately libidinous aristocratic woman and an even more volatile and violent Italian, exactly the sort of woman anti-Jacobin Britain loathed and feared. Between Smith's publication of *Emmeline* in 1788 and Dacre's publication of *Zofloya* in 1806, Britain had undergone a political and social sea change. Liberal sympathies that were tolerated before the French Revolution, the Terror, and Napoleon, were no longer viewed with bemused detachment. Emotional excess, unbridled adulterous passion, greed, pride, and lust were viewed with intense loathing by a new bourgeoisie that privileged what I have labeled "professional femininity," a masquerade of emotional restraint, fidelity, and a calm and reasonable decorum. And crucial to supporting this new social edifice was the bourgeois mother, a paragon of domestic virtues and disinterested goodness. When Wollstonecraft advocated a new system of education for women in order to prepare them better for their roles as wives and mothers, she could never have anticipated the virtual parody of her ideas that Dacre would pen just a decade later.

---

11. Identifying and verifying as historically specific the exact works of Austen's famous listing of gothic titles was first accomplished by Michael Sadlier, "The Northanger Novels: A Footnote to Jane Austen," English Association pamphlet, 1927; reprinted as "'All Horrid?': Jane Austen and the Gothic Romance," in his *Things Past* (London: Constable, 1944), 167–200. Sadlier concludes that the listing of novels "was rather deliberate than random, [and] was made for the stories' rather than for their titles' sake."

Dacre, in effect, takes Wollstonecraft's argument and turns it on its head. She concludes by blaming the mother for all the accumulating social and spiritual ills plaguing contemporary society. One might be tempted to say that she blames adulterous mothers for causing all of the social and political turmoil that led to and resulted in the French Revolution, so extreme is her vituperation against the openly sexual and lustful mother in *Zofloya*. At one of at least two dozen places in the text she lets loose with this sort of statement: "Unhappy Laurina! whose criminal desertion of thine offspring entailed upon them such misery and degradation. In this early career of their lives, behold the guilt and unworthiness for which thou art amenable. Yet, darker still, and disfigured by greater crimes, will be the days which are to come. Faultless example would have shamed into efforts of virtue, the proud and violent nature of thy daughter. . . . Tremble, unfortunate and guilty mother, for longer and more gloomy becomes the register of thy crimes!" (136). But there are three women in *Zofloya* who bear close scrutiny—the sexual mother, her flamboyantly evil daughter Victoria, and Victoria's rival and double, the blonde and dainty Lilla. Each one stands as a gendered cliché of overdetermined and hyperbolic femininity, and each one embodies the melodrama that was the construction of woman in early nineteenth-century Britain.

Zofloya, or the Moor was Dacre's second novel, written when she was twenty-four years old (or so she claimed) and the beautiful toast of London literary circles. Her first novel, *The Confessions of the Nun of St. Omer,* was written when she was eighteen, or twenty-eight, depending on which biographical source one credits, and in the grip of an infatuation with the excessive gothicism of Lewis's *Monk.* Dacre's novels by 1809 were ridiculed as "lovely ROSA's prose" by Byron, who went on to mock the novels as "prose in masquerade, / Whose strains, the faithful echoes of her mind, / Leave wondering comprehension far behind" (*English Bards and Scotch Reviewers,* lines 756–58). Despite their improbabilities or more likely because of them, *Zofloya* was also an early influence on Percy Shelley, whose two youthful gothic novels, *Zastrozzi* (1810) and *St. Irvyne; or The Rosicrucian* (1811), bear a number of clear resemblances to Dacre's works.[12] She and her four novels

---

12. We know little about Charlotte Dacre Byrne, not even her birth date. A summary of the contested biographical sources surrounding her life is provided in Adriana Craciun, "'I hasten to be Disembodied': Charlotte Dacre, the Demon Lover, and Representations of the Body," *ERR* 4 (1995), 90–91. The standard sources on her life include the contradictory introductions provided for her works by Montague Summers, Devendra Varma, Donald Reiman, and Sandra Knight-Roth. To my knowledge, the most recent and extensive work on Dacre is the unpublished doctoral dissertation by

and two-volume book of poetry are virtually forgotten today, but all of these works—most particularly *Zofloya*—are important historical documents for understanding how literature participated in the larger culture's attempt to rewrite appropriate feminine behavior as passionless, passively domestic, and pious. Dacre was no feminist, but as the daughter of a well-connected Jewish banker and supporter of radical political causes who was friendly with William Godwin, she certainly had every opportunity to absorb the gothic and feminist ambiences. And she clearly would have had access to Wollstonecraft's writings. We know very little about Dacre's life, but one fact remains: in *Zofloya* she produced a virtual parody of Wollstonecraft's works and as such introduced Wollstonecraft's ideas, albeit in perverted form, to a larger reading audience.

Zofloya is also, however, racist, xenophobic, and misogynistic—as politically incorrect as any early nineteenth-century text. And although the action is set in late fifteenth-century Italy, the novel holds up for our view the popular consciousness of early nineteenth-century bourgeois England. It reveals how thoroughly this class felt besieged by the sexually and financially voracious demands of women. It reveals that this was a culture looking for someone to blame for the social, familial, political, and economic transformation it was experiencing. It chose to blame the devil in league with a sexually demanding woman. Not an original plot, to be sure, but one that epitomized a culture's intense dread of maternal and feminine sexuality as so viciously evil and unnatural that in its force it rivaled the blackness of Satan's dark deeds themselves.

The novel begins with an address to "the historian who would wish his lessons to sink deep into the heart, thereby essaying to render mankind virtuous and more happy" (39), and there is throughout the entire three-volume text an attempt to advocate a behavioral agenda predicated on appropriate character traits (having the right sort of "virtuous" "heart").[13] Actually, however, Dacre pursues her social agenda by presenting the consequences of a lack of virtue on the family, one's immediate society, and the larger political

---

Knight-Roth, "Charlotte Dacre and the Gothic Tradition," Dalhousie University, 1972. Also see Byron's *English Bards and Scotch Reviewers* in *The Poems of Lord Byron*, ed. Jerome McGann, vol. 1 (Oxford: Oxford University Press, 1980).

13. Charlotte Dacre, *Zofloya, or the Moor: A Romance of the Fifteenth Century,* ed. Adriana Craciun (Ontario: Broadview, 1997). All quotations are from this edition, with page numbers in parentheses in the text. According to the scanty biographical information we have about her, Dacre had three children before her lover was widowed and finally able to marry her, making it possible for their children to be baptized. There is more than a bit of irony (and perhaps self-defense) in her composition of texts that position her narrative voice as a paragon of domestic and maternal purity.

state. And she begins, as virtually all female gothic authors begin, with the absence or corruption of the mother as the cause for all the subsequent misery in the novel. The mother in this work is named Laurina di Cornari, wife for the past seventeen years of the Marchese di Loredania. Still in possession of "unexampled beauty, and rare and singular endowments," Laurina appears to be a prime candidate for a seventeen-year itch. She is vain and in particular suffers from "too great a thirst for admiration, and confidence in herself" (39).

Laurina is, in short, flawed, and has failed most grievously to effectively raise and discipline her two children, "the lovely and haughty" Victoria and her handsome brother Leonardo, "ever haughty and turbulent in his manners" (39). The two are coded as defective aristocrats, with the fifteen-year old Victoria described as "proud, haughty, and self-sufficient—of a wild, ardent, and irrepressible spirit, indifferent to reproof, careless of censure—of an implacable, revengeful, and cruel nature, and bent upon gaining the ascendancy in whatever she engaged." Leonardo, sixteen years old, is described in equally severe terms: "he was violent and revengeful; he had a quick impatient sense of honor" (40). These two naturally violent children should have been carefully educated by a loving and devoted mother, but their youthful mother, married at age fifteen, was too busy admiring herself to pay any attention to her children. Dacre tells us that "brilliant examples of virtue and decorum" would have "counteracted the evils engendered by the want of steady attention to the propensities of childhood" (40), but these examples the siblings were not fortunate enough to possess. Their natural vices as aristocrats and Venetians were exacerbated by their mother's self-absorption and neglect.

The mother's most serious fall occurs, however, when she allows herself to be seduced by an experienced rake, Count Ardolph, a German nobleman who travels around Europe on the prowl to break up happy marriages. Although she initially repulses Ardolph's "naturally vicious inclinations," she finally succumbs when he feigns illness at her continued rejections (43). The affair causes her to leave her husband and children and move to a villa with her lover. One day several months later, the innocent husband stumbles on Ardolph, impetuously challenges him to a duel, and is killed by a swift blow from a dagger.

But Laurina's guilt is not complete. She has not only caused the death of her husband but has also caused both of her children endless misery. Leonardo flees Venice in disgrace, and Victoria swears vengeance on the human race for her mother's fall and her father's death. Playing the sexual mother to her new lover, Laurina sinks into the deepest form of vice imaginable to this society. She not only actively seeks out and enjoys sex with Ardolph, she compounds the perversity of the affair by casting him, at least initially, in the terms of a son dependent on his mother-lover's body. The blatant identification of Ardolph with her children becomes even clearer when Laurina early in the affair confesses to her lover that she would leave her husband if it were not for the children. Ardolph melodramatically responds, "'May those children *witness*—nay, *perpetuate* my destruction, should ever my heart become cold towards thee!'" (47). At the conclusion of the novel, as this piece of heavy-handed foreshadowing indicates, Ardolph is found beating Laurina and is killed by Leonardo, who has become the king of an outlaw band of robbers. Leonardo dies by his own hand rather than face capture by the Italian police, but his sister Victoria faces an even more horrendous fate. She quite literally goes to the devil.

Zofloya traces the melodramatic adventures of Victoria, and to a much lesser extent her brother. Whereas Leonardo's fall is gradual and tragically familiar within the gothic universe, Victoria's is spectacular. Initially taken by her fallen mother and Ardolph to an elderly aunt's estate for safekeeping, Victoria manages to escape by tricking a female servant into exchanging clothes with her and then leading her to the edge of the aunt's wooded estate. From there it is nothing to walk back to Venice where Victoria quickly sets about seducing a rich aristocrat, Berenza. Ironically, Berenza decides to marry Victoria after she is stabbed trying to defend him against a dagger-wielding assassin. The attacker turns out to be Leonardo, who was at this time living with Berenza's former mistress, Megalina Strozzi, a Florentine prostitute. Megalina too was prone to using daggers to settle her scores, and she originally sent Leonardo to kill Berenza, not aware that Berenza would be in bed with Leonardo's sister.

Because Victoria was willing to take a knife in the shoulder for him, she earns the undying love and trust of Berenza. He marries her, and they spend the next five years in comparative harmony. But that is shattered when Berenza's younger and more handsome brother, Henriquez, arrives for a visit. Victoria suffers an intense and lustful infatuation for him immediately, but he finds her repulsive. Indeed, on more than one occasion she is described as odious to Henriquez because she is "masculine," "harsh and fierce," and an "untameable hyena" (190, 211, 75). Henriquez instead is enamored of his lovely little thirteen-year-old orphaned friend, Lilla, thrown on his protection by the deaths of her parents. Lilla is as blonde as Victoria is dark, as prepubescent, passive, good, and obedient as Victoria is the opposite.

Lilla, in other words, is the new bourgeois ideal of the "civilized" domestic idol, the professionally feminine girl-woman. Victoria embodies the earlier, uncivilized, aristocratic woman—vain, lustful, libidinously aggressive, actively and openly sexual, and violent. According to the code of the ideology, Lilla should live and triumph over Victoria. The opposite occurs in this work, perhaps the most eccentric female gothic ever penned.[14]

Before we move to Lilla's murder scene, however, it is necessary to examine the other protagonist in the novel—Zofloya, or the Moor—the titular and presumably the most important character in the work. Zofloya is initially presented to us as Henriquez's black servant, acquired in Spain after Zofloya's master was killed in a battle. Matthew Lewis had portrayed another powerful and vengeful black servant named Hassan in his gothic drama *The Castle Spectre* (1798), and he had chosen to use Hassan to embody the dualistic characteristics that blacks (and, we might add, Italian women in gothic novels) were thought to possess: a superficial eagerness to please combined with a tendency, when injured, to plot a violent and extreme revenge. As did Lewis's *Journal* that described his visits to his own Jamaican plantation, the gothic drama presents black slaves as only too quick to flip the master-slave dialectic and deal in Obeah poisonings and slave uprisings. Sensational press accounts of the maroon wars of the 1790s in Jamaica and the bloody revolution in Haiti made the issue too immediate to ignore. Significantly, when Hassan swears that he will have his vengeance, he uses language that implies the sexual threat implicit in his very presence in this society: "'Am I not branded with scorn? am I not now despised? What man would accept the negro's friendship? What woman would not turn from the negro in disgust? Oh! how it joys me when the white man suffers!'"

Dacre responded to Hassan's query by creating a white woman who would not turn from the black man in disgust. By the conclusion of the novel, Victoria and Zofloya are living together as lovers, Zofloya having initially appeared to Victoria in her dreams the night she first met Henriquez and decided that she must sexually possess him or die. Victoria's dreams, which occur throughout the novel and always accurately present the next major action of the text, remind us of the dreams in Radcliffe's *Romance of the Forest*. Dreams in Dacre's work, however, suggest a new level of psychological sophistication we have not seen in the female gothic. Victoria's

---

14. There are scattered and brief discussions of *Zofloya* throughout the gothic bibliography but the most useful are in Craciun's introduction to the novel; Ann Jones, *Ideas and Innovations: Best Sellers of Jane Austen's Age* (New York: AMS, 1986); and Robert Miles, *Gothic Writing*.

dreams present us with the possibility that the character we recognize as "Zofloya" is actually less a real personage than a representation of the dark and demonic forces within Victoria's own psyche. The confluence here of the sexually predatory woman and the black male servant is revealing for what it says about early nineteenth-century British attitudes toward both gender and race. A woman who would sexually pursue not simply one man but two—and brothers at that—is a woman who has to be full of the devil. And the devil is not simply represented as black, of a lower class, and foreign; he is empowered by functioning in league, as one, with a corrupt aristocratic and foreign woman.

But if we can also consider for a moment this novel as a document operating within a larger colonialist project, I think we can uncover Dacre's complicity in what Homi Bhabha has labeled "the strategy of social and political control": "The black is both savage (cannibal) and yet the most obedient and dignified of servants (the bearer of food); he is the embodiment of rampant sexuality and yet innocent as a child; he is mystical, primitive, simple-minded and yet the most worldly and accomplished liar, and manipulator of social forces. In each case what is being dramatized is a separation—*between* races, cultures, histories, *within* histories—a separation between *before* and *after* that repeats obsessively the mythical moment of disjunction" (90). Bhabha appears to be uncannily describing the many shifting roles Zofloya actually plays in this novel toward his alter ego, Victoria, and what we might ask, does such a configuration signify in regard to the female gothic's participation in the colonialist project? In an age that was anxiously confronting the foreign as a threat, blackness was the ultimate fear, while attempts to contain and commodify it emerge in a number of literary texts, including James I's *Daemonology* (1597), Aphra Behn's *Oroonoko* (1688), and Edward Long's *History of Jamaica* (1774). It is Long who writes, "[Negroes] are represented by all authors as the vilest of human kind, to which they have little more pretension of resemblance than what arises from their exterior forms." But it is precisely the exterior form, the skin, that draws the obsessive gaze of Victoria to Zofloya. In fixating on his blackness, Dacre defines one aspect of the colonialist discourse as a cross-classificatory, discriminatory knowledge that attempts to objectify and thereby control the object of colonialism's regulatory power; in other words, Dacre attempts to make Zofloya a subject of racial, cultural, and national representation that she and by extension the white bourgeois world could ultimately control.

Zofloya and Victoria are both inhabiting not simply a gothic universe but what Bhabha has called the "not quite/not white" world of the margins where "the *founding objects* of the Western world become the erratic, eccentric, accidental *objets trouvés* of the colonial discourse. . . . [where] black skin splits under the racist gaze, displaced into signs of bestiality, genitalia, grotesquerie, which reveal the phobic myth of the undifferentiated whole white body" (91). The conjunction in this novel of a white woman with a black male servant is most peculiar unless we read it as a sign of the ambivalence that some middle-class white women had toward what they actually recognized on some level as a similarity in their social positions. As Winthrop Jordan has observed in his classic study *White Over Black*, "it is scarcely surprising that Englishmen should have used peoples overseas as social mirrors and that they were especially inclined to discover attributes in savages which they found first but could not speak of in themselves" (40). For Englishmen and women, according to Jordan, the black subject represented essentially three forces they wanted to deny in themselves and their society: first, the beast within themselves; second, illicit desire and the loss of control over the baser passions; and third, the breakdown of proper social ordering (144).

But we also might point out that women, like blacks, have cultivated mimicry and double consciousness in order to survive. As Bhabha points out, "the ambivalence of colonial authority repeatedly turns from *mimicry*— a difference that is almost nothing but not quite—to *menace*—a difference that is almost total but not quite. And in that other scene of colonial power, where history turns to farce and presence to 'a part' can be seen the twin figures of narcissism and paranoia that repeat furiously, uncontrollably" (92).[15] *Zofloya* recapitulates what we can only view as the farcical aspects of an alliance between the hyperbolically feminine and white Victoria and her very black and demonic ally and lover, Zofloya. The menace inherent in the text is not simply the menace of white women taking black men as illicit lovers. The deeper threat appears to be the social and economic alliance of dispossessed subject populations working together, recognizing their mutual alienation and objectification, and banding as one in a maniacal and deadly pursuit of the great white father and his property.

When the unlucky Berenza proposes to Victoria, they have been living together for some time, and he has been hesitant to marry her, not because

---

15. See Homi K. Bhabha, *The Location of Culture* (London: Routledge, 1994), 90–92; Winthrop Jordan, *White Over Black: American Attitudes Toward the Negro, 1550–1812* (Baltimore: Penguin, 1969) (Edward Long is cited in Bhabha, 90); and H. L. Malchow, *Gothic Images of Race in Nineteenth-Century Britain* (Stanford: Stanford University Press, 1996), for provocative background material on the effect of race and colonialism on British traditions.

of her mother's scandalous behavior but because of the excesses Berenza has observed in Victoria's character. In proposing to her, however, he alludes to his delay in soliciting her hand and attributes it to her "unworthiness" due to her mother's fall. Suffice it to say that Berenza sealed his own death warrant with that statement. Victoria smiled and "harmonized her features," but "sudden hatred and desire of revenge took possession of her vindictive soul. . . . Unhappy Berenza! all thy delicacy, thy forbearance, and nobleness of mind, will not save thee from the consequences of having proceeded thus far" (138–39). Although she marries him and feigns love and devotion, Victoria is merely waiting for the right moment to hand her husband his punishment—death followed by an adulterous affair with his brother. The fact that she waits for five years, silently nursing her grievances against him, should not surprise us. In Italy a well-known maxim states that revenge is a dish best served cold.

But Victoria is as passionate in her lust as she is in her vengeance, and indeed the aristocracy would appear to be an antiquated breeding ground for such extreme and dangerous emotions. As immediate as her lust for Henriquez is, her hatred for Lilla is almost instinctual. Victoria senses and hates in Lilla not simply the latter's goodness but what she recognizes as the arrival of a new feminine ideal, a type that will supplant the volatile Victoria and her ilk. And considering Dacre's influence on both Byron and Percy Shelley, it is interesting to speculate just how thoroughly and quickly this new feminine ideal made her way into canonical Romantic poetry through Haidée, Emily, Cythna and Asia. Once again Dacre takes this occasion to blame the mother for all of Victoria's weaknesses. We are told that "the curses of Laurina were entailed upon her daughter." The naturally "fickle and unregulated mind" of Victoria was "from her infancy untaught, therefore unaccustomed to subdue herself"; unable to control her emotions and a stranger to "self-denial," Victoria rushes headlong into her pursuit of Henriquez. But the blame for her behavior is placed squarely on her mother: "Education had never corrected the evil propensities that were by nature hers: hence pride, stubbornness, the gratification of self, contempt and ignorance of the nobler properties of the mind, with a strong tincture of the darker passions, revenge, hate, and cruelty, made up the sum of her early character. Example, a *mother's* example, had more than corroborated every tendency to evil" (143). Because of her stunted emotional faculties and her failure to recognize let alone appreciate goodness, Victoria can only despise the orphan Lilla, the epitome of an emerging British domestic ideology transplanted rather clumsily to fifteenth-century Italy. Lilla's mind, we are told, is "pure, innocent, free even from the smallest taint of a corrupt thought." She is physically described as "delicate, symmetrical, and of fairy-like beauty," while her soul is possessed of "seraphic serenity and angelic." This paragon of bourgeois innocence and domesticity has "long flaxen hair [that] floated over her shoulder" (144). In short, Lilla is just asking to be tortured and murdered by Victoria, and such is her fate in alarmingly short order. But first Victoria has other business to transact. She has to poison her husband, seduce Henriquez, and cause Henriquez's suicide.

The slow murder of Berenza occurs in his remote castle, Torre Alto, in the Appennine Mountains (reminiscent of *Udolpho*), where Victoria has persuaded the family to relocate to better conceal her assault on Henriquez and Lilla. But the murder of Berenza by a series of increasingly potent poisons provided by Zofloya is a most diabolical act, meant to prey on the anxieties of Dacre's readers about the innate perversion of sexually predatory wives. Victoria first forms the idea of killing Berenza in a dream, suggesting that her unconscious has slipped the slight yoke of social control that her conscious mind had managed to cultivate. In this first dream she sees Henriquez and Lilla initially in a garden and then in a church on the point of marrying. The black Moor suddenly appears and asks Victoria, "'Wilt thou be mine? . . . and none then shall oppose thee. . . . and the marriage shall *not be!*'" The moment Victoria assents, she is transported into Lilla's position as bride and "Berenza, suddenly wounded by an invisible hand, sunk covered with blood at the foot of the altar!" (146). All of these events come to pass, although the murder of Berenza by a series of incrementally stronger poisons introduced by Victoria into his drinks results in his bloodless but immensely painful and disfiguring death. Leaving the body of Berenza at the foot of the altar suggests that in Victoria's mind his crime has been to marry her, to enslave her.

But even more ominously we are told that Victoria possesses a "masculine spirit" (190) and "bold masculine features" (211), and whereas conventionally or bourgeois-coded masculine traits such as reason, calmness, and taciturnity are generally presented positively when they are associated with female gothic heroines, here there can be no doubt that "masculine" refers to Victoria's murderously violent streak, her aristocratic propensity to seize what she wants by wielding the knife as calmly as any man. It is Lilla, the ultrafeminine ideal, who is coded in the text as the appropriate female role model, and yet she is Victoria's next victim. The ideology goes something like this: if women fail to be effectively educated by their mothers, if they fail to embrace their proper feminine roles as docile, passive, and dependent on the rightful claims of the patriarchy, then we will witness women as monstrous as Victoria—masculine and destructive of both men and women. This particular maternal ideology, as I have suggested, merely exaggerates in its extremely crude form the celebration of the mother and the centrality of the mother's role as educator that Wollstonecraft had advocated in *A Vindication of the Rights of Woman.*

After poisoning both Berenza and Lilla's elderly aunt-chaperon, Victoria is ready to dispose of her rival Lilla, whom she and Zofloya drug and then carry to a remote stone cavern for safekeeping. In this dark and ominous cave there just happens to be "a massy chain, which though fixed to the opposite side of the wall, extended in length to the sloping irregular ascent" (203). The chain is affixed to Lilla's wrist and she, like the besieged wife in Siddons's melodrama, finds herself yet another female victim chained in the stone cavern of a corrupt patriarch, slowly starving to death. But such a fate does not satisfy Victoria for long. She procures another magical potion from Zofloya, this time one that causes Henriquez to confuse Victoria for Lilla. After a wedding banquet and a night of wild sexual revelry, Henriquez wakes up to discover the loathed Victoria in his bed. When he realizes that he has been duped and has betrayed his beloved Lilla, he promptly falls on his sword.

Victoria now stalks her real prey, the orphan Lilla, chained and defenseless in the stone cave. The confrontation between the two women is one of the most bizarre in the history of the female gothic, and is coded in stereotypical gendered terms, loaded with representations of an intermingling of feminine sexuality and perversity. When Victoria descends on the innocent Lilla, she finds Lilla sleeping on the floor of the cave surrounded by "coarse fragments of scanty food" and clothed only in "a mantle of leopard skin, brought her by Zofloya." The leopard skin, so incongruous in fifteenth-century Italy, represents the descent this very civilized domestic paragon has made into the animal realm. Upon awakening, Lilla clasps "her thin hands upon her polished bosom, and with some of her long tresses, still in pure unaltered modesty, essaying to veil it, she raised her eyes, of heavenly blue, to the stern and frantic countenance of her gloomy persecutor, appearing, in figure, grace, and attitude, a miniature semblance of the Medicean Venus" (218). Lilla here is presented as an icon, a statue, "polished," that is, too polite or civilized to survive, a "Medicean Venus," while at the same time she is coded as the embodiment of domestic virtues and characteristics: modest, blue eyes, long blonde hair. Her iconic, fetishistic qualities are further accentuated as she begs Victoria not to murder her, as if she were negotiating forgiveness for a piece of broken china: "'Alas! Victoria, in what then have I offended you, that you should hate me thus?—Ah, consider I am but a poor and friendless orphan, who can never do you ill'" (218). Lilla's presentation of herself as an orphan, bereft of patriarchal protection, reminds us of Smith's Emmeline and the entire tradition of orphaned female gothic heroines struggling to defend themselves against the terrific forces of a corrupt patriarchy.

The fact that Lilla is killed not by a corrupt monk or a greedy usurping uncle but by a lustful, vengeful, and passionate aristocratic woman suggests that by 1806 the female gothic genre had shifted sufficiently to present women as inveterate enemies of each other. Competing for the same man, Victoria and Lilla are archetypal female rivals, both pursuing the same limited goods—the same man. But the "castle" is no longer the object of the orphan's struggle for ascendancy; the focus now is on the man and marriage to him, possession of his body. It is interesting that Victoria disposes of her own husband, the heir to several large holdings in Italy, in order to sexually pursue the younger son, who has no wealth or estates in his own right. Both dispossessed women shun property and wealth in favor of the sexuality of Henriquez himself, suggesting a significant shift in the history of women's fiction. When sexual passion is viewed as more important than economic gain and social status, then women have become openly sexualized to a degree found dangerous and threatening to a culture that is predicated on their sexual discipline and control.

Victoria drags her victim to the top of a cliff, leaving Lilla's "blood red traces at every step," and announces that she will "push thee headlong" because "no art could root [thee] from the breast of Henriquez." Terrified by the view, Lilla makes her next appeal to Victoria, the sentimental one: "'Oh, sweet Victoria, remember we have been friends.—I loved thee! nay, even now I love thee, and believe that thou art mad!—Oh, think, think we have been companions, bedfellows!'" (219). Bedfellows? Somehow one cannot imagine any reason why Victoria would have crawled into bed with Lilla. This appeal to the cult of female friendship is also scornfully rejected by Victoria, who now announces to Lilla that Henriquez is dead.

At this point, Lilla makes another appeal to Victoria. She asks that she be killed the same way Henriquez was, by a stiletto through the heart, and to this Victoria agrees. The first plunge wounds "only her uplifted hand, and glanc[es] across her alabaster shoulder, the blood that issued thence, slightly tinged her flaxen tresses with a brilliant red" (220). As much is made of Lilla's shed blood as is made of her blonde tresses. The imagistic mingling here of the two is significant as a representation of soiled innocence. The horror of the scene has to be located in its unnaturalness, the violent murder of one woman by another. And again we are reminded that this nightmare of women feeding voraciously on the flesh of each other resulted because of a mother's sexual fall into an adulterous affair.

Thinking that all verbal appeals will be in vain, Lilla resorts to her final option, she starts running. But she is no match for Victoria, who catches up to her on the uttermost edge of a ridge of mountains. The two women now grapple hand to hand, and Lilla makes one final appeal, reminding Victoria that she is Lilla's hostess: "'Barbarous Victoria!—look down upon me, behold what thou hast done, and let the blood thou hast shed appease thee. Ah! little did I think, when a deserted orphan, invited by thee to remain beneath thy roof, that such would be my miserable fate! Remember *that*, Victoria—have pity on me—and I will pray of heaven to forgive thee the past!'" (220). But appealing to codes of hospitality means nothing to a woman who would serve poisoned drinks to her own husband. And the appeal to God and a religious system of belief is equally ineffectual. Victoria has sold her soul to the devil for one night in Henriquez's bed. When Lilla sees there is no hope, she flings her final taunt in her rival's face: "'Take then my life Victoria—take it at once,—but kill me I implore, with that same dagger with which you murdered Henriquez, because he loved me more than he did you!'" This insult fires Victoria's arm and the murder is described in a sort of pornographic frenzy: "With her poignard [Victoria] stabbed her in the bosom, in the shoulder, and other parts:—the expiring Lilla sank upon her knees.—Victoria pursued her blows—she covered her fair body with innumerable wounds, then dashed her headlong over the edge of the steep.—Her fairy form bounded as it fell against the projecting crags of the mountain, diminishing to the sight of her cruel enemy, who followed it far as her eye could reach" (220–21). Although victorious, Victoria has a difficult time returning to the castle. She cannot escape the feeling that she is haunted and pursued by the "mangled form of Lilla, risen from the stream. . . . those fair tresses dyed in crimson gore, that bleeding bosom" (221). The bloody hair and bosom have functioned throughout the entire scene as fetishistic part-objects of the besieged commodity Lilla. To despoil the blonde hair and the white bosom of Lilla is to attack the domestic feminine ideal at its most potent core—the promise of innocent and nurturing motherhood. Dacre intended her readers to see that the crime of Laurina affected not only her own children but untold other children, who now will be unborn because their potential mother has been destroyed most cruelly.

By this time Victoria has no hope of escaping the consequences of her many crimes. Her husband's body, which Zofloya had hidden in an old casket in a deserted wing of the castle (again we are reminded of *The Romance of the Forest*) has been discovered, as has Henriquez's. Victoria has no choice but to beg protection from Zofloya, who now makes her his mistress. Dacre's sexual and racial nausea as well as her ambivalent attraction to such a situation can barely be concealed, and much is again made of Zofloya's "blackness." We are reminded at this point of Edmund Burke's discussion of the association of blackness with the sublime. Burke tells us the "very curious story of a boy, who had been born blind and continued so until he was thirteen; he was then couched for a cataract, by which operation he received his sight. . . . some time after, upon seeing a negro woman, he was struck with great horror at the sight." For Burke, the boy's horrifying response is proof of the power of blackness to cause terror and by extension to produce a sense of the sublime.

The unfortunate Victoria and her black lover Zofloya have sunk as low as living beings can, and they now find themselves living in the Italian mountains with a band of banditti led by Victoria's brother Leonardo and his analogously dark mistress Megalena. To make the dysfunctional family circle complete, Laurina and Ardolph suddenly arrive as captives, and Leonardo murders Ardolph when he realizes who he is and that he has been beating Leonardo's dying mother. The only earthly authority figures feared by Victoria are the Venetian Council of Ten, Il Consiglio de Dieci, the political arm of the state, and the powers of the Roman Catholic Church as represented by the Inquisition (*The Italian* and *The Monk* are recalled here). Whenever Zofloya wants to threaten or intimidate Victoria, he refers to the "familiars of the holy inquisition" and Il Consiglio as the only forces from whom he could never protect or shield Victoria. Of course, these very forces descend on the mountainous hideout and Leonardo and Megalena both kill themselves rather than be taken alive.

Once again Victoria asks Zofloya to save her, and this time he announces that he can do so only if she will travel with him to his abode, hell. He strips away the appearance he has assumed on earth, and appears before her as he actually is: "a figure, fierce, gigantic, and hideous to behold!—Terror and despair seized the soul of Victoria; she shrieked, and would have fallen from the dizzying height, had not his hand, who appeared Zofloya no longer, seized her with a grasp of iron by the neck!" (254). Racism demanded a demonization of difference, and as H. L. Malchow has suggested, the gothic genre offered "a language that could be appropriated, consciously or not, by racists in a powerful and obsessively reiterated evocation of terror, disgust, and alienation. But the gothic literary sensibility itself also evoked in the context of an expanding experience of cultural conflict, the brutal progress of European nationalism and imperialism, and was in part a construct of that phenomenon."[16]

But sexism also demands a demonization of difference, and this we can see when Victoria quite literally goes to the devil. The moral Dacre pens on her last page makes the mother's guilt and responsibility for all this clear: "Over their passions and their weaknesses, mortals cannot keep a curb too strong. . . . Either we must suppose that the love of evil is born with us (which would be an insult to the Deity), or we must attribute them (as appears more consonant with reason) to the suggestions of infernal influence" (254–55). If the devil is an active presence in the world, then the angelic mother, sexless and nurturing, must do battle with him for the souls of not only her children but of future generations of children. If the mother indulges her sexuality and scorns her educational duties to her children, then she is actively working in league with the devil. Wollstonecraft may not have put the maternal ideology so crudely, but its popularized extension led to works like *Zofloya*.

Parody or camp, self-conscious deflation or hyperbolic ideological ruminations run amok, female gothic authors found themselves resorting to such extreme and extravagant positions largely, I would claim, because the idealized maternal ideology was so potent, so socially and sexually charged. Control of the female body through marriage followed by the regulation of the mother's sexuality were the basic foundations on which bourgeois Britain constructed its hegemony. Catherine Morland's history is similar, although her passivity is the object of Austen's satire in this most blatant parody of the genre. In Dacre's novel the parodic Victoria embodies every vice that bourgeois Britain found itself repulsed by in the safely distanced Italians. Victoria is the excessive and hyperbolic aristocratic woman who has finally waged open war on bourgeois values and received her just punishment. Aristocratic and sexually threatening women will surface again in Charlotte Brontë's portraits of Blanche Ingram and Bertha Rochester in *Jane Eyre*. But the type of femininity that this woman represents—sexually

---

16. Edmund Burke, *A Philosophical Enquiry into the Origin of Our Ideas of the Sublime and Beautiful*, ed. Adam Phillips (Oxford: Oxford University Press, 1990), 131–33. See the more extensive discussion of this connection among race, gender, and the sublime in Barbara Claire Freeman, *The Feminine Sublime: Gender and Excess in Women's Fiction* (Berkeley and Los Angeles: University of California Press, 1995).

promiscuous, passionately aggressive, openly adulterous—was consigned to the nether reaches of hell in 1806 when Victoria descended into the "awful abyss" in the arms of her demon lover.

IV

As the daughter of Mary Wollstonecraft and William Godwin, Mary Wollstonecraft Godwin Shelley was destined to be an overdetermined personality. A fearful intellectual burden rested on her slight shoulders, and for the most part she fulfilled that expectation by not only marrying extravagantly but by writing well. In fact, her marriage to Percy Shelley may have been her greatest literary performance, her real and imagined victimization at his hands being only slightly less than the sufferings experienced by her fictional heroines. And although her husband's presence haunts all of her works, the real heroes of Mary's life were always her parents, who recur obsessively in various mutated forms in virtually everything she wrote. As a writer Mary Wollstonecraft may have left us only some inadequately realized fictions and A Vindication, but she also left Mary Shelley, in many ways destined to complete and fulfill her mother's aborted philosophical and literary visions.[17] If Wollstonecraft failed to understand the full implications of her suggestions for women—that they effectively "masculinize" themselves and shun "feminine" values as weak and debilitating—her daughter understood all too well the consequences of such behavior for both men and women. Mary's major work, Frankenstein (1817), stands paradoxically as a gothic embodiment of the critique of gothic feminism. If Wollstonecraft could barely imagine a brave new world for women inhabited by sensitive Henrys, Mary Shelley puts her fictional women into that world and reveals

---

17. The relationship, real and imagined, between Mary Shelley and her dead mother and flawed father is explored most revealingly in William St. Clair's Godwins and the Shelleys: The Biography of a Family (New York: Norton, 1989). Sandra M. Gilbert and Susan Gubar, in The Madwoman in the Attic (New Haven: Yale University Press, 1979), discuss Mary's relationship with her mother and its influence on her works (213–47), as does Janet M. Todd, in "Frankenstein's Daughter: Mary Shelley and Mary Wollstonecraft," WL 4 (1976), 18–27. On the influence of Godwin on her works, see Katherine Powers, The Influence of William Godwin on the Novels of Mary Shelley (New York: Arno, 1980), and on Mary's relationship with her father, see U. C. Knoepflmacher, "Thoughts on the Aggression of Daughters," in The Endurance of Frankenstein, ed. U. C. Knoepflmacher (Berkeley and Los Angeles: University of California Press, 1979), 88–119. Several recent biographies of Mary Shelley explore the parental influence on her writings. In particular, see Anne K. Mellor, Mary Shelley: Her Life, Her Fiction, Her Monsters (London: Routledge, 1988); Emily Sunstein, Mary Shelley: Romance and Reality (Boston: Little, Brown, 1989); and Muriel Spark, Mary Shelley (London: Constable, 1988).

that the sensitive male hero has always been a mad egotist intent on usurp-ing feminine values and destroying all forms of life in his insane quest for phallic mastery. Such is obviously the theme of her masterpiece, *Frankenstein,* but *Mathilda* (1819) also critiques in startling ways the female gothic formula as it had been developed by the time Mary was writing. For instance, *Mathilda* rewrites *Frankenstein,* turning the prior text inside out to reveal the incestuous core of the gothic feminist fantasy as Mary experi-enced it. Everyone in Mary's corpus is a victim, but her female characters are the victims of victims, and thus doubly pathetic and weak.

We do not think of Mary Shelley as a feminist by contemporary stan-dards, nor did she think of herself as one. She once stated, "If I have never written to vindicate the rights of women, I have ever befriended women when oppressed—at every risk I have defended & supported victims to the social system—But I do not make a boast." It would appear that Mary understood all too well what her mother failed to grasp—that women's pro-tection was in their studied pose of difference and weakness. In fact, she went so far as to observe, "the sex of our [woman's] material mechanism makes us quite different creatures [from men]—better though weaker."[18] But Mary's notion of the social system—the legal, financial, class, religious, and educational superstructure that undergirded nineteenth-century British culture—was finally codified and symbolized by her in the patriarchal bour-geois family. Her fathers are not simply demigods of the family hearth, they are representatives of a larger oppressive patriarchal system. They inherit and bequeath wealth because they represent and embody that lucre them-selves in their persons.[19] The body of the male in Mary Shelley's fiction is

---

18. The full text of Mary's well-known journal confession read, "With regard to the 'good Cause'—the cause of the advancement of freedom & knowledge—of the Rights of Woman, &c—I am not a person of opinions. . . . Some [people] have a passion for reforming the world:—others do not cling to particular opinions. That my Parents and Shelley were of the former class, makes me respect it. . . . I was nursed and fed with a love of glory. To be something great and good was the precept given me by my Father: Shelley reiterated it. Alone & poor, I could only be something by joining a party—& there was much in me—the woman's love of looking up & being guided, & being willing to do anything if any one supported & brought me forward, which would have made me a good partizan—but Shelley died & I was alone. . . . If I have never written to vindicate the Rights of women, I have ever befriended women when oppressed" (October 21, 1838). See *The Journals of Mary Shelley,* ed. Paula R. Feldman and Diana Scott-Kilvert (Oxford: Clarendon, 1987), 2:553–54. The second Shelley quotation is taken from her letter of June 11, 1835: *Selected Letters of Mary W. Shelley,* ed. Betty T. Bennett (Baltimore: Johns Hopkins University Press, 1995), 257.

19. Analyzing fathers and mothers in Mary Shelley's fiction has been a persistent focus in the lit-erary criticism of her work. A useful overview of the critical history on this topic can be found in Jane Blumberg, *Mary Shelley's Early Novels: 'This Child of Imagination and Misery'* (Iowa City: University of Iowa Press, 1993).

always a commodity of worth, an object to be valued, reconstructed, reassembled, and salvaged, while the bodies of the women in her texts are always devalued, compromised, flawed, and inherently worthless.

At the core of all Mary Shelley's works, however, is the residue of what Freud has labeled, in "A Child Is Being Beaten" (SE 17:179–204), as variations on the infantile beating fantasy, but for Mary Shelley the psychic terrain is complicated in that she as a woman writer typically seeks to elide gender by assuming the position of a male protagonist. The basic beating fantasies we see throughout her works—the attacks the "creature" makes on various members of Victor Frankenstein's family or the incestuous attack on Mathilda by her father—all represent variations of the beating fantasy, expressing the child's ambivalence and impotence when confronted with the power and mystery of the parental figures.

Incest hovers over Mary Shelley's gothic works in ways that do not occur quite so self-consciously in the works of other female gothic writers, while her heroines are always defined and self-identified as daughters first, wives second, mothers only briefly. Another way of addressing these issues is to ask why Mary Shelley sent the text of *Mathilda*, a shockingly graphic (for its time) portrayal of a father's incestuous love for his daughter, to her own father? And why would she then be surprised when he failed to arrange for its publication?[20] Writing on the margins of her unconscious obsessions, Mary Shelley played the role of dutiful daughter to the end, leaving the ashes of Percy in Rome and having herself buried with her parents and son in England. In many ways, Percy was as ephemeral a presence in her life as she was in his. It appears from a reading of their letters and journals that both were playacting at love with ideal objects of their own imaginary creation. Unfortunately, as Mary learned too late, the real loves in both their lives were their parents, for Percy loved and hated his parents with an intensity that matched Mary's for hers. Percy's *Prometheus Unbound* stands as one of the

---

20. Mary sent the manuscript of *Mathilda* to Godwin by their mutual friend Maria Gisborne in May 1820. After almost two years of fruitless inquiry, Mary finally concluded that Godwin would not help see the manuscript into publication, so she began trying to recover it. She never succeeded, and the novella was not published until 1959. Terence Harpold explores the incestuous core and motivation of *Mathilda* in his article "'Did you get Mathilda from Papa?': Seduction Fantasy and the Circulation of Mary Shelley's *Mathilda*, SR 28 (1989), 49–67. Harpold concludes that the novel "represents a fantasy of seduction," and that the submission of the novel to Godwin "signals Mary's effort to engage him in the seduction fantasy, but to acknowledge the authority of his desire in the primal scene which determines her understanding of herself and her relations with each of her parents" (64). Another recent reading of the psychodynamic structure of *Mathilda* can be found in Tilottama Rajan, "Mary Shelley's *Mathilda*: Melancholy and the Political Economy of Romanticism," SNNTS 26 (1994), 43–68.

most blatant meditations on parricide ever penned, and note that he wrote it in Italy, a safe enough distance from the overbearing Sir Timothy and the lovely Elizabeth.[21]

Written after *Frankenstein* and not published until 1959, *Mathilda* is one of those lost fictions that surfaces more than a century later and suggests new possibilities and openings for understanding a writer's career.[22] A short novel about a father's incestuous love for his daughter, his suicide, and the daughter's decline into melancholia and early death, *Mathilda* was written out of intense ambivalence toward both Godwin and Percy by a young woman who had seen her father and her husband disappoint her and three of her own young children die by the time she was twenty-two. Like her mother's thinly veiled autobiographies, *Mary* and *Maria*, *Mathilda* reads all too much like Mary Shelley's own fantasy rewrite of her life: the dead but perfect mother, the absent but all-loving father willing to kill himself rather than hurt his beloved daughter, the bright but grieving daughter pursued by the handsome, rich, and famous young poet. Mathilda wills her own early death, but before that event occurs in the final pages of the novella, she depicts for her idealized audience of one (the poet Woodville) her life and the history of her emotions. The young idealized heroine has had very little external life, very few events outside the claustrophobic confines of the idyllic bourgeois family. The only adventure of Mathilda's life is the discovery and brief recovery of her father. That recovery, unfortunately, kills them both.

In the first and rejected version of the novel, "The Fields of Fancy," Mathilda is only one of several characters met by the narrative consciousness in a sort of Dantean dream vision. Mathilda as a character probably

---

21. Percy Shelley's relationship with his parents has recently been explored by Barbara Gelpi in *Shelley's Goddess: Language, Maternity, and Subjectivity* (Oxford: Oxford University Press, 1992). Mary Shelley's relationship with Percy as a formative influence on her life and writing is best explored in William Veeder's *Mary Shelley and Frankenstein: The Fate of Androgyny* (Chicago: University of Chicago Press, 1986), while the interconnections between Percy's *Cenci* and Mary's *Mathilda* are provocatively treated in Caroline Gonda, *Reading Daughters' Fictions: 1709–1834* (Cambridge: Cambridge University Press, 1996), 162–73: "the reader of female Gothic is put in the position of the bewildered child attempting to make sense of an intimidating and outsize adult world overstocked with unpredictable and often baleful authority figures. . . . The authority for secrecy is situated not in the agonized heart but in the paternal voice. . . . To write from the father's position is an impossibility, given the power-structures of Gothic, in which paternal tyranny seems as arbitrary and threatening as the supernatural—and as difficult to exorcise" (173).

22. All quotations from the novel are from *Matilda*, ed. Janet Todd (London: Penguin, 1992), with page numbers in parentheses in the text. This edition also contains Wollstonecraft's *Mary* and *Maria*, and has a valuable introduction that places all three works within a familial context.

originated out of Mary's reading of Dante's *Purgatorio*, which she was studying (in February and then again in August 1819) both before and after her son William's death. In the literary source, Mathilda is Dante's guide through the Terrestrial Paradise when Virgil is no longer able to accompany him. It is Mathilda who leads Dante to the waters that allow him to forget evil and remember only good, but it was Mary Shelley who was cursed with a memory that never forgot pain and had less and less good to remember. In "The Fields of Fancy" we are also presented with a character named Diotima, drawn from Plato's *Symposium*, which Percy Shelley had translated only a few years before. Mary's reading of Diotima is less platonic than it is personal. The description of this idealized mother figure, "a woman about forty years of age, her eyes burned with a deep fire and every line of her face expressed enthusiasm and wisdom," recalls the portraits of Wollstonecraft that we have, particularly the one that hung above the Godwin fireplace throughout Mary's childhood. Fingering the mother's face, even if that face is only a dusty and dimly remembered portrait, shapes the daughter's wound, her lack, as well as her adult consciousness and identity. Mathilda knows herself and who she is because of who and what her mother was. But unfortunately the destiny that the mother passes to her daughter tells a tale of obsessive and consuming love and tragic and early death. If Mathilda is to survive and thrive she has to reject the mother's legacy, as well as her father's encroaching and all-consuming passion. The fearful burden that the romantic daughter inherits concerns the task of parthenogenesis. Unless she can give birth to herself, she is doomed to the same cycle of generation that killed her mother and caused her father to turn inward and love only his own production, his daughter.

In *Mathilda*, the final version of "The Fields of Fancy," Mary strips away the mother figure as guide to present her heroine Mathilda as a motherless quasi orphan in a strangely gothic landscape—the bourgeois home dominated by an absent father. The mother's absence from the heroine's life appears to be the first and greatest trauma of Mathilda's life. This first wound is repeated when she recovers her father's love, only to be forced to repudiate it within a year. The final traumatic catastrophe occurs when the father commits suicide following his confession of incestuous love for Mathilda. Mathilda's passivity or rather her ostensible lack of control over any of these events suggests the nature of trauma, as well as the posture or pose of gothic feminism. The daughter effectively destroys both her parents simply by being; her very ontology is fatal. But there is no inheriting of the paternal estate, and there is no marriage or celebratory new generation to redeem the disappointments of the earlier generation. Mary Shelley's gothic feminism ends in futility and waste, total devastation both for the older and for the younger generations. This is a community that is so tired, so enfeebled by the incestuous struggle that it can only turn on itself and feed on its own tail. The wheel turns in Mary Shelley's fiction, but it goes nowhere. We end where we began—in death and disappointment.

Mathilda begins her tale in the winter, living in a frozen and sterile landscape: "a lone cottage on a solitary, wide heath." On the point of death, totally isolated, and "joyous," Mathilda has finally reached the endpoint of her journey: she has written her "tragic history" and captured its "sacred horror": "It is as the wood of the Eumenides none but the dying may enter; and Oedipus is about to die" (151). If Mathilda self-consciously styles herself as a female Oedipus, she is telling us by the second paragraph of the novel that this is a narrative of incestuous horror and can be read only if, as in *Frankenstein*, we understand the code, that "male" is to be read as "female," at least as far as the central consciousness is concerned.[23] If Mathilda thinks of herself as Oedipus, then surely that would suggest some conscious action on her part, some share of guilt in the crime and horror of incestuous passion and parricide. Oedipus, after all, murdered his father in a fit of rage, albeit unknowingly, and married his mother, also unknowingly. Both actions fulfilled the prophecy he and his parents took such great pains to avoid. The spiral of fate and free will twined around all three of them until

---

23. Criticism of *Mathilda* is scarce, although the text is gaining a critical following, and more work is certainly forthcoming. As mentioned, the text was first published in 1959 by Elizabeth Nitchie, *SP*, extra ser., 3 (Chapel Hill: University of North Carolina Press, 1959). Todd reprints this edition, modernizing the title of the work as *Matilda*. I have chosen to follow Nitchie's spelling, as does everyone else who has published on the novella. Nitchie concludes that the work is largely an autobiographical document, motivated by Mary's "horror" at her emotional estrangement from Percy after the death of their daughter Clara. The other biographical factor, according to Nitchie, was Mary's "sorrow over her alienation from her father" caused by his continual demands for money from Percy: "Like Mathilda, she had truly lost a beloved but cruel father, a loss all the more poignant because of what she later acknowledged to Mrs. Gisborne was her 'excessive romantic' attachment to him" (457–59). Also see Nitchie, "Mary Shelley's *Mathilda*: An Unpublished Story and Its Biographical Significance," *SP* 40 (1943), 448–49; Nitchie, appendix to *Mary Shelley* (New Brunswick: Rutgers University Press, 1953; reprinted Westport, Conn.: Greenwood, 1970); and Kate Ellis, "Subversive Surfaces: The Limits of Domestic Affection in Mary Shelley's Later Fiction," in *The Other Mary Shelley*, ed. Audrey A. Fisch, Anne K. Mellor, and Esther Schor (New York: Oxford University Press, 1993). Most recently the work has been analyzed by Susan Lanser, who reads it as a failed attempt to denounce the basic incompatibility between feminism and masculine romanticism, in *Fictions of Authority: Women Writers and Narrative Voice* (Ithaca: Cornell University Press, 1992), 168–72; and by Katherine Hill-Miller, who reads it within an autobiographical context, in *My Hideous Progeny: Mary Shelley, William Godwin, and the Father-Daughter Relationship* (Newark: University of Delaware Press, 1995).

they were strangled in its inextricable knots.

But Mathilda ostensibly does nothing. Her birth kills her mother, while her existence causes her father to love her with a love that dared not speak its name. We are tempted to observe that Mathilda is not Oedipus; she is Mary Shelley. And notice that she describes herself to Woodville, the recipient of the tale, as guilty of "no crimes." Her only "faults may easily be pardoned; for they proceeded not from evil motive but from want of judgement." In fact, she goes even further to vindicate herself, but here I think she protests too much: "I believe few would say that they could, by a different conduct and superior wisdom, have avoided the misfortunes to which I am the victim. My fate has been governed by necessity, a hideous necessity" (152). We can recall that Godwin had made his philosophical reputation writing of necessitarianism, and Percy believed so strongly in necessity that he made it a central character in his *Prometheus Unbound* and called "him" Demogorgon, the only force powerful enough to destroy tyranny.

When Mathilda recounts her origins she presents her father as "a man of rank," fatherless and "educated by a weak mother with all the indulgence she thought due to a nobleman of wealth" (152). Shades of Wollstonecraft's class critique emerge in this description, as does the depiction of his love for the decidedly middle-class Diana, the daughter of "a gentleman of small fortune who lived near his family mansion" (153). The valorization of the shabby genteel heroine, the castigation of the upper-class male heir—these are motifs we recognize from Wollstonecraft's two novels. But in Mary Shelley's version Diana, the beloved childhood friend, becomes the wife within a year of her mother-in-law's death. She marries as if to replace the mother only to die herself within a year, leaving a daughter as surrogate for herself. Women spiral around each other in just this way throughout the fiction of Mary Shelley, suggesting in an uncanny manner the sameness of all women, their fetishistic replaceability, their interchangeable natures. But if women are generic in their roles and identities, men are nameless. We never learn the name of Mathilda's father. Indeed, he changes his name after his wife's death, and even his own sister does not know his new identity or his whereabouts. To Mathilda he is simply "my father" or a "towering spirit" (156) throughout the text. That is, he is less an individual than he is a role, the phallic embodiment of status and prerogative, privilege and patrilineal descent. He makes decisions, while Mathilda lives with the consequences of those decisions. Such a situation would appear to be the simplest definition of the difference between male and female power in the female gothic universe.

But where the mother Diana grew up motherless as a child, raised by a doting father, Mathilda is not so fortunate, growing up both motherless and fatherless. As a consequence, Mathilda describes herself as possessing the "greatest sensibility of disposition. I cannot say with what passion I loved every thing even the inanimate objects that surrounded me" (157). Mathilda's extreme affectivity is most likely the result of emotional deprivation in her childhood home. Raised by a dour Scottish aunt and a servant who "never caressed" her, Mathilda falls prey to the "good nurse"/"bad servant" syndrome, a version of the "good mother"/"wicked stepmother" dynamic that lies at the root of the family romance. Only in Mathilda's case, when her "real" father finally does arrive on the scene when she is sixteen, he is all too ready to play the part of the "false" seducer. In the family romance as described by Freud, the child imagines that her parents are not her real parents. Instead, she fancies that she is the child of royalty, mistakenly placed in the home of benighted peasants, who misunderstand and devalue her. *Mathilda* can be read on several levels as a working out of Mary Shelley's own fantasy of the family romance turned nightmare. The worm at the core of Mary Shelley's version, however, consists of her own displaced and elided incestuous desires, concealed from her consciousness by the use of the characters in *Mathilda* as screen memories, fictively blocking her from viewing her own parents as objects of desire. But if the "peasant" family she presents in *Mathilda* is decisively rejected by the heroine-surrogate, then Mary is in the uncomfortable position of seeing as "royal" her "real," biological parents. The "royal" parents that she so desires for herself are in fact her idealized reconstructions of Godwin and Wollstonecraft, two literary and intellectual giants, two "masculine" presences that she could never fully satisfy.

Like Wollstonecraft's Mary and Maria, however, Mathilda is educated in the tradition of a sentimental/gothic heroine. She has little contact with the outside world and her imagination is fed by literature rather than life: "As I grew older books in some degree supplied the place of human intercourse: the library of my aunt was very small; Shakespeare, Milton, Pope and Cowper were the strangely assorted poets of her collection." In addition to developing a bookish imagination, Mathilda is also taught to play the harp amidst natural scenes. Her favorite childhood sport is to "form affections and intimacies with the aerial creations of my own brain" and to "cling to the memory of my parents; my mother I should never see, she was dead: but the idea of my unhappy, wandering father was the idol of my imagination." Gazing longingly at the miniature of her father, Mathilda amuses herself with the fantasy that "disguised like a boy I would seek my father through the world. My imagination hung upon the scene of recognition; his miniature, which I should continually wear exposed on my breast, would be the means and I imagined the moment to my mind a thousand and a thousand times" (159).

Mathilda imagines herself searching for her father disguised as a boy, and we could say that such is the case because only boys have the freedom to travel, but we should also recognize here the desire of a girl to change her sex so that she will be more acceptable to the father. The use of the minia-ture as a talismanic identifying tag suggests a rewriting of *The Italian* in interesting and ironic ways that reverberate throughout this text, for Ellena's miniature garnered her only a false father, producing a sadistic spin on the family romance as nightmare. When Mathilda imagines her reunion with her father, it occurs sometimes in a desert, sometimes in a populous city, sometimes at a ball, sometimes on a vessel. He always speaks first, and always his words are exactly the same: "'My daughter, I love thee!'" (159). The loca-tion—sometimes empty, sometimes crowded—suggests that the core of the incestuous fantasy for the child concerns numbers; that is, when she imag-ines the reunion, she refigures it as a denial of the reality of encroaching oth-ers in what is for her essentially a dyadic relationship. For Mathilda, any competition for the father is fearful and needs to be eliminated. The father is allowed to reappear only when Mathilda is sixteen and at the height of her youthful beauty. With her mother safely dead and no siblings as rivals, Mathilda does not need to brook any competition from anyone. When her father magically appears in a forest to claim her, she is clad in a symbolically virginal white frock with a fetching tartan accent.

Mathilda reads at this and other points as an embarrassingly personal fan-tasy. We have here Mary Shelley's attempt to rewrite her life as if her father had not remarried and had a favorite son named William. In the fantasy world that Mary inhabited, Godwin had no need to marry the odious Mrs. Clairmont in order to gain a caretaker for his children. In Mary's fantasy, she was the only child because she was the only child of Godwin and Wollstonecraft. Fanny Imlay did not signify; Claire, William, none of them was as real to Mary as she was to herself. This intense myopia is perhaps the real issue for all romantic solipsists—Mary Shelley as well as Percy. We are tempted to conclude that Mary understood Percy so well because she was prey to the same sort of solipsistic fantasies herself. If Percy could immerse himself in the world of *Alastor,* a realm where the poet-hero travels through-out the Orient in search of truth, Mary could present a domesticated version of the same man in Mathilda's father. This man recounts his travels to Mathilda, sounding very much like the *Alastor* poet: "He had passed the sixteen years of absence among nations nearly unknown to Europe; he had wandered through Persia, Arabia and the north of India and had penetrated among the habitations of the natives with a freedom permitted to few Europeans" (161). During his travels the father admits that initially he missed his little daughter and imagined himself returning to claim her. But as time went on, he found he was quite content to live with his own psychic construction of Mathilda. This child was the perfect idea of a child, a "fairy form," a "spirit" of "consolation" and "hope" (161). This child was a version of the woman within as infantile, safe, and ultimately nonthreatening because nonsexual. She was, in short, a childlike version of Percy's epipsyche.

If the father invented his ideal construction of Mathilda as a substitute for his dead wife while traveling abroad, he was also exposed to some unusual moral and religious teachings as well. Although Mary Shelley does not make the connection explicit, she certainly suggests that he learned his tendencies to rationalize incest somewhere in the extremely suspect regions of the Orient: "He had seen so many customs and witnessed so great a variety of moral creeds that he had been obliged to form an independent one for himself which had no relation to the peculiar notions of any one country" (161). Father-daughter incest, as Mathilda's father would have learned, is a ritualized "rite of passage" for young women in several Asian and African countries, just a different "custom" that our narrow "moral creeds" have prohibited. Percy Shelley himself experimented with literarily presenting sibling incest in *Laon and Cythna,* the first and unpublishable version of *The Revolt of Islam.* For both Shelleys, shocking the narrow sexual prejudices of the bourgeoisie was great sport, and surely Mary's *Mathilda* has to be read on some level as yet another attempt to expose and attack the flaws of the inwardly focused patriarchal family. In depicting the incestuous love of a widowed father for his nubile daughter, Mary reveals in this text another way that the middle-class domestic abode can be seen as a haven for fostering perverse and perverting love.

Although Mathilda cannot name it, she senses immediately that there is something odd about her father. First she tells us that "a curious feeling of unreality [was] attached by him to his foreign life," as if what he did or learned in foreign countries was less real than what he did in England. Next she notices that he "talked of my Mother as if she had lived but a few weeks before." This, she knows, is strange: "In all this there was a strangeness that attracted and enchanted me." He tells her that it is as if he were awakening from a "long, visionary sleep," only to discover, like a male Sleeping Beauty, that his daughter "was all that he had to love on earth" (162). The "sleep" that the father has undergone during the past sixteen years, since the death of his wife, represents a sort of latency period for him, a time of static anticipation of his daughter's ability to step into her dead mother's role as potential sexual partner and love object. This is a man—Mary implies—like all men compelled to love that which he has created and therefore can control. Father and daughter live for a brief time in Scotland in "Paradisiacal bliss," divinely happy for three months until they are rudely shut out of this garden by the death of Mathilda's aunt.

It is while living in London, a more sophisticated urban landscape, that the father at last is forced to confront the true nature of his incestuous desires. Mathilda, who had earlier imaged herself as a female Oedipus, now fancies herself a "Psyche[, I] lived for awhile in an enchanted palace" (163). This enchanted palace, the idyllic paternal home, is magical because the beloved only child is the sole love object within. Like Psyche, however, she does not understand the true nature of her lover. Mathilda thinks she is innocently loved by a father's pure and selfless devotion, not suspecting that she is actually loved by a monster father. Mathilda's situation is similar only to the story Psyche's sister tells her, precipitating her later trouble and quest. The role of Psyche's sister, the troublemaker, is played in Mathilda's narrative by the unwelcome suitor, "a young man of rank, well informed and agreeable in his person." From this man's sudden absence, Mathilda is able to date her father's drastic change in mood. No longer the loving god Eros, he has suddenly become "the king of hell." In yet another mythic displacement, Mathilda now compares herself to "Proserpine, who was gaily and heedlessly gathering flowers on the sweet plain of Enna, when the king of hell snatched her away to the abodes of death and misery. Alas!" (164).

Content to resort to literary displacement yet one more time, Mathilda next compares herself to the biblical David: "Sometimes I said to myself, this is an enchantment, and I must strive against it. My father is blinded by some malignant vision which I must remove. And then, like David, I would try music to win the evil spirit from him" (165). Oedipus becomes Psyche becomes Proserpine becomes David. The transformation in associations and mythic archetypes suggests that Mathilda sees herself alternately as male or female, sometimes victimizer and sometimes victim of forces beyond her control. All of these mythic characters, however, have two traits in common: they were all wounded and traumatized repeatedly and yet all used their special talents to do battle against a potent and threatening familial figure or figures. Again we can recall what Freud has described as the core of surviving a deep psychic wound: Is trauma to be understood as the direct and immediate brush with death or is trauma the experience of surviving that near fatal disaster and yet being forced to relive it repeatedly in dreams and painful memories? As Caruth has noted, "in the oscillation between the crisis of death and the crisis of life" we get "a kind of double-telling," a narrative that exists "between the story of the unbearable nature of an event and the story of the unbearable nature of its survival."[24] In Mathilda's case she conceals the initial wound—the mother's death and her own survival—only to have that original lack, the primordial trauma, reactivated when her father loves and then deserts her.

Mathilda suggests, albeit unconsciously, that she understands the nature of her struggle with her father when she next tries to discuss Alfieri's tragedy "Myrrha" with him. "Myrrha" had been one of Byron's favorite dramas, reputedly one of the sources for his own incestuous closet drama *Manfred*. If Byron chose to tell his tale of incest punished from the male point of view exclusively, then in *Mathilda* it is as if Mary chooses to allow Astarte to live and speak. But as this novel is structured around gaps of knowledge, Mathilda does not know that her father's drastic change in mood is caused by a conversation that occurred between him and her erstwhile suitor, in which the suitor pointedly accused the father of unnatural desires for his daughter. Mathilda only knows that her father bristles when she praises Myrrha, the daughter who dies because of her father's incestuous love for her.

This most literary of frustrated couples next takes up residence in Yorkshire, at the paternal estate where Mathilda's parents had lived briefly before. Soon after arriving, in a futile attempt to distinguish mother from daughter, the father asks Mathilda to read Dante to him, "'When I was last here your mother read Dante to me; you shall go on where she left off.' And then in a moment he said, 'No, that must not be; you must not read Dante.'" The command and then the sudden repudiation of the repetition compulsion suggest that the father is dimly struggling to comprehend his own need to construct and then deconstruct the mother and daughter as the same. When he asks Mathilda to pick her own book for reading aloud, she rather perversely chooses Spenser's description of Sir Guyon's descent into the halls of Avarice (167). The Yorkshire estate, Mathilda dimly recognizes, stands at the gates of hell itself. Her ownership of it and the riches the estate represents could only be purchased by an unlawful and unnatural deed, incest with the patriarch himself. But behind the reference to Spenser is the sug-

---

24. Cathy Caruth, *Unclaimed Experience*, 7.

gestion that the gates of hell will be opened only when the hero is brave enough to face his most fearsome opponent and temptation. Struggling to confront the truth about her father's change of attitude, Mathilda forces her father to take her to the gates of hell. She demands that he tell her his secret: "and when I know his secret then will I pour a balm into his soul and again I shall enjoy the ravishing delight of beholding his smile" (169).

This optimistic version of events is belied by the horror of the secret, which surely by this time must have been intuited by Mathilda. Styling herself as a heroine of melodrama, Mathilda cannot see herself except through the lenses of literary conventions. Sometimes she is a Greek mythological figure, sometimes a biblical hero, sometimes a Renaissance ideal, but finally she is never simply herself. In fact, one is tempted to say that she has not developed a sense of self, a sense of separation from others that would allow her to approach her father as an equal. She can only be his inferior and his part object, a cathectic reminder of his earlier passion for his dead wife. She exists, in other words, as the living embodiment of *his* wound, his loss of his wife. Because we read the text completely from Mathilda's point of view, it is easy to overlook the fact that the father is as wounded, if not more so, than his daughter. The narrative relates a doubled trauma, as if father and daughter were confronting each other in a dream and simultaneously asking, "Father/Daughter, don't you see that I am burning?" When Mathilda finally forces the "truth" out of her father, she is really confronting less the horror of incest than the fact that she has never been real to him. He sees her as the living embodiment of an earlier and more fulfilling relationship. He does not see her, but then he never did. He has simply been too wounded, too caught in his own saga of loss to see her as anything other than the living residue of his dead wife.

The theories of Nicolas Abraham are relevant here, particularly his notion of the "phantom," which he labels an "invention of the living" designed to objectify "the gap that the concealment of some part of a loved one's life produced in us. The phantom is, therefore, also a metapsychological fact. Consequently, what haunts are not the dead, but the gaps left within us by the secrets of others." Mathilda, therefore, would appear to be pursued by the phantom of her mother, but in actuality she is haunted by the gap in her living father's consciousness, his secret sexual dislocations. This syndrome is identified in the case studies of Abraham, and his description bears an uncanny resemblance to the metapsychological dynamics of Mathilda and her father: "Because the phantom is not related to the loss of a loved one, it cannot be considered the effect of unsuccessful mourning, as is the case of melancholics or of all those who carry a tomb within themselves. It is the children's or descendants' lot to objectify these buried tombs through diverse species of ghosts. What comes back to haunt are the tombs of others. The phantoms of folklore merely objectify a metaphor active within the unconscious: the burial of an unspeakable fact *within the loved one*."[25]

When Mathilda confronts her father, she begs to be informed of his "secret grief" (171), and she dares to claim that she is addressing him as a "friend and equal" (170). We know, however, that she is neither in his eyes. Her melodramatic posturings in this scene drip with the irony that pervaded the popular stage dramas of the time. Everyone is in the know except the heroine. The reader of the novel surely knows by this time what Mathilda herself has been hinting at in her allusions to Oedipus, Proserpine, Myrrha: that she herself is also a victim of unnatural paternal lust. When her father responds by begging Mathilda to drop her prying quest, he cautions her to "wait in submissive patience the event of what is passing around you" (171). Advising gothic heroines to practice submissive patience had long been standard in stock sentimental and melodramatic literature, and we have seen that no gothic feminist worth her pedigree would actually practice patience and be long-suffering. Mathilda is no different.

She responds to her father in ironic tones and then moves to the heart of the issue: "'Am I the cause of your grief?'" (171). Her father, no longer able to sustain this linguistic sexual teasing, blurts out, "'Yes, you are the sole, the agonizing cause of all I suffer, of all I must suffer until I die. Now, beware! Be silent! Do not urge me to your destruction. . . . beware!" (172). The syntax here is revealing, for it suggests a blaming of the victim that pervades the consciousness of most female gothic works. Mathilda *causes* her own destruction, the father suggests, by being lovable. Women, Mary implies, deserve to suffer because something within them causes fatally excessive emotions in the men closest to them. This supposed passion pretends on the surface to be "love," but the many references to "hate" throughout these pages speak to the fact that Mary Shelley recognized—as few female authors of her time did—that women cause an extreme and dangerous ambivalence in men, and this oscillation between love and hate, victim and victimizer is what is explored in muted form throughout the text.

The climatic scene between Mathilda and her father, their last conversation before he dies, is suffused with intensity, sexual frustration, anger,

25. Nicolas Abraham, "Notes on the Phantom: A Complement to Freud's Metapsychology," trans. Nicholas Rand, *CI* 13 (1987), 287, 289.

betrayal, a frenzy of sadomasochistic posturing between father and daughter seldom seen in literature before or since. She approaches; he retreats. She taunts and tempts; he denounces and warns. The dueling and sparring, resembling the verbal gaming that occurred in Renaissance and Restoration drama, suggest a power struggle that can only consume one participant utterly. The father's hold on power consists in his ability to deny and not speak the unspeakable. He is safe as long as he keeps silent about his secret lust. In other words, he is placed in a traditionally feminine posture in relation to the more aggressive, demanding Mathilda. The woman here relentlessly pursues knowledge; she sadistically and knowingly leads her father into a confession that will destroy them both: "I was led by passion and drew him with frantic heedlessness into the abyss that he so fearfully avoided" (172). Her final trump is to accuse the father of hatred: "'you no longer love me. I adjure you, my father, has not an unnatural passion seized upon your heart? Am I not the most miserable worm that crawls? Do I not embrace your knees, and you most cruelly repulse me? I know it—I see it—you hate me!'" (172). We are surely meant to read this plea as ironic. We are meant to recognize that the "unnatural passion" that has seized the father's heart is incestuous love, not hate. But if we read perversely, if we read this passage as if the irony is a cover for Mary's own ambivalence toward Godwin, then we will recognize that the real passion motivating the relationship between father and daughter is hate. We recall here that Mary's first and rejected work of fiction was entitled "Hate." Mary touches the wound, the pain, more clearly than even she perhaps realized when she has her heroine Mathilda accuse the father of "hate." But note that the accusation works both ways. If Mathilda can accuse her father of hate, it is because she hates him as well. The projection is complete when we recognize that both father and daughter are caught on the wheel of familial duty and claustrophobic emotions. Both love as much as they hate or hate as much as they love.

When confronted with the truth of his ambivalence, the father initially concedes the truth, which we are meant to take as untruth: "'Yes, yes, I hate you! You are my bane, my poison, my disgust! Oh! No! . . . you are none of all these; you are my light, my only one, my life.—My daughter, I love you!'" (173). The text has moved inexorably to this moment of climax, this confession of unnatural and incestuous passion. But the confession of love follows within a few breaths from an outburst of hatred. To say that the love confession is compromised by the passage about hatred would be to recognize the obvious. Mathilda's immediate response is to sink to the ground, "covering my face and almost dead with excess of sickness and fear: a cold perspiration covered my forehead and I shivered in every limb" (173). The nausea that attacks her here is repeated at the end of the text, as she waits to die from a self-induced fever. But the illness from which she truly suffers and has suffered throughout the text is hatred toward her father and guilt for that hatred. His early desertion and long absence are never forgiven. His eccentricity, his jealousy of the vague suitor, his "strangeness"—all of these are repeated or elided so consistently that we can only conclude that Mathilda hates her father and longs to escape with an idealized and phantom mother. The negative Oedipus complex is perhaps clearer in this scene than in any other, except perhaps Radcliffe's *Italian*.

But recall Abraham's theory of the phantom yet once more. Children are haunted by the unresolved and secret sexual and psychic histories of their parents in such a way that the children themselves come to embody the tombs that are enclosed within the psyches of their parents:

> The phantom is a formation of the unconscious that has never been conscious—for good reason. It passes—in a way yet to be determined—from the parent's unconscious into the child's. . . . *The phantom which returns to haunt bears witness to the existence of the dead buried within the other.* A surprising fact gradually emerges: the work of the phantom coincides in every respect with Freud's description of the death instinct. . . . [T]he phantom is sustained by secreted words, invisible gnomes whose aim is to wreak havoc, from within the unconscious, in the coherence of logical progression. Finally, it gives rise to endless repetition and, more often than not, eludes rationalization. (291)

If anyone is in the grip of the death instinct it would appear to be Mathilda, who ends up recapitulating her father's drive toward self-extinction. And note the repetition compulsion evidenced in the continual use of literary allusions to distance herself from the pain of actual life. Do either Mathilda or her father understand the psychic abyss into which they have fallen? It would seem that neither is able to rationalize the dilemma and so both continue to sink.

The father's love precipitates the last great melodramatic outpouring of the novel when he realizes that he has confessed his love and Mathilda yet lives. He declares himself first a "Monster," then a "fallen archangel," and finally a "devil" (173). Claiming that he loves his daughter "as one who was never before loved: and she knows it now," he begs to be allowed to die in her arms (173). With her father lying insensate at her feet, wallowing like the worm she had earlier felt herself to be, Mathilda responds as any melodramatic heroine would in such a situation: "I tore my hair; I raved aloud; at one moment in pity for his sufferings I would have clasped my father in my arms; and then starting back with horror I spurned him with my foot; I felt as if stung by a serpent, as if scourged by a whip of scorpions which drove me—Ah! Whither—Whither?" (173). Mathilda leaves her father wallowing in the misery that she created, knowing that she is leaving him to "his grave" (173). Once again she lapses into literary allusion as a means of hyperbolic self-dramatizing and emotional distancing, this time styling herself as Boccaccio's "Sigismunda" weeping over Guiscardo. But she also realizes that she has now awakened from her "life as from a dream." Her "father was as dead to [her]"; in fact, she now recognizes him as her "greatest enemy" (174). Significantly, her first fantasy of escape is to envision life in a convent, "not for religion's sake, for I was not a Catholic, but that I might for ever be shut out from the world. I should there find solitude where I might weep, and the voices of life might never reach me" (175). And perhaps with a bit of luck she could find her long-lost mother in that convent.

Instead, Mathilda curses her father, dooming both of them to the self-generating cycles of reproach and bitterness: "This is my curse, a daughter's curse: go, and return pure to thy child, who will never love aught but thee" (175). But while protesting to love her father still with a pure heart, Mathilda is suddenly placed in a most gothic situation that very night. Much past midnight she hears her father's footsteps approach her bedroom, pause at her door, and then, after a few moments, retreat. This gothic leitmotif, the heroine besieged in her own bedroom on a dark and stormy night by a potential rapist, precipitates the most anxious emotions in Mathilda: "That he should be restless I understood; that he should wander as an unlaid ghost and find no quiet from the burning hell that consumed his heart. But why approach my chamber? Was not that sacred? I felt almost ready to faint while he had stood there, but I had not betrayed my wakefulness by the slightest motion, although I had heard my own heart beat with violent fear" (175). This nocturnal visit causes Mathilda to have a particularly unpleasant dream or rather nightmare about her father. Like most dreams in gothic texts, this one is an overdetermined warning and foreshadowing of what lies in the future for the heroine. It is also, like the dreams of Adeline in *The Romance of the Forest,* a repetitious reenactment of trauma. Freud emphasizes that there is a complicated relation between trauma and survival precisely because of the indirect nature of psychic woundings. What causes trauma, according to Freud, is a sudden shock that actually acts very much like a bodily, physical threat but is instead a rupture in the psyche's experience of time: "We may, I think, tentatively venture to regard the common traumatic neurosis as a consequence of an extensive breach being made in the protective shield against stimuli. . . . And we still attribute importance to the element of fright. It is caused by lack of any preparedness for anxiety" (*SE* 18:31). Shortly after this passage, Freud points out that it is in dreams that we attempt to compensate for having directly missed the traumatic event. As Caruth points out, "The return of the traumatic experience in the dream is not the signal of the direct experience but, rather, of the attempt to overcome the fact that it was *not* direct, to attempt to master what was never fully grasped in the first place. Not having truly known the threat of death in the past, the survivor is forced, continually, to confront it over and over again. For consciousness, then, the act of survival, as the experience of trauma, is the repeated confrontation with the necessity and impossibility of grasping the threat to one's own life" (62).

In her ominously foreshadowing dream Mathilda finds her father "deadly pale, and clothed in flowing garments of white. Suddenly he started up and fled from me" (176). The chase ensues, with Mathilda vaguely aware that her father means to kill himself unless she can rescue him first. Just as she reaches him and catches a part of his robe, he leaps to his death off a cliff. Recall that Mathilda first met her father in a wood clothed in a flowing white garment, and notice now that the power dynamic between them has shifted. Now it is the father who is dressed in white, less a virgin than a sacrificial victim. Now it is in the daughter's hands to give life and happiness, not the father's. The apprehension and resentment that the child feels at her powerlessness to win and keep the father's affections has turned into the opposite emotion. Now it is the child who can doom the father with her rejection of him. There is guilt and sorrow in the dream, but ultimately there is also anger and revenge: a wish fulfillment that appears to say, "Daddy, don't you see that you are dying?" The wages of the father's earlier desertion of the child are death now by that child's hands.

The dream stands clearly as a wish fulfillment, and the very next day the dream will be enacted with the expected fatal consequences. When Mathilda awakes the next morning, she learns that her father has fled the estate, leaving behind a maudlin and self-justifying letter. This missive wallows in masochistic posturings and melodramatic beating scenarios of punishment and abasement: "I have betrayed your confidence; I have endeavoured to pollute your mind, and have made your innocent heart acquainted with the looks and language of unlawful and monstrous passion. I must expiate these crimes, and must endeavour in some degree to proportionate my punishment to my guilt" (177). In the melodramatic universe of the female gothic text, the only punishment appropriate for the crime of loving (read: hating and wounding) one's daughter excessively is suicide. But the letter is significant also for its extreme literariness. Mathilda's father claims to see a pattern of causation in their fates, and that pattern conforms to literary types we recognize as derived from Dante and Plato. After imagining his daughter for sixteen years as the living embodiment of feminine loveliness, he finally meets her and is compelled to project onto her all his fantasies: "At length I saw you. You appeared as the deity of a lovely region, the ministering Angel of a Paradise to which of all human kind you admitted only me" (178). Mathilda is Beatrice; the father is Dante; both are caught in idealizing fantasies of their own creation. Neither wants to believe that the other has a physical body. Neither wants to admit that others can intrude into the tight domestic paradise they have created for each other.

Mathilda's father claims that his love for her was one of "sinless passion. . . . I loved you as a human father might be supposed to love a daughter borne to him by a heavenly mother." Human as opposed to what? He provides the answer in the next line, which suggests that the world of Greek mythology supplies for this family an endless treasure trove of analogies. Comparing himself to Anchises, he presents himself as the father of Aeneas, suggesting that his daughter Mathilda is now for him a masculine warrior and conqueror. The father has been destroyed, not by the specter of his dead wife, who he claims haunts his consciousness, but by the living presence of a potential male rival for the daughter, the erstwhile suitor: "But when I saw you become the object of another's love; when I imagined that you might be loved otherwise than as a sacred type and image of loveliness and excellence; or that you might love another with a more ardent affection than that which you bore to me, then the fiend awoke within me; I dismissed your lover" (179). When Mathilda reads this portion of the letter she is struck dumb in amazement. If she had a "lover" she was never aware of it. Clearly, the "lover" is the central enigma in the text. He is unnamed, shadowy, mysterious. We might be tempted initially to claim that he embodies the father's long-repressed incestuous desires, functioning as a screen memory onto which he can project his hitherto unconscious longings for his daughter. But it is also possible to claim that the male suitor's mysterious presence and sudden absence reveal a homoerotic tendency in the hysterical father that he cannot admit to himself. The struggle that takes place over the body of Mathilda actually represents a displaced attraction between the two men that must undergo a hysterical abjection. While claiming to "love" his daughter is odious to the father, the other possibility, that he "loves" the suitor, is much more objectionable. We can recall here Eve Sedgwick's observation in *Between Men* that, in any erotic triangle, "the bond that links the two rivals is as intense and potent as the bond that links either of the rivals to the beloved" (21). Soon after the expulsion of the third party, however, the father finds himself consumed with "self-anger," "despair," and "unimaginable sensations" (179). He desperately tries to "awaken in [his] heart the grief [he] had felt at the loss of your mother." But all of his efforts are to no avail. He can no more love a dead woman than he can love a living one. He recognizes that all of his attempts to reject his incestuous love for Mathilda result only in "this guilty love more unnatural than hate" (179).

"Hate" recurs throughout this letter so often that we know it is the real issue between father and daughter. The final lines suggest as much: "Farewell, Matilda, I go with the belief that I have your pardon. Your gentle nature would not permit you to hate your greatest enemy and though I be he, . . . yet you will forgive me" (181). After writing his letter, Mathilda's father promptly leaves and dutifully walks off the very cliff Mathilda had foreseen in her dream. His death march to the sea is punctuated by a lightning flash that rends an oak, a bell that sounds like a death knell, all of the gothic props that had occurred in Matilda's dream of the night before. Following her father just too late to save him, she finally locates his dead body in a cottage near the sea: "the bed within instantly caught my eyes, something stiff and straight lay on it, covered by a sheet; the cottagers looked aghast" (184). The father has become that which he spent his life fleeing: an object on a bed, stiff, straight, the subject of shock and disgust for innocent onlookers. In short, the father has become a phallic spectacle. Mathilda can only collapse on the side of the bed, having escaped the bed, having escaped the fate of her mother. A fear and loathing of the body is evidenced here, both in the father and in Mathilda. The bed of life is also the bed of death, and it is a lucky child who is born and not consumed by her parents in the process of life.

In the final section of the text, Matilda constructs a life for herself as a survivor of the female gothic nightmare. Initially she is puzzled that she feels "no horror" at the death of her father, only the need to conceal her "secret" at all costs (184–85). Like all gothic feminists, she is compelled to "be silent lest my faltering voice should betray unimagined horrors." Further, she must cultivate "false smiles and words, cunning frauds, treacherous laughter and a mixture of all light deceits," all designed to hide her father's guilt that lives on still in her "glazed eyes" (185). Comparing herself to Job, Mathilda now sees that death or pretending to be dead is her only escape from the tainted legacy that her father has bequeathed her. Gothic feminists have played several games in their attempt to shape ideology and energy to their own purposes, but Mathilda now plays dead in a particularly perverse manner. When she realizes that she can easily fake her death and construct a new life for herself on her own terms, she remarks, "Oh, this was a delicious life quite void of guile! I with my dove's look and fox's heart: for indeed I felt only the degradation of falsehood, and not any sacred sentiment of conscious innocence that might redeem it" (186). This life of "innocent deceit" allows Mathilda to imagine that she is happily waiting reunion with her father in the spiritual world, where they will be free to love each other because neither will be burdened by the inconvenient demands of fallen and physical bodies. Women have known for centuries that looking like the dove allows them protective coloration in a hostile environment. The later allusion to Coleridge's *Christabel,* in which a split woman plays both dove and serpent effectively, is surely no coincidence.

The literary posturings, however, come thick and fast as the narrative draws to a close. While in London and walking among falling leaves, Mathilda compares herself to Coleridge's Ancient Mariner blessing the water snakes. Next she compares herself to the "unfortunate Constance," and then to a "youthful Hermitess dedicated to seclusion, and whose bosom she must strive to keep free from all tumult and unholy despair" (187–88). Describing herself as "an altered creature," she disappears and begins wearing a "fanciful nunlike dress." Her earlier fantasies about becoming a nun or at least posing as one have finally been realized. But Mathilda is a particularly Rousseauesque nun, worshipping the "moonshine, the bright stars, the breezes and the refreshing rains," surrounded by "many books and a harp with which when despairing I could soothe my spirits" (188). While claiming to be at peace with her choice, Mathilda admits that she is often prey to "despair and melancholy; gloom that nought could dissipate or overcome; a hatred of life." She quotes Wordsworth to express her increasing desire to be dead: "Before I see another day / Oh, let this body die away!" (189).

After two years Mathilda is visited by a rich and famous poet named Woodville, who becomes her dear and devoted friend. His life exactly mirrors Mathilda's; indeed we might think of him as the male version of her, much in the same way Percy Shelley created a visionary maiden as love object for his poet-hero in *Alastor.* Like Mathilda's mother, Woodville's father was poor and exceptionally gifted. Mathilda's description of Woodville reads as a covert description of her own fantasy life: Woodville "was glorious from his youth. Every one loved him; no shadow of envy or hate cast even from the meanest mind ever fell upon him. He was, as one the peculiar delight of the Gods, railed and fenced in by his own divinity, so that nought but love and admiration could approach him" (191). His aborted romance with Elinor, ending in her tragic death, mirrors Mathilda's own relationship with her father (not to mention presenting a sanitized version of Percy's disastrous first marriage to Harriet). Like Mathilda, he also seeks to restore his damaged spirits by communing with the beauties of nature, and it is in the countryside that these two kindred spirits meet. Dressed in her "whimsical nunlike habit," Mathilda causes Woodville's horse to throw him, and thus begins a beautiful gothic friendship. Mathilda very quickly makes it a point to tell us that Woodville does not in any way remind her of her father: "He was younger, less worn, more passionless than my father and in no degree reminded me of him; he suffered under immediate grief yet its gentle influence instead of calling feelings otherwise dormant into action, seemed only to veil that which otherwise would have been too dazzling for me" (195). Woodville attracts her because he is "passionless" and because his sufferings have effectively castrated him. Woodville is yet another example of the feminized gothic hero who has been wounded by life, making no emotional or sexual demands on the heroine. He effectively rewrites the father's passion out of the text, while he revises human history so that he represents a world in which a different sort of human being lives, not the "strange, complicated" men that we now know, but different men, "glorious" beings who live through the "power of their minds" (195).

But it is too late for Mathilda to find love or happiness with any living man, particularly one whose philosophical opinions bear such an uncanny resemblance to Percy Shelley's own ideas. Again citing Dante to her beloved Woodville, Mathilda decides to reject him because he cannot "drive the fiend from [her] soul and make [her] more human." She admits to herself that Woodville probably finds her amusing to visit because she has become for him the living embodiment of a melodramatic cliché. After all, even she considers herself as nothing more than a literary character in a tragedy. Woodville, she thinks, visits her in order to see a character act out a tragic part: "now and then he gives me my cue that I may make a speech more to his purpose; perhaps he is already planning a poem in which I am to figure. I am a farce and play to him, but to me this is all dreary reality: he takes all the profit and I bear all the burthen" (199).

But "bearing all the burden" is only too comfortable for the gothic heroine.

Mathilda decides that she will play the tragic or melodramatic heroine to the hilt and actually stage a double suicide with Woodville. She purchases laudanum and places it in two glasses on a table decorated with flowers. She prides herself, she tells us, on "decorat[ing] the last scene of [her] tragedy with the nicest care" (200). But when she invites Woodville to partake of her repast, he demurs. Mathilda quotes Mary Shelley's maternal grandmother's dying words, which also functioned as a leitmotif in Wollstonecraft's fiction: "A little patience, and all will be over." Afterwards she resorts to citing the words of Despair in Spenser's *Faerie Queene,* all to no avail. The literary playacting continues when Woodville rejects Mathilda's offer by saying to her, "Come, as you have played Despair with me I will play the part of Una with you and bring you hurtless from his dark cavern. . . . We know not what all this wide world means; its strange mixture of good and evil. But we have been placed here and bid live and hope" (202). It is, however, too late for Mathilda to hope for anything but death. She feels herself marked with the sign of Cain (203), a freak produced by her father's "unnatural love." Woodville cannot save Mathilda for life. In fact, he flees from her, conveniently called in the nick of time to the sickbed of his beloved mother. Always the claims of parents are paramount in Mary Shelley's fiction, and always they are resented.

Singing her father's favorite song and quoting Dante's description of Matilda gathering flowers, Mathilda actively seeks her death amid the world of nature that she claims to love so much. Catching her death of cold, she reminds us of the characters in Wollstonecraft's *Mary* who die after a carriage ride in damp air. Sinking into a rapid consumption, Mathilda muses on Wordsworth's Lucy and her imminent reunion with the Universal Mother (207): "In truth I am in love with death; no maiden ever took more pleasure in the contemplation of her bridal attire than I in fancying my limbs already enwrapped in their shroud: is it not my marriage dress? Alone it will unite me to my father when in an eternal mental union we shall never part" (208). The nun's garb has only to be slightly altered in styling to become a shroud, and the would-be bride of Christ has become the bride of her dead father. Living in an "eternal mental union" is as far as the sexes can get from the reality of their fallen and gendered bodies, while it is the dead father who is the love object, the ultimate goal at the end of the daughter's quest. Not Woodville. He is almost too quickly forgotten. If father-daughter-suitor have triangulated not once but twice in this novel, it is revealing to notice that the second attempt to procure a viable suitor for the daughter was even less real than the first.

In her final death throes, Mathilda muses on her strange and sad fate: "Again and again I have passed over in my remembrance the different scenes of my short life: if the world is a stage and I merely an actor on it my part has been strange, and, alas! tragical.... The earth was to me a magic lantern and I a gazer, and a listener but no actor; but then came the transporting and soul-reviving era of my existence: my father returned and I could pour my warm affections on a human heart.... This was the drama of my life" (208–09). According to Mary Shelley, the gothic feminist can only find herself in the peculiarly passive position of playacting in a life whose greatest crisis centers on the oedipal drama. Four years after her father's return and three years after his springtime death, in yet another May, Mathilda dies, a victim of oedipal love.

The father, who hovered so amorphously in *Frankenstein,* emerges in *Mathilda* to reveal himself as a ravening, lustful, perverse presence. Polymorphously perverse, he would appear to be in the grip of a homoerotic attraction-repulsion compulsion toward the male suitor disguised in his consciousness as an unnatural and incestuous desire for his daughter. Screen memories function throughout this text, suggesting that Mary reveals more than she perhaps knew in this work. Surely she suspects a core of sexual bonding between men that effectively shuts women out of this homoerotic circle. Frankenstein, his father, his best friend, all of them live in a world where women are subsidiary and inferior, both as intellectual and sexual companions. Mathilda fears that she inhabits the same sort of world, a world where women can only be acceptable as love objects if they are dead. Initially rejecting her mother's fate, Mathilda finally is drawn to the dream of death and the phantom female body, all mind and spirit.

After *Mathilda,* the most gothic example to be found in Mary's fiction may be "The Mortal Immortal: A Tale" (1833), one of the many short stories Mary wrote for money in her later life. This work in its title plays with ambiguity and impossibility, suggesting that there may be a way to make mortals immortal, just as Mary desperately wanted to believe that there may be a way to equalize women with men. But the fear and loathing of the female body that activated *Frankenstein* and *Mathilda* recur as the dominant motifs of the majority of Mary's short fiction, not simply in this story.[26]

---

26. See my discussion of "Mary Shelley and Gothic Feminism: The Case of 'The Mortal Immortal,'" in *Iconoclastic Departures: Mary Shelley After 'Frankenstein,'* eds. Syndy Conger and Frederick Frank (Rutherford: Fairleigh Dickinson University Press, 1997), 150–63. And for a very different reading of the female body in Shelley's works, see Sonia Hofkosh, "Disfiguring Economies: Mary Shelley's Short Stories," in *The Other Mary Shelley: Beyond Frankenstein,* ed. Audrey A. Fisch et al., 204–19.

Mary Shelley punished every female body in *Frankenstein,* scarring and disfiguring all female attempts to rewrite the generative body as sacred and whole. The experiments of Victor Frankenstein replace the maternal womb with chemical and alchemical artifice, only to blast masculine attempts at procreation as futile and destructive. In *Mathilda* the male principle once again would appear to be the only effectual parent, but as in the earlier work the father produces his progeny only to consume it, feeding on his daughter as a vampire feeds on victims in order to sustain a perverse form of death-in-life.

The dream of desire is the same at the end of virtually all Mary Shelley's texts: to escape the corrupted body and live in the realm of pure mind. Like her mother, Mary Shelley was a reluctant sensualist. She needed philosophically to embrace free love and open marriage, but her disappointments in her philandering husband could not be concealed. Claiming to support free love is easy as long as one has a monogamous husband. But finally a deep revulsion towards the female body emerges as clearly in Mary's works as it does in Wollstonecraft's. Gothic feminism for Mary Shelley entailed the realization that women would always be life's victims, not simply because social, political, economic, and religious conventions placed them in inferior and infantilizing postures, but because their own bodies cursed them forever to serve the wheel of physical corruption. Being a mother, bringing to life a child who would die, and perhaps would die soon, condemned women to serve a merciless god—the cycle of generation, birth, and death—in a way that men did not. The nightmare haunting Mary Shelley's life was not simply that she caused the death of her mother but that she recapitulated a reversed version of the same tragedy with three of her own children. She experienced her life as a sort of curse to herself and the ones she loved, and why? She understood that her life, her very physical being, fed on her mother's body parasitically, cannibalistically consuming it. Later she watched her children wither, unable to be sustained by her. These recurring nightmares fed her fictions, but they also spoke to a deeper fear that has continually plagued women.

Gothic feminism seeks to escape the female body through a dream of turning weakness into strength. By pretending that one is weak or a passive victim, one essentially camouflages oneself in a hostile terrain, diverting attention from one's real identity. Mary Shelley knew that on some level she was no victim; she knew her strength and intelligence were more than a match for anyone's. But she also feared that strength or at least experienced it ambivalently, fearing that it caused the deaths of others. The freakishness of the creature in *Frankenstein,* "his" oddly assembled body and his continual rejection by everyone he seeks to love, figure Mary's own sense of herself and all women as diseased, aberrant, and freakish composites of the hopes and dreams of other people. Gothic feminism for Mary Shelley is embodied in the sense of herself and the female body as a void, an empty signifier, a lure into the cycle of painful birth and disappointing death. Railing against the female body—sometimes disguised as male and sometimes blatantly presented as female—is finally the only position that Mary Shelley could take. She could laud the bourgeois family, she could valorize community and what we now label "family values," but ultimately she could not escape the mortality that gives the lie to everything she sought to praise. She inhabited a female body; she bled and caused bleeding in others, and those unfortunate facts defined for her and her fiction the gothic feminist nightmare in its starkest terms.

FIVE

The Triumph of the Civilizing Process

The Brontës and Romantic Feminism

One suffers in silence so long as one has the strength
so to do, and when that strength gives out one
speaks without too carefully measuring one's words.
—CHARLOTTE BRONTË

I

By 1847 the female gothic genre had virtually disappeared among fashionable London literary circles, but fortunately word had not yet reached an isolated Yorkshire parsonage where three young sisters and their rather eccentric brother, wrapped in a classic cocoon of gothic vestiges, were reworking their childhood readings in Charlotte Smith, Ann Radcliffe, Mary Shelley, and (I suspect) Charlotte Dacre. With a dead mother and two dead sisters hovering over the household, with an overbearing father and a substance-abusing brother very much underfoot, Charlotte, Emily, and Anne Brontë lived the gothic fantasy. They loved and resented their father as much as any gothic patriarch has ever been both loved and resented, and with a brother like Branwell—need I say more? Life could never have lived up to the gothic expectations they brought to it.

If their childhood home was isolated from literary fashion, it was also filled with religious angst and spiritual fervor. As children, the Brontës slipped into a curiously discursive world, made even more overwhelmingly powerful because of their physical isolation. Not simply avid readers as children, they became precocious and compulsive authors of an immense amount of juvenilia (the Angrian and Gondal sagas). These narratives of sexual obsession and adultery, barely concealed incest, parricide, and matricide run rampant, provide us with an uncanny glimpse into—shall we be blunt?—childhood neurosis. Telling the same story of love, betrayal, adultery, and murder again and again, the Brontë children drew on their own wounds and losses, as well as on their readings in the gothic fiction of their own and past generations. Charlotte Dacre's antiheroine Victoria would have felt right at home in the juvenilia universe of the Brontës.[1] But we will examine instead in this chapter only those classics of late gothic feminism—*Wuthering Heights, Jane Eyre,* and *Villette*—each of which can be read as an extended gloss on the conventions, poses, obsessions, and anxieties of the female gothic novel tradition. But finally each of these novels stands as an indictment of the limitations of gothic feminism in their examination of various gothic feminist strategies—rejection of motherhood, control of the patriarchal estate, struggle with tyrannous religious forces, overthrow of the suffocating and claustrophobic nuclear family, the celebration of education for women—and each novel concludes on a compromised note. Women sometimes survive in the Brontë universe, but sometimes they do not. They may try to shape their destinies, as Jane Eyre most aggressively does, but in the end their own efforts do not seem to have been the factors that made the difference. Brontë heroines live in a world of stark fate and even starker possibilities for failure. Brontë heroines live or die according to chance and their own limited efforts to control their destinies. The Brontës existentialize the female gothic heroine, and as such they introduce her to the modern world.

The Brontës are, perhaps more than any other female writers, a composite group, a writing consortium, not simply individuals writing in some sort of neutral or transhistorical setting.[2] Their fiction represents the recurrent

---

1. A modern critical edition of Charlotte's juvenilia is being prepared by Christine Alexander, *An Edition of the Early Writings of Charlotte Brontë* (Oxford: Blackwell, 1983). Three volumes have been published thus far, with another one projected: *The Glass Town Saga, 1826–32* (Oxford: Blackwell, 1987); *The Rise of Angria, 1833–34* (Oxford: Blackwell, 1991); and *The Rise of Angria, 1834–35* (Oxford: Blackwell, 1991). Emily Brontë's juvenilia has been published as *Gondal's Queen: A Novel in Verse,* arranged by Fannie Ratchford (Austin: University of Texas Press, 1955).

2. See Helena Michie, "'That Stormy Sisterhood': Portrait of the Brontës," in her *Sororophobia* (New York: Oxford, 1992), for a recent discussion of the Brontës as a familial writing unit mediated by Charlotte's stronger and surviving presence. The recent trend to discuss the family as a composite writing unit is reflected in some of the biographies: Rebecca Fraser, *The Brontës: Charlotte Brontë and Her Family* (New York: Crown, 1988); Tom Winnifrith, *The Brontës* (London: Macmillan, 1977) and

obsession with family dynamics that we know forms the structure and meaning of gothic fiction. But as I have noted before, the female gothic presents a belief in the family structure that bears more than a passing resemblance to what Freud was later to label the "uncanny." The family is literally horrendous for female gothic authors because it graphically illustrates that each of us is replaceable by a younger, more idealized version of ourselves. As Freud was later to point out, however, the uncanny is not simply about repetition; it is also about the return of the repressed (*SE* 17:220–49). And the repressed that seems to recur most frequently within the family unit is precisely the specter of the fragmented or incomplete self. What Freud meant by this is that an individual within a family is never simply an individual; he or she has a role that continually shifts and is finally replaced altogether by the next generation. Valorizing love—the platonic type that urged participants to believe that they were reuniting with their divided soul mates—became the dream that motivated and ultimately destroyed the Brontë heroines.[3]

One of the most striking examples of this phenomenon in literature is the elder Catherine in *Wuthering Heights* who begins as a daughter, becomes a wife and mother only long enough for her daughter to replace her as daughter, wife, and, implicitly, a mother who in her own turn will be replaced. This pattern replicates the fact that all family members are fragments of the whole and that the whole is always greater than the value of any one part. As readers we also realize, as did the Brontës, that the family is an assemblage of selves whose identities are dependent on their shifting relationships to one another. It is in the nature of family members to use and abuse power over one other, while it is in the nature of families to struggle over the issue of generational survival. Further, it is in the nature of families to be sites of pain, scenes of suffering. Idealizing a form of heterosexual passion became for Catherine I her means of escaping the gendered warfare that she experienced as her family. She was destroyed in the effort to shape Heathcliff into her best solipsistic imagining of him—"Heathcliff is me!" What Catherine learned too late was that the wounded gothic villain could not also play the part of the sentimental hero. It was as if Emily Brontë

The Brontës and Their Background: Romance and Reality (New York: Barnes, 1973); and Juliet Barker, *The Brontes* (New York: St. Martin's, 1995).

3. Freud's theory of the uncanny was based on his reading of Hoffman's story "The Sandman." See his essay on "The Uncanny" (1919) in SE 17:219–56, as well as the provocative analysis of the valorization of the visual and its complicity in "the phallic gaze" in Peter Brooks, "The Body in the Field of Vision," in *Body Work* (Cambridge: Harvard University Press, 1993), 88–122.

attempted to graft the characters from a gothic novel onto the plot of a sentimental one, and then wondered why everything was muddled and everyone was unhappy. What I am calling the "romantic feminism" that characterizes the Brontë novels grew out of their heroines' frustrated attempts to escape the female body that we have seen operating in other practitioners of gothic feminism. The Brontë heroines believe they can escape gendered warfare through the love of a feminized version of themselves, but as we will see, their efforts are ambivalent at best.

If the family, according to late eighteenth- and early nineteenth-century bourgeois novelists, was the only sure and certain reality in a perilously shifting world of values, then it is possible to see why the gothic, particularly as it was developed in works by women, would seek to discredit or at least redefine the family. Established and reinforced in order to ensure inheritance rights based on legitimacy and male supremacy, the patriarchally marked family functions as a sacred totem in society, an order that is not only above the law; it is the basis of the legal system.[4] What gothic fiction by women attempts to do, in a conscious albeit covert manner, is to subvert the privileges and assumed prerogatives of the family as a patriarchal institution. Much is made, therefore, of incest, matricide, patricide, intense sibling rivalry, symbolically cannibalistic tendencies in the parents, and dreams of escape by pursued and persecuted children. The gothic family is a theater in which members enact both a mythic struggle for species survival as well as a more personal quest for individual validation. The female as author, narrative voice, and protagonist participates in a literary fantasy formation by which she totally reshapes or annihilates human history in tracing the fate of one family. The dream that motivates much of *Wuthering Heights* is the fantasy that families will ultimately self-destruct and that women will be allowed to live and function as individuals first and foremost.

But this family-less world is never achieved and all of the Brontës' novels end in bowed submission to the power, primacy, and ultimate indestructibility of the patriarch and his bastion. Women as gothic feminists attempt to rewrite the family out of existence, but we can only conclude that

---

4. Setting the Brontë novels within their historical ambience has long been standard critical practice. For instance, see Margaret Lenta, "Capitalism or Patriarchy and Immortal Love: A Study of *Wuthering Heights*," *Theoria* 62 (1984), 63–76. An overview of the Brontës as writers within their particular family structure can be found in Maurianne Adams, "Family Disintegration and Creative Reintegration: The Case of Charlotte Brontë and *Jane Eyre*," in *The Victorian Family: Structure and Stresses*, ed. Anthony Wohl (London: Croon Helm, 1978), 148–79; and Jerome Bump, "*Jane Eyre* and Family Systems Therapy," in *Approaches to Teaching 'Jane Eyre,'* ed. Diane Long Hoeveler and Beth Lau (New York: MLA, 1993), 130–38.

their efforts are limited at best, futile and self-destructive at worst. Lucy Snowe tries to create a new world through her school; Jane Eyre tries to find the perfectly balanced life by retreating into an isolated forest with a weak and wounded husband and a dependent son; Catherine Earnshaw dies trying to bring a child into something other than a family. When Catherine II sits in front of a fire trying to instruct Hareton in how to read, we know that we are being confronted with a new Eve trying to construct a new Adam, an Adam who has not yet learned that women are evil and the cause of all the suffering in the world. Gothic feminism teaches its readers that women will be able to effect change only through the gradual reform of education, both for women and for men. In writing new visions of the world, women authors were trying to construct new vistas for both the sexes. No longer trapped in stifling domiciles that teach both sexes that they are fallen and flawed, the new gothic feminist attempts to offer a different message: that education and perception control the way we see our world and its possibilities. Lucy Snowe, Jane Eyre, and Catherine II may not have been particularly gifted instructors, but they were all teachers and that is the important fact for the mid-nineteenth-century female gothic vision.

Finally, in the Brontes' consistent practice of what Barthes has labeled "neither-norism" or what Hertz has labeled "double surrogation," we can see one possible explanation for the allegorical elements that recur throughout all their novels.[5] The doubled heroes in *Wuthering Heights*, both of them ultimately destroyed, suggest a compulsion to erase both the "bad" and the "good," the aristocracy and the lower classes, while the Bertha Mason/Helen Burns dichotomy in *Jane Eyre* suggests something similar. The fact is that the Brontës tried to resuscitate in their mature writings the sweeping melodramatic romantic feminism they practiced in their juvenile works, but their maturity and adult sensibilities caused them to undercut the enterprise while they were compelled to recapitulate the same scenarios, or more specifically, the same traumas, the same wounds.

The Brontës rewrote gothic feminism for a newly emerging bourgeois class of women: governesses and wives and mothers responsible for the education as well as the care of their charges. The Brontës, by necessity more practical than either Radcliffe or Austen, saw that social, political, and economic changes for women would occur only when the visions of Wollstonecraft and her followers were widespread, well known, and accepted

---

5. Barthes, "Neither-Norism," in *Mythologies*, trans. Annette Lavers (New York: Hill, 1972), 81–83; and Neil Hertz, *The End of the Line* (New York: Columbia, 1986), 224.

throughout the reading population. Brontë novels are filled with scenes of instruction, vignettes of reading, appeals to the power of the logos, the word, to shape both character and destiny. The final manifestation of the gothic feminist is as a schoolmarm leading her charges in the subversive activity of imagining a new world in which women are equal to men, and not because they are victims or posing as victims. The Brontës professionalize gender. Their texts eradicate once and for all the lure of the sexually overt aristocratic woman, making the bourgeois world safe for governesses and schoolmarms. The "civilizing process" described by Elias reaches its peak when Bertha Mason Rochester leaps from the roof of the aristocratic estate, thereby making room for the appropriation of a reformed aristocracy by the newly professional girl-woman. In this, the ultimate beating fantasy, the middle-class heroine professionalizes and codifies what we would now recognize as an appropriate model of "femininity." In Jane's triumph, we see the apotheosis of the professionally feminine gothic feminist, valorized for her homely, plain, small, and nondemanding nature, while the openly libidinous and aristocratic women in the text are all not simply punished but written out of existence. The fantasy is a potent one, and it has survived well into our own century. Witness *Rebecca*.

II

Emily's Brontë's portrait in *Wuthering Heights* of the perverse and indestructible nature of family relations functions on several levels as a severe indictment of patriarchy. We can initially begin our analysis by examining the character of Emily Brontë's first version of the gothic feminist heroine, Catherine Earnshaw, as she undergoes an emotional and sexual struggle without ever being aware of any of the forces conditioning her to accept familial and social conformity. Even as a very young child, Catherine does not fit the Victorian standards of the docile, submissive child. She is described at this stage as a "wild, wicked slip" whose "spirits were always at high-water mark," "spirits" that are in evidence in her dealings with all the others at the Heights.[6] As Nelly Dean observes, "she never was happier than when she was defying us with her bold, saucy look, and her ready words"

---

6. Emily Brontë, *Wuthering Heights*, 3rd ed., ed. William M. Sale, Jr., and Richard Dunn (New York: Norton, 1990), 32. All subsequent quotations from *Wuthering Heights* are from this edition with page numbers in parentheses in the text.

(33). These sharp words even strike the hallowed figure of her father, who is continually harassed by what he considers her impudent ways. The night he dies he finds her docile and gentle, which causes him to remark, "'Why cant thou not always be a good lass, Cathy?'" Cathy's reply would have been unheard of from the typical Victorian child-heroine: "'Why cannot you always be a good man, Father?'" (34). This is not the voice of a child who fears being the object of a beating. Remember that her one request from her father's shopping excursion was that he bring her home a whip for playtime activities.

From this brief description of Catherine as a child, the Victorian reader familiar with novels like Dacre's *Zofloya*, not to mention the underground pornographic novels of the day, would have immediately identified and typed Catherine as a future specimen of the "Bad (read: passionate) Woman."[7] This ideological construction concerned a high-spirited girl who was led to indulge her passions with a lover who subsequently considered it his duty to betray her and marry a virgin. This fate does not await Catherine because she chooses the other alternative proffered by her society—the idealization of sexual repression and its sublimation in a "safe" marriage. In other words, Catherine chooses the path of the Radcliffe heroine; she marries a safely feminized man but unfortunately she does not live happily ever. Brontë subverts our expectations by demonstrating the inadequacies of the Radcliffean formula; she forces her heroine to actually live with her weak husband and actually become pregnant, and the indignity of childbirth is not suffered lightly by most gothic feminists (Wollstonecraft's Maria comes to mind). But by continuing where Radcliffe chose to conclude her narrative, Emily Brontë exposes the falsity and futility of "love and marriage" as the "happy ending" for women. Her heroine dies and the next generation barely survives, having learned very little from the errors of her predecessors.

The representation of Heathcliff, however, is essential at this point to a fuller understanding of the personality and familial dilemma of Catherine. As a child he too is depicted as socially rebellious and unacceptable. Physically, he is a "dark-skinned gipsy," as "rough as saw-edge and hard as whinstone" (5, 27). The implication is clear: Heathcliff is a force of nature, a wild and untamable embodiment of pure, diffuse sexual energy. His influence on Catherine is strong, and Nelly has to admit that "they both promised

---

7. Pornography was widely read and easily accessible during the Victorian period. This topic is discussed in numerous sources, most recently in Iain McCalman, *Radical Underworld: Prophets, Revolutionaries, and Pornographers in London, 1795–1840* (Cambridge: Cambridge University Press, 1988).

to grow up as rude as savages. . . . [They] grew more reckless daily . . . [becoming] unfriended creatures" (36). But what was considered by Victorian standards to be the most threatening aspect of both Catherine and Heathcliff is their unchanneled and unleashed energy that appears to take on a vaguely sexual character. That Catherine and Heathcliff should have become initially attracted to each other seems obvious to us, both from a psychological and a literary perspective. Freud notes that "the choice of a [sexual] object . . . has already frequently or habitually been effected during the years of childhood. The simplest course for the child would be to choose as his sexual objects the same persons whom, since his childhood, he has loved with what must be described as damped-down libido" (*SE* 7:225). The gothic genre frequently depicts a quasi-incestuous attraction between pseudosiblings, and in several ways that characterize the gothic novel, the early relationship between Catherine and Heathcliff is meant to suggest a primitive pseudomarriage, a union of soul mates who do not engage in a sexual relationship but who act and think of themselves as a dyadic, androgynous unit.[8]

Catherine and Heathcliff sleep in the same bed as children and join as allies against Earnshaw and his young wife, as well as that other, equally perverse "couple" in the family, Nelly and Joseph. The novel, in fact, is filled with displaced marital relationships, suggesting that the need to form "families," surrogate or biological, is a distinctly human need, found in all people who can only define themselves if they are in relation to others. The early childhood "marriage" of Catherine and Heathcliff is rudely sundered by two events: the death of Mr. Earnshaw and contact with an alien and oddly civilized world, Thrushcross Grange. During one particularly ominous evening ramble when they stumble on the Linton household, both of the children, now budding adolescents, view this effeminate household as a bizarre aberration of human interaction, with its tea cups and polite conversations. This opinion is confirmed when there is a sudden assault on Catherine—as real as it is symbolic. A guard dog literally drags Catherine, kicking and screaming, into the other, proper world, with its other, proper husband. The dog senses that Catherine is its appropriate prey, not the unregenerate Heathcliff. And it is the animal in Catherine that is seized and wounded by the Linton dog.

---

8. For varieties of "Freudian" readings of *Wuthering Heights*, see Wade Thompson, "Infanticide and Sadism in Wuthering Heights," in *Wuthering Heights: An Anthology of Criticism*, ed. Alastair Everitt (London: Cass, 1967); and Michael D. Reed, "The Power of *Wuthering Heights:* A Psychoanalytic Examination," in *PsR* 1 (1977), 21–42.

When the Linton children welcome Catherine into their household they ritualistically wash her feet, and we can see from this action that Catherine is being constructed as the scapegoat who will be offered up for the continuance of their bourgeois world. Indeed, Catherine is initiated into this new realm through gifts of cakes and a ritualistic combing of her hair (the taming of her free and wild tresses suggests a disciplining of her sexual energy). Catherine becomes for the Lintons a sort of fetish, a feminine icon, a new object that they can shape into social conformity, and they appear to succeed admirably.[9] After several weeks of social recuperation and brainwashing, Catherine returns to Wuthering Heights a demure, fashionable little lady who has been reformed by "fine clothes and flattery." Nelly observes that Catherine is no longer a "wild, hatless little savage," and although Heathcliff makes one effort to be accepted by this other society ("'make me decent, I'm going to be good. . . . I wish I had light hair and fair skin'"), he is unable to be assimilated because he will not or cannot deny his nature as easily as Catherine has (40, 43–44).

Catherine's "civilizing process," her conversion to bourgeois values, however, is far from complete. Nelly notices that Catherine is now "full of ambition, [which] led her to adopt a double character without exactly intending to deceive anyone." Unable to transform her natural and wild spirit, nor to accept completely the imposed politeness and repression of the Lintons, Catherine is torn between Heathcliff and Linton, passion and its denial. When Nelly tells us that Catherine has been forced to "adopt a double character" (52), we recognize the guise of the gothic feminist all too clearly. The masquerade of passive-aggression, the posing and counterposing for effect, the appearance of compliance while one actively and covertly subverts, these have always been the characteristics of the professionally feminine woman. The gothic feminist has always been torn between her own nature and her own best social, economic, political interests, her own impulses and her own survival, hence her "double character."

---

9. Charlotte Brontë herself began the critical denigration of Heathcliff as something less than human in her comment, "Whether it is right or advisable to create beings like Heathcliff, I do not know: I scarcely think it is." See her "Editor's Preface to the New Edition of Wuthering Heights," reprinted in *Wuthering Heights* (New York: Norton, 1972), 12. More recent critical essays on Heathcliff's problematic status in the novel include Patricia Parker, "The (Self-)Identity of the Literary Text: Property, Propriety, Proper Place, and Proper Name in *Wuthering Heights*," in *Identity of the Literary Text*, ed. Mario J. Valdes and Owen Miller (Toronto: University of Toronto Press, 1985); John Allen Stevenson, "'Heathcliff is Me!': *Wuthering Heights* and the Question of Likeness," *NCL* 43 (1988), 60–81; and Steven Vine, "The Wuther of the Other in *Wuthering Heights*," *NCL* 49 (1994), 339–59.

On the one hand, Catherine's pseudomarriage to Heathcliff is a denial of the traditional, patriarchal family, a relationship in which she is not defined by her father or his status. It is a relationship that they have entered freely, as equals, and it is a relationship that she has entered into without the intercession or involvement of her father or brother as broker. As a pseudomarriage, it denies the practice of "traffic in women." In a freely chosen alliance with a nameless and illegitimate young man, Catherine finds a means of repudiating masculine and specifically patriarchal values. With Heathcliff she is beyond social norms and conventions; she is not a daughter, a sister, or a wife; she fancies instead that she is an individual who has found an idyllic escape from the realities of repressive roles. But just as history begins with the establishment of names, defined clans, and powerful totems or claims on turf, so must history begin for Catherine with her realization that human beings, particularly women, do not exist apart from the men who can provide them with names and status. In this new world there can be no room for Heathcliff the nameless, as he continues to represent the freedom and aboriginal rebellion that must be denied as well as destroyed before society can progress.

After his only and feeble attempt to reform and conform, Heathcliff reverts even further into his "heathenism." Lately, Nelly observes, he has seemed "possessed of something diabolical" (51). His disdain for the Lintons as rivals for Catherine has been established, and he pleads with her not to turn him out "for those pitiful, silly friends of yours!" (54). But Catherine cannot fail to notice the social and economic superiority of Linton to Heathcliff, although the contrast—which is actually financially based—is represented as physical or even topographical. Linton, she notes, is similar to "a beautiful, fertile valley," while Heathcliff in contrast reminds her of a "bleak, hilly, coal country" (54). And although Catherine is seduced by Edgar's money, position, and manners, she knows in her heart that such a choice is "wrong," for its price is the fulfillment of her sexual nature. She exchanges the fire of Heathcliff for the frost of Linton, a choice that all Brontë heroines are forced to confront. We can recall here the contrast between the fiery Rochester and the icy duty of St. John Rivers. Catherine, however, denies her sexual nature and marries against herself or at least against her body's best interests. The sorrows and follies that ensue are the result of this unnatural choice, and yet, Brontë suggests, this is the best choice that has been held out to women, not simply by their society but by women authors like Radcliffe and Wollstonecraft. Brontë's indictment of the "reasonable woman" is also an indictment of the entire tradition of splitting head and heart and valorizing the former at the expense of the latter.[10]

After her famous "I am Heathcliff" speech to Nelly, a set piece that effectively sends up the absurdity of the Shelleyan epipsyche and the Byronic sister-muse at the same time it reifies the ideal, Catherine confesses that she loves Heathcliff but would be embarrassed to be his wife. Heathcliff flees, hearing only that Catherine has decided to marry Linton. A violent storm of nature occurs at just this point in the text to emphasize a similar state in the human realm. The lightning that splits the tree and knocks down part of a chimney clearly foreshadows the fate of the estate and paternal legacy of both the Heights and the Grange; both will be threatened if not destroyed later by Heathcliff's vengeance (66).

But what are we to make of the novel's gothic antiheroine, Isabella? She is clearly meant to be Catherine's double or foil, a class-based critique of Catherine's more natural and wild temperament. But her marriage to Heathcliff, so painfully detailed, is little more than a beating fantasy with the other woman as the victim, Catherine as the voyeur, and Heathcliff as sadistic and paternally displaced aggressor. The episode also seems to suggest that for Brontë marriage is a form of institutionalized torture and sexual depravity for women. Isabella's wallowing in masochistic postures at Heathcliff's feet suggests her need not simply to humiliate her brother's class-based snobbery but to debase herself as well.

All of my remarks thus far have been examples of fairly traditional readings of the book's mechanics and theme. And on a literal level the novel is a fairly straightforward romance, using standard romance devices (betrayal, separated soul mates, thwarted sexual longings) with a few gothic touches for effect (Catherine as the ghost haunting Lockwood, Heathcliff as cannibalistic vampire-usurper of the Earnshaw estate). But the initial and instigating motivation of the novel, the choice of Linton over Heathcliff, forms the first crucial act that inaugurates the establishment of the patriarchy over the anarchy and sexual energy that Heathcliff represents. Seen from another perspective, however, what we are witnessing in *Wuthering Heights* is the

---

10. I am obviously indebted to Gilbert and Gubar's influential reading of *Wuthering Heights*, "Looking Oppositely: Emily Brontë's Bible of Hell," in *The Madwoman in the Attic*, 248–308. I also admire the discussion of the novel to be found in Terence Eagleton's *Myths of Power: A Marxist Study of the Brontës* (London: Macmillan, 1975), 97–121. For discussions of the specifically female configuration of Emily Brontë's creativity, see Margaret Homans, *Bearing the Word: Language and Female Experience in Nineteenth-Century Women's Writing* (Chicago: University of Chicago Press, 1986), 68–83; and Patricia Yaeger, *Honey-Mad Women: Emancipatory Strategies in Women's Writing* (New York: Columbia University Press, 1988), 177–206.

return and revenge of the earlier and repressed sentimental tradition and its
hero, Edgar Linton, who triumphs over the gothic literary movement and
its representative, Heathcliff. The novel pits these two genres against each
other in a bifurcated attempt to resolve the popular literary heritages that
have shaped women's romantic attitudes for the past century. It is as if the
sentimental erupts into this gothic text and will not die. The sentimental
hero wages a life or death battle with his nemesis, the gothic antihero, and
he wins a partial victory. In other words, the sentimental will not die in
Wuthering Heights, but then neither will the gothic. The reconciled and chastened couple in the last scene of the book, Catherine II and Hareton, exist
as residual vestiges of both traditions. They would appear to embody
Brontë's final suggestion: that the sentimental needs passion to be authentic while the gothic needs taming, but both impulses finally bring women
only to the pages of a book, which is where, after all, they both began.

Let us return, however, to the beginning of the novel and recall that Mr.
Earnshaw originally brings Heathcliff into the family by introducing him as
a substitute for an earlier, dead son with the same name. Supposedly
Earnshaw found the child an orphan in Liverpool, but there is always about
Heathcliff the suggestion that he is actually Earnshaw's illegitimate child,
and certainly Catherine's query to her father on the night of his death, "why
cannot you always be a good man?" suggests some sense on her part, if only
unconscious, that her father has not been the paragon of sexual virtue that
he might have been. The entry of Heathcliff into the family results in his
intense rivalry with Catherine's "real" brother, Earnshaw, for the love and
attention of the father. The fact that the father is unable to mediate between
the factions that form over Heathcliff's new status suggests that the family
as a unit is a fragile and shifting entity that requires continual vigilance lest
it be destroyed or mutated.

Why does the elder Earnshaw bring an interloper into his home and why
does he insist that Heathcliff, with that strange adopted single name, be
accepted as his son? These are questions that are obviously meant to be
unanswerable, but they suggest depths of paternalistic insecurity and paranoia. Was Earnshaw afraid to die with only one male heir? Was Heathcliff
his insurance policy should his "real" son prove either weak or unsuitable?
Ironically, the introduction of Heathcliff into the family creates both the
problems and the solution to those problems. Heathcliff wreaks havoc on
the estate of Wuthering Heights, but he also strengthens the second
Catherine and the eventual heir, Hareton, through his sheer negative presence. By being such an effective blocking figure, he tempers and shapes both

their characters more than their own parents were capable of doing. As the embodiment of the bête noire, Heathcliff becomes the active evil force that has to be confronted and overcome if the gothic feminist is to shape and redeem the old world into something vibrant and new. Heathcliff reminds us of Montoni or General Tilney or many of those dark brooding slightly Byronic gothic tyrants who do not deserve to hold their estates. His corruption is more sympathetically presented by Brontë, who sees her gothic villain as himself a victim of class prejudice, but finally Heathcliff has to be destroyed if the world is to be safe for the daughters of gothic feminists. Heathcliff, like the rest of those earlier gothic patriarchs, stands as an anachronism.

All of this is not meant to suggest that Heathcliff is not first and foremost a literary character. He is but he is also somewhat of a principle (and surely the fact that he is both is not contradictory, although it has spawned a vast critical debate). As a literary character, Heathcliff is a foundling, exuding the aura of illegitimacy and sexual rebellion, a sort of Byronic gothic antihero intent on destroying others as well as himself. But as a principle, he embodies many other dark and fearful aspects of the human mind. In particular, he represents the family's fear and revulsion toward open or aggressive sexuality. He appears to represent the untamed, uncivilized male principle at war with the increasingly potent forces of feminine domesticity, but he also paradoxically represents the very forces that would destroy patriarchy and the entire system of male privilege.

After Catherine decides to marry Edgar, changes begin to develop in both Heathcliff's and Catherine's personalities. His bitterness and frustration turn him into the "devil" and "ghoul" that he is later seen to be by Nelly and his wife Isabella. The change in his sexual nature is predictable. Consider Freud's observation: "sexuality in most males contains an element of aggressiveness—a desire to subjugate; . . . there is an intimate connection between cruelty and the sexual instinct. . . . this aggressive element of the sexual instinct is in reality a relic of cannibalistic desires" (*SE* 7:159). To claim that Heathcliff is in some symbolic manner a throwback to our cannibalistic heritage is, perhaps, a bizarre claim. But there is some justification for this interpretation if we consider the dominance of oral imagery throughout the text, the profusion of scenes in which food is literally oppressive and the characters are depicted as either starving (Catherine I and the dying Heathcliff) or gluttonous (Lockwood and Joseph). In several ways the urge to metaphorically consume the beloved lies within the gothic and the romantic traditions. This urge originates from the ethos established by Percy Shelley and Byron—a desire to be one with one's spiritual and physical complement.

Part of the incestuously driven Byronic legacy concerns just this urge on the part of the male to absorb the feminine and thus to be become androgynous—at least that is the dream if not the accomplished reality of Romantic poetry by men. That Brontë has written her novel as an extended gloss on *Manfred*, as well as on *Frankenstein*, has been noted by other critics.[11] But the novel also needs to be situated within the gothic family saga tradition that emphasizes and explores perverse sexual and generational relations. Heathcliff in the latter part of the novel is not much different from Ambrosio, Lewis's obsessed monk, or Walpole's mad Manfred, with his mania to produce yet one more male heir. But whereas these works by men explicitly develop the theme of familial and dynastic ruin, Brontë's approach is distinctively covert. She would like to destroy the foundations as well as the generational power of the family, and her scathing depictions of all the marriages in the novel stand as her clearest attempt to do so. Emily Brontë dreams of a world in which there is neither marrying nor giving in marriage; she dreams of a world populated by passionate but nonsexual forces of energy. She dreams of a world not dependent on the use and abuse of female bodies. She has her heroine Catherine dream, quite literally, of heaven. But dreams, as we know, are always sites of repeated trauma and reenactments of woundings that live on indefinitely in the psyche. Catherine's repetitious dreams reenact over and over again the sundering of her original union with Heathcliff.

If Heathcliff has been sexually mutated by his rejection by and forced separation from Catherine, so has she. This fact becomes evident in her sudden development of hysteria and her eventual death by anorexia complicated by pregnancy (a death that eerily foreshadows Charlotte Brontë's own demise). Freud sees the development of hysteria in women as caused by repression in adolescence, and it seems that Catherine I might have recently been seen by Freud, for her symptoms sound ominously like his diagnosis. The fever Catherine suffers after Heathcliff runs away leaves her "saucier and more passionate and haughtier than ever," while the doc-

---

11. Gilbert and Gubar in *Madwoman* situate *Wuthering Heights* in a line of descent that originates with *Frankenstein* (249); they also compare the novel to *Manfred* (259). Joseph Wiesenfarth, "*Wuthering Heights:* The Gothic Tradition Domesticated," in his *Gothic Manners and the Classic English Novel* (Madison: University of Wisconsin Press, 1988), sets Heathcliff within the tradition of gothic villains, comparing him to both Zofloya and Mathilda in Lewis' *Monk* (77), while Robert Kiely places the work within the "romantic" tradition in his study *The Romantic Novel* (Cambridge: Harvard University Press, 1972).

tor's orders are to allow her "whatever she pleased to demand, and generally [to avoid] aggravating her fiery temper" (69). But Catherine's health is finally destroyed by her pregnancy. We learn of her condition almost indirectly, as if the author were as embarrassed about it as Catherine appears to be. And our response to the pregnancy is amazement—somehow we are unable to imagine a sexual relationship between Catherine and the effeminate Linton. So between her bodily distortion and willful starvation, Catherine effectively destroys herself while in the act of creating her biological successor, her mirror-image daughter who will bear the same name and eerily reenact another version of the same feminine destiny.

Heathcliff's return to the Heights after a three years' absence begins the final and inevitable working out of the fates of Catherine and Heathcliff. Catherine's process of repression and forced socialization has proceeded far enough so that she is able to describe Heathcliff as "an unreclaimed creature, without refinement, without cultivation, an arid wilderness of furze and whinstone . . . a fierce, pitiless, wolfish man" (79–80). This is the supposedly civilized Heathcliff, the Heathcliff who has spent three years amassing money and a veneer of cultivation, the Heathcliff who has returned to compete on an equal footing with Linton for the affections of Catherine. Catherine is not particularly interested in this new, monied Heathcliff. She is more interested in the aboriginal Heathcliff, the man who provided her with the appearance of amorality and antisocial deviance, all safely controlled, of course, by the incest taboo operating on them. Seeing herself as "dirty" and of the lower classes is a sort of game with Catherine, a posing for effect while she retreats safely into the world of privilege whenever she wants. On the night of Heathcliff's return, Catherine coaxes Edgar to receive him by setting up two tables, one for the siblings Edgar and Isabella as the "gentry," and one for the pseudosiblings Catherine and Heathcliff as the "lower orders" (74).

The amusement and happiness of Heathcliff's return, however, do not last long. Heathcliff accuses Catherine of having treated him "infernally" and swears revenge, though not on her directly (87). He calls Linton "this lamb . . . a sucking leveret . . . the milk-blooded coward . . . the slavering, shivering thing" (89–90). His overt implication to Catherine is that she has replaced Heathcliff's sexual superiority with Linton's impotency. Catherine not only appears to recognize the error of her choice, but she admits to suffering, to being "tormented . . . haunted" (94). Catherine, however, never really had the freedom to choose Heathcliff as a mate, and to cling to that idea is a delusion at best. The social and economic facts are such that an intelligent young woman does not choose to marry a nameless, illegitimate pauper as a husband, no matter what the sexual attraction. In gothic novels written by men, the female character often insists on marrying the man of her choice, no matter what his social or economic status. The intense desire to follow her passion into the abyss of social rejection is a potent male fantasy, one that recurs throughout gothic novels written by men.[12] But female authors do not indulge their female characters in such a manner, for they understand all too well the consequences of familial power. As an adult woman, Catherine is game playing; she wants to be the wife of the propertied and secure Linton, but she wants to play at being a social outcast with Heathcliff. There is never any question about whom or what will be chosen at the conclusion of the game.

Although Catherine's waking life may be under her control, her unconscious life as manifested in her dreams is not. In the first dream she describes to Nelly, she has died, has gone to heaven, and is unhappy there because she is not with Heathcliff. She finds herself thrown out of heaven to wander on the moors around the Heights, unable to accept the world of the body or the world of the spirit (62). The dream fingers the wound of her separation from Heathcliff and her marriage to an alien, nonfamilial man, but it is also prophetic in at least two ways. Catherine's vision of heaven proves to be very much like the condition of her marriage to Linton. Patriarchal codes told her that she would find happiness in such a marriage, yet she finds none because the cost of the marriage is the denial of both her sexual and her second self. When Catherine says, "'Heathcliff is more myself than I am,'" or "'I am Heathcliff,'" she expresses that he is the masculine component of her nature, a component that society has taught her to fear and repress (62, 64). Her unhappiness in a heaven without Heathcliff is as inevitable as her unhappiness in a union with Linton. She wants incompatible social realities; she wants passion and respectability, and it is Brontë's point that such a combination is not possible for repressed and successfully socialized Victorian women.

Catherine relates another dream after her hysteria-produced illness, a dream that focuses on the quasi-incestuous oak-paneled bed at the Heights. She describes herself in this dream as aching with "some great grief" and discovers that she cannot remember the last seven years of her life. This dis-

---

12. For instance, Joseph Andriano discusses the female figure as a Jungian-inspired anima who haunts gothic literature written by men in his *Our Ladies of Darkness: Feminine Daemonology in Male Gothic Fiction* (University Park: Penn State Press, 1993).

covery about her unconscious reveals that her sexual development as a woman abruptly stopped when she was "converted at a stroke into Mrs. Linton . . . wife of a stranger: an exile, and outcast, thenceforth, from what had been my world" (97). Catherine's unconscious mind will not allow her to dupe herself into believing that she ever successfully converted her fiery nature into the frosty restraint that the Lintons required. Catherine longs to awaken from the nightmare that is her life: "'I wish I were a girl again, half savage and hardy, and free . . . and laughing at injuries, not maddening under them! Why am I so changed?'" (97). The processes of repression and socialization have taken their toll. Her only hope of escape lies in death and a future reunion with Heathcliff in the spiritual realm: "'they may bury me twelve feet deep, and throw the church down over me, but I won't rest till you [Heathcliff] are with me'" (98). It would appear that the memory of symbiotic oneness with Heathcliff in that oak-paneled bed is the most potent of Catherine's life. Heaven for her can only be imaged as a return of the repressed, a resurrection of the childhood bed and a return to a womb-like existence with one's split-off and fragmented self.

After Catherine's recovery from her attack of hysteria, Heathcliff arrives for what turns out to be their final meeting. Nelly notes that Catherine has been changed physically by her illness, or more probably, by her attempt to conceal and reject her pregnancy. She is "unearthly," "dreamy and melancholy," while she seems to "gaze beyond, and far beyond . . . out of this world" (121). In their final meeting it is evident that their life-long frustrated love can find release only in causing pain, torture, or destruction to each other. This species of sadomasochistic love glories in knowing that each is the cause of the other's suffering. Catherine says, "'I care nothing for your sufferings. Why shouldn't you suffer? I do,'" while Heathcliff knows that Catherine will not be at peace, and that heaven will "be a land of exile to her," while at her death he will be plunged into the "torments of hell" with his "soul in the grave" (123, 125). Heathcliff's final indictment of Catherine's treachery touches the core of the social dilemma she faced: "'Why did you betray your own heart, Cathy? . . . You have killed yourself. . . . What right had you to leave me? What right—answer me—for the poor fancy you felt for Linton?'" Catherine's answer, unfortunately, does not reveal the extent of the social and familial pressures she faced, nor is she particularly aware of all the facets of her choice. She replies, "'I've done wrong, I'm dying for it'" (125).

Death is the only release for Catherine and she accepts that death with a "calmness" and "peace" that have been unknown in her last seven years of marriage. It is surely no coincidence that Nelly describes Catherine's death as "like a child reviving" (129). Death is Catherine's only possible return to childhood and the free innocence she had experienced with Heathcliff in a sort of polymorphously perverse realm of infantile sexuality. Her salvation comes in escaping a society that could accept her only if she denied her nature and assumed an alien one. Like Catherine, Heathcliff's only escape is through death. His death is the inevitable working out of the spiritual principle that both he and Catherine embodied, and which worked to unite them in spirit after death. The happiness that was denied Heathcliff in life by a society that was threatened by his anarchical presence is obtained by him in death. Heathcliff knows his fulfillment is in a union with Catherine's spirit, not in any socially acceptable conception of an afterlife. His last words are almost identical to the sentiment expressed by Catherine's dream of heaven without Heathcliff: "'I have attained *my* heaven, and that of others is altogether unvalued and uncoveted by me!'" (253). The Tristan/Isolde impetus here—the love/death spiral—suggests the basic pessimism implicit in the "melodramatically tragic" strain in female gothic novels. Sexuality and heterosexual passion lead to death for both Heathcliff and Catherine I, because the genre was in the grip of tragedy's replacement, melodrama, the need alternately to celebrate and punish victims. Both Heathcliff and Catherine certainly had unique psychic configurations that led to a predisposition toward incest and dreams of parricide, but finally both are simply characters in a novel and have no real childhoods because they have no ontological existence. Both are signs—coded manifestations of "masculinity" and "femininity"—and the interaction between the two is what the novel as a text is about.

When Emily Brontë chose to retell the Heathcliff/Catherine I narrative, this time with two slightly different constructions of gender, she presented a "happy ending." But that ending has always puzzled or angered its readers, and most critics agree that the second half of the book is its weak section, a sort of extended afterthought.[13] I think not. The second ending tells us that the bourgeois civilizing process has worked and triumphed. Women may be forced to marry oafish men, but those men will turn out to be, after all, educable. Men will continue to exist in female gothic texts, but these men

---

13. The general critical consensus that the second half of the novel represents an adulteration of the first half, not only in characterizations but in its control of narration and theme, has been most recently discussed by Bette London, "*Wuthering Heights* and the Text Between the Lines," *PLL* 24 (1988), 34–52; and Anita Levy, "The History of Desire in *Wuthering Heights*," *Genre* 19 (1986), 409–30.

will not be the dark, brooding, and sexually potent gothic heroes we saw in Heathcliff. They will be a sort of amalgam of sentimental Werthers with just a touch of fire. The final world that Emily Brontë depicts for us at the conclusion of *Wuthering Heights* is a world of readers or would-be readers sitting calmly before the hearth as domestic altar, with the professionally feminine girl-woman as Sophia, goddess of wisdom and savior of the civilizable man.

III

Charlotte Brontë was writing *Jane Eyre* as her sister Emily was composing *Wuthering Heights,* and much has been made over the past century about the competition between them to out-Byronize each other. *Jane Eyre* appears to have won the contest, for its popular status has been immense over the past century. Unlike *Wuthering Heights,* which is fairly stark and uncompromising and at points almost painful to read, *Jane Eyre* has become the canonical female gothic text, reproduced over and over again in films, an archetypal dream of the little woman finding love and a home with a fatherly beast, ritualistically tamed and shorn of his aristocratic lust and pride.[14] Jane has become the embodiment of the gothic feminist par excellence, and it is this heroine who has come to represent the genre as a whole, as if Emily and Ellena and all the rest had never existed.

But they did exist, and Jane Eyre took her cues from the stock devices of all gothic feminist heroines as she set her sights on Rochester and disposed of and replaced his inconvenient mad wife at the same time. Jane begins life as an orphan, without property or status, love, support, or a family behind her, but she concludes her narrative with a wealthy but safely wounded husband and a first-born son and heir in tow. If her narrative is self-congratulatory, it is only because she has earned the right to crow. She has done what every gothic feminist has had to do: she has created a new family with herself in a matriarchal and unchallenged position of power. Jane appears to be the only gothic feminist who survives childbirth and lives with her gothic

---

14. The canonical status of *Jane Eyre* as the paradigmatic "woman's text" was insured and institutionalized when it was reprinted in full—to the consternation of many critics—in *The Norton Anthology of Literature by Women,* ed. Sandra M. Gilbert and Susan Gubar (New York: Norton, 1985), 347–735. Gilbert and Gubar's influential analysis of *Jane Eyre,* "A Dialogue of Self and Soul: Plain Jane's Progress," in *The Madwoman in the Attic,* 336–71, remains the most frequently cited discussion of the novel.

hero to tell the tale, but as everyone knows, her gothic hero has been tamed and ritualistically wounded. Blind in one eye, missing a hand, and prone to lean heavily on his beloved helpmate, Rochester is the ultimate embodiment of the masculine victim in the female gothic fantasy. He is daddy wounded; he is the safe husband; he is the punished patriarch; he is man. Or rather, he is the weakened man that the gothic feminist must have if she is to live with a man at all.

In order to appreciate how *Jane Eyre* functions as a gothic feminist text, it is necessary to begin by examining how Jane's character was shaped by her early childhood experiences and her "education" at the illustrious Lowood Academy. Like most gothic heroines, Jane is an orphan raised by an evil aunt who resents her presence among her own unpromising children. Not surprisingly, Jane's character is formed in opposition to the aunt and these three siblings, all of whom engage in some form of abuse—physical, emotional, or psychic—toward the heroine. Her cousin John kindly informs her that she "ought to beg, and not to live here with gentlemen's children like us" (8), while the maid Abbot tells her that she is "less than a servant" (9) because she does not even work for her bread.[15] Even her ally in the household, Bessie, tells Jane that she is "the most wicked and abandoned child ever reared under a roof" (23). Later Bessie warns Jane that she could be turned out of the house at any moment if she is not cooperative and properly docile: "My first recollections of existence included hints of the same kind," Jane tells us. The threat of abandonment is never far below the surface in Jane's psyche. She tells her reader, "[t]his reproach of my dependence had become a vague sing-song in my ear; very painful and crushing" (10). The young Jane has "only bad feelings surging in [her] breast," having been "poisoned" by her desire for vengeance against her enemies. One would not predict success for a child who fit this description. Already crushed by life, this girl appears doomed, wounded beyond repair. Childhood pain and emotional woundings only strengthen the gothic feminist because her will, her desire, her energy are stronger than those of her opponents. They are mere mortals; she is the heroine and in the melodrama of vindication, the heroine always triumphs.

But before we arrive at Jane's self-narrated and self-constructed apotheosis, she has to undergo fearful trials by fire, bullyings and brutality, and all manner of subtle and not so subtle humiliations before she triumphs over

---

15. All quotations from *Jane Eyre* are from the Norton Critical Edition, 2d ed., ed. Richard J. Dunn (New York: Norton, 1987), with references to page numbers in parentheses in the text.

everyone who has ever hurt or belittled her. Her first serious nemesis is her cousin John Reed, who abuses Jane "not two or three times in the week, nor once or twice in the day, but continually: every nerve I had feared him, and every morsel of flesh on my bones shrank when he came near" (7). Apparently cowed by his sheer physical bulk, Jane—like Emily and Ellena before her—learns that bullies will always self-destruct if given enough time and space. As an adult, John Reed drinks, eats, and gambles himself into an abyss that only his suicide allows him to escape. His sisters, like Cinderella's sisters, suffer similarly disastrous fates. Georgiana, like her brother John an orally greedy child, grows up to be a fat and unhappily married matron, while Eliza, anal retentive and compulsive, ends her days in a French convent. We are reminded of the fates of the antiheroines in *Emmeline* as well as *Udolpho*. All three of their pitiable lives caused by the errors of a self-indulgent, careless, and lazy mother stand in direct opposition to the success and energy that Jane manages to create in her own life. If a male heir and two wealthy women (read: the aristocracy) have every advantage in society, Brontë seems to be saying, they still have to discipline themselves and work if they are to succeed, and this is what John Reed and his pathetic sisters were not able to do. The bourgeoisie and its work ethic triumph in this novel with a vengeance.

Jane may feel that as a child she had "no appeal whatever" against John's bullying "menaces" and "inflictions" (8), but these early lessons in abuse teach her a valuable lesson that she will employ later at Lowood: to endure and bide her time. Her aunt—the supposed authority figure in the household—refuses to defend or protect her, while the servants are as helpless and as hopeless as Jane. Jane learns a valuable lesson, however, by seeing the impotence and corruption of the family's authority figure. She learns very early that power structures like families function essentially as protection rackets, and she, like Emmeline before her, has no protector. The impetus of Jane's narrative is propelled by her desire to locate and claim her own protector, but one who will be ultimately in her complete control. If the young Jane moans that it seems "useless to try to win any one's favour" (12), the mature Jane knows that "favour[s]"—protection and rewards—are finally the only objects worth winning. Jane may lead "a life of ceaseless reprimand and thankless fagging" as a child, but as an adult she is never corrected and has a rich husband and his servants to wait on her. The fairy-tale dynamics operating here—the lowly brought to triumph and the lordly brought low—suggest that *Jane Eyre* as a novel functions like so many female gothic texts, as a species of wish fulfillment.

The grandiose ego writing the script we call the novel, however, needs to have odious enemies because their fall and punishment will be that much sweeter as a vindication for the heroine. Life is only rewarding when there has been a struggle, and gothic feminists love nothing more than a struggle against vicious predators, particularly when the heroine knows she is going to win. Jane is able to become a female gothic heroine because she is able to turn her abusive childhood outward onto scenarios of disaster for others to suffer in her place. Does Bertha suffer a crushing blow? So much for Jane's unruly passions. Does Helen Burns die a miserable death? So much for Jane's tendency to immolate and punish herself. In this very allegorical novel, almost all of the characters act as split-off tendencies within the heroine's psyche, allowing the safely adult narrator Jane to emerge intact and pristine, or at least appear to do so. But notice also that such a device merely serves to highlight Jane's wounds. It is as if she wears her pain on her sleeve and then justifies herself to anyone foolish enough to cross her. Living "without one bit of love or kindness" from anyone, Jane spends the first ten years of her life trying to master a battery of defense strategies (31).

Like most female gothic heroines, Jane escapes first into books, but Jane's tastes in literature are more than a bit morbid and odd.[16] When she looks at *Bewick's Birds*, we know, as evidenced in her later painting, that she is actually brooding on imagined dead bodies—perhaps fantasized reconstructions of her parents—and cormorants. Even at this early date Jane appears to be lost in an abusive psychic landscape, imagining herself either as the object of a variety of birds of prey or, more unconsciously, positioning herself as the attacker. When Mrs. Reed demands that Jane exhibit a "franker, more natural manner," Jane can only respond by hiding behind a curtain in front of the window seat (5). This is a child who wants to hide because she does not trust what she herself feels toward others—aggression, hostility, anger, and revenge. Jane would like, that is, to think of herself as the innocent victim of large looming birds of prey—her aunt and her cousin John. But it is Jane who actually experiences herself as if she were preying on them, living off them like a parasite lives off an unwelcoming host.

What is occurring here is a version of the victim/victimizer scenario, the

---

16. For an analysis of the literarily dense text of *Jane Eyre*, see Mark Hennelley, Jr., "Jane Eyre's Reading Lesson," *ELH* 51 (1984), 693–717. For very different readings of both Jane's and Charlotte's immersion in the world of romantic and gothic texts, see Karen Rowe, "'Fair Born and Human Bred': Jane Eyre's Education in Romance," in *The Voyage In: Fictions of Female Development*, ed. Elizabeth Abel, Marianne Hirsch, and Elizabeth Langland (Hanover: University Press of New England, 1983), 69–89; and Jerome Beaty, *Misreading 'Jane Eyre'* (Columbus: Ohio State University Press, 1996).

beating fantasy, that we have seen time and again in female gothic texts. The strange symbiosis that occurs between victim and victimizer suggests that once the cycle of abuse has begun, there is no longer any way of telling who began the pain, who is the victim and who the victimizer.[17] From Jane's point of view, she is the victim. She tells us about herself: "What a miserable little poltroon had fear, engendered of unjust punishment, made of me in those days!" (26). John Reed calls Jane "Madam Mope," and clearly the young Jane suffers from a depression that would now be recognized as in need of clinical treatment. She is, as she admits herself, the victim of a "habitual mood of humiliation, self-doubt, forlorn depression" (13). Jane is correct in seeing herself as the victim of injustice. But from Mrs. Reed's vantage, Jane is not "sociable and childlike"; she is instead "a compound of virulent passions, mean spirit, and dangerous duplicity" (14). The charge of "duplicity" was made against Catherine I, and it will be made later against Lucy Snowe. Gothic feminists are forced to be "duplicitous" or at least appear to be duplicitous in the eyes of their enemies in order simply to survive. If a woman is not duplicitous, she will be defamed, slandered, and constructed into oblivion by the same forces that will take her estate, her family, and finally her life.

When Jane seeks refuge in the breakfast room window seat to peruse *Bewick's History of British Birds*, she is not only cocooning herself within a safe, warm, and food-filled haven but imaginatively retreating into her own self-created world of victims and victimizers, the birds and their prey. To be broken in upon by John Reed at this moment, to be assaulted with the book, the instrument of her gothic imaginings and escape, is too much to bear. Jane explodes and at first verbally attacks John and accuses him of cruelty and wickedness. He hits her again and this time, finally, Jane strikes: "I received him in frantic sort. I don't very well know what I did with my hands, but he called me 'Rat! rat!' and bellowed out aloud" (9). The beating fantasy merges with the castration fantasy here in a real physical assault. No longer a voyeur or passive participant, Jane is being beaten and finally strikes back.

The only aspect of this incident that should surprise us is that it took Jane

---

17. Michele Massé has explored the psychic dynamics of victimization as caused by actual systemic discrimination against women in her book *In the Name of Love*. Her chapter on *Jane Eyre* is quite appropriately titled "Looking Out for Yourself: The Spectator and Jane Eyre," 192–238. Other discussions of *Jane Eyre* within the gothic ambience of victim fiction include Joanna Russ, "Somebody's Trying to Kill Me and I Think It's My Husband: The Modern Gothic," in *The Female Gothic*, ed. Juliann Fleenor (Montreal: Eden, 1983), 31–56; and Peter Bellis, "In the Window-Seat: Vision and Power in *Jane Eyre*," *ELH* 54 (1987), 639–52.

ten years to explode given her abusive treatment. Bessie observes that she cannot understand Jane's outburst because "'she never did so before.'" Abbot, on the other hand, subscribes to the Reeds' view of Jane as an incipient lower-class revolutionary: "'it was always in her'" and besides "'She's an underhand little thing: I never saw a girl of her age with so much cover'" (10). "Cover" is just what the gothic feminist in training needs to develop. We might call it protective camouflage, the sort of coloration that butterflies adapt to blend in with their surroundings. But Jane is no butterfly; she is desperate and resolves "to go all lengths" to settle the score with her oppressors. Like a Luddite revolutionary, she experiences the mood of the "rebel slave." We will recall that the description here of Jane echoes her later portrait of the desperate Bertha, caged like an animal by Rochester. Bertha *is* Jane's aggression, her rage, her class-based attack on a system of barter that places her, like all women, in dependent and subsidiary positions. Jane's evolving attitude at the age of ten, however, is "a new thing" for her, and she resolves to escape either through flight or self-imposed starvation (9). Neither option is open to her; instead her punishment at her aunt's hands is quick and sadistic.

Jane's sojourn in the Red Room is perhaps the first clearly gothic set piece in this very self-consciously late gothic text. The ghost of her dead uncle, the brother of her dead and disinherited mother, presides over this room the way patriarchs always preside over the residues of their power. This particular patriarch, however, hovers over his large, imposing, and empty bed, the seat of his reproductive labors, and it is the specter of generation and childbirth that emerges in this tableau to haunt the young, prepubescent Jane. We suspect that Jane is haunted and nauseous in the presence of her uncle's bed, because it suggests vaguely to her not only the horror of her aunt as a sexually desirable woman but of her own parents' sexual activity. The dim and only vaguely sensed presence of one's parents as sexual beings is always so repulsive to female gothic heroines that it throws them into a frenzy, and this we see enacted in the Red Room scenario. We are reminded also of the dead father's ghostly presence emerging for his daughter from the text he composed while awaiting his murder in *The Romance of the Forest.* Clearly, Brontë in this episode plays on our knowledge of gothic tropes both to present Jane as an incipient gothic heroine in training and to undercut her position as

---

18. Evidence that Brontë read and was influenced by Ann Radcliffe's works, particularly *The Italian*, is recorded in the exchange between Caroline Helstone and Rose Yorke in her novel *Shirley,* ed. Herbert Rosengarten and Margaret Smith (Oxford: Clarendon, 1981), 398–99.

such. Jane is self-haunted in a way that Radcliffe's heroine is not.[18] Or rather, Jane works herself up into a frenzy that is instead imposed on Radcliffe's heroines by an ontological reality that does not exist in this later text.

Jane places herself once again within the iconography of *Bewick's Birds* and imagines a victim/victimizer scenario, this time with the ghost of Uncle Reed descending on his wife and children in order to avenge the wrongs committed by them against Jane. Imagining that she can see the ghost, she screams and begs her aunt for escape. When her aunt refuses and sadistically shuts her up in the room for the entire night, Jane swoons into unconsciousness, the victim of a hysterically self-induced fit. Ironically, in succumbing to the excesses of female passion, Jane attracts medical help and gains her first patriarchal ally—her first living father figure—the apothecary Mr. Lloyd. The sympathetic and astute Lloyd manages to get Jane sent to Lowood rather than the poorhouse, and she begins that arduous journey that will lead her to Rochester and eventually the master bedroom of Ferndean. The Red Room, in other words, figures the first of many enclosed spaces that the heroine has to rewrite in order to script herself out of the limitations imposed on her by her orphaned and classless status.

But Jane is not a silent sufferer the way other gothic feminists have been. She talks back and launches a veritable verbal assault on her aunt after the Red Room disaster. Whereas the Radcliffe heroine usually suffers in silence, Jane plays the guilt card, asking her aunt, "'What would uncle Reed say to you, if he were alive?'" Jane has learned, in short, that gothic heroines have few if any resources beyond their tongues. They can hurt and engage in name-calling, which are the child Jane's earliest responses to her aunt's continual abuse, or they can construct narratives that essentially rewrite history and present themselves as the innocent victims of tyranny and abuse. Jane's novel—*Jane Eyre*—is an example of the latter. When aunt Reed tells the visiting Mr. Brockelhurst that Jane is a liar, Jane responds by calling Mrs. Reed "bad," "hard-hearted," and "deceitful"; she swears that when she is able she will tell everyone far and wide how "the very thought of you makes me sick, and that you [Mrs. Reed] treated me with miserable cruelty" (31).

The tongue is used here as an instrument of revenge. Jane promises to defame the reputation of Mrs. Reed in much the same way that Emmeline was defamed by the Crofts. The anachronistic aristocratic tradition that suffuses this novel is apparent in this vignette. Reputations are property and to sully someone's reputation is to seize property and worth from them by the sheer force of one's tongue. Using her newfound verbal aggression allows Jane to "exult" in her new "sense of freedom, of triumph" (31). Realizing that the weak are despised and harassed as easy targets, Jane ventures off to school determined to fear nothing and no one. In reading the childhood of Jane, more than any other gothic feminist, we realize that she has been schooled in dodging the slings and arrows of systematic psychic and emotional abuse. She is one of life's walking wounded, and as such the text she constructs for us can stand only as an elaborate template that has been written in order to conceal her pain.

The educational idyll that characterizes so many female gothic texts is inverted in Brontë's description of life at Lowood, the school from hell run by an evil man who is as cruel as he is incompetent. In the Reverend Mr. Brockelhurst we see a hypocritical religious toadie, a Dickensian villain, a Protestant spin on the evil genius presiding over a Radcliffean gothic convent. In publicly branding Jane a liar and in instructing the other girls to reject her, Brockelhurst is acting as the minion of Mrs. Reed, much as Schedoni was willing to serve as the tool of Vivaldi's mother in their mutual persecution of Ellena. Again, the class issue surfaces, with the religious clergy only too willing to persecute nubile women who threaten to usurp attention and resources from the older, sexually sullied gothic mother. But Mrs. Reed is not simply a version of the fairy-tale evil stepmother. She is finally a domesticated version of all of those gothic antiheroines who conspire with rogue priests to do away with the virtuous and more potentially marketable gothic heroine. Mrs. Reed sends Jane to Lowood because she wants her to die there. Her actions are not much different from those of Sleeping Beauty's stepmother, who sends her into the forest. Gothic heroines are always sent into this quagmire we call life and expected to emerge unscathed, which—magically—they do. Jane is no exception. While the other girls die around her at an alarming rate, Jane is untouched by the influenza that ravages the merely mortal. She sleeps in Helen Burns's arms and arises from Helen's deathbed a stronger, albeit chastened, young woman. At Lowood Jane walks through the valley of the shadow of death and emerges ready to face her most formidable opponent—her potential husband.

But before Jane is able to leave Lowood, site of her ritual maiming, she must face the challenges presented there and overcome her adversaries. After her stigmatization by Brockelhurst, she feels "crushed and trodden on" and actually hopes "to die" of her shame: "'I would rather die than live—I cannot bear to be solitary and hated.'" But she is revived first by the friendship of Helen Burns and then by the support of Miss Temple. Helen is a virtual embodiment of the sentimental heroine come back to life after many years. Like Clarissa, she pines for the afterlife with a vengeance. She warns Jane that it is dangerous to value "too much the love of human beings," and she advises Jane to live within her own conscience, not the opinions of others" (60). Helen is, in short, too good for this fallen world and the world makes quick work of her. The odious Miss Scatcherd beats Helen for daydreaming, and without a father to protect her, Helen is fair game in the predatory feeding frenzy that is life at Lowood. Deserted by her biological father, Helen worships instead at the shrine of the "mighty universal Parent," a vaguely androgynous godhead who "waits only the separation of spirit from flesh to crown us with a full reward" (71, 60–61). Helen's religion is a natural outgrowth of the sentimental ideology, and it is, unfortunately, as dangerous and outdated in this text as it was for Clarissa.

One of the primary reasons that Jane survives and Helen does not, however, concerns Jane's ability, nay compulsion, to tell over and over the "tale of [her] sufferings and resentments" (50) to a close friend or confidante. Bessie, her earliest audience, is succeeded by Mr. Lloyd, then Helen and Miss Temple. In verbally constructing herself as the blameless victim of tyranny and cruel oppression, Jane learns the first lesson that every gothic feminist has to learn to survive and thrive: the power of narrative. At Lowood Jane learns that she will remain locked forever in her childhood narrative of victimization unless she can find a way out, and that means of escape appears to be her powerful desire for "Liberty, Excitement, Enjoyment" (75). Living at Lowood as an overaged schoolgirl, Jane the young adult craves "the real world" that she imagines is "wide" and filled with "a varied field of hopes and fears, of sensations and excitements." Like the feisty gothic feminist that she fancies herself to be, Jane wants to have the "courage to go forth into its expanse, to seek real knowledge of life amidst its perils" (74), but Jane is not a gothic adventuress. There will be no trips to the Italian Alps for her. Jane finds herself praying instead for "a humbler supplication: for change, stimulus," but even that prayer is moderated, so that finally Jane begs for the known and familiar: "a new servitude!" (74). This is a young woman who simply cannot trust herself because no one has ever really trusted her. She imagines that she desires "life and movement," but she fears getting into a "scrape." She fears that the sort of scandal that destroyed her mother will be her fate, and so she wants "above all things" to be "respectable, proper, *en règle*" (77). Jane is, in short, a field of desire and energy at odds with herself.

Jane Eyre, however, is also filled with what Virginia Woolf has called

---

19. Woolf's reaction to and condemnation of the "feminist outbursts" in *Jane Eyre* are recorded in her essay "*Jane Eyre* and *Wuthering Heights*," in *The Common Reader* (New York: Harcourt, 1925), 219–27.

"feminist outbursts,"[19] and the first one occurs in chapter 12. After Jane has resolved to accept the position of governess at Thornfield, she contrasts her limited and narrow lot with her lived circumstances. She is miserable but soothes her misery by thinking of the millions of other women who, like her, suffer from "too rigid a constraint, too absolute a stagnation" and are "in silent revolt against their lot" (96). Gothic feminism conforms fairly closely to this pattern of verbal behavior at the expense of real action. It raises whining to an art form. Jane, like other gothic feminists, has the chance to be independent and to pursue adventures, but she chooses out of her sense of inadequacy and fear to retreat into the safety of an upper-class estate. It is one of the contrivances of the plot that she is presented with adventures and mysteries to solve within the enclosed confines of the domestic abode. Luckily, she manages to find a gothic hero, a mad gothic antiheroine, and an estate to be claimed right in her own backyard.

The romance of Rochester and Jane is, like the romance of Heathcliff and Catherine I, a staple tableau of women's fiction, a well-worn iconic terrain that hundreds of critics have analyzed since both books were published in 1847. Neither Jane nor Rochester is conventionally attractive, and initially that appears to have been the basis of their mutual attraction to each other. Jane needs to read Rochester as a Byronic hero, and thus she notices his "decisive nose," his "grim mouth, chin, and jaw" (105). He is a "fierce falcon" (167) compared with the conventionally handsome Mr. Mason. And similarly, Rochester needs to construct Jane according to the melodramatic scenario of the fairy tale. To Rochester, Jane is a princess pretending to be a governess, a singular person who is "cast in a different mould to the majority" (118). Neither of them, in other words, sees the other. They see literary and fairy-tale conventions operating and then insert themselves into ready-made formulas in a complementary role. But Jane can only play a subsidiary role in this scenario, since she has very few life adventures to share with Rochester, beyond surviving a brush with a childhood bully and the typhus epidemic. It is Rochester who now comes to the fore, and it is his adventures that Jane lives out vicariously through the safely distanced medium of his personal narration.

When Rochester recites to Jane his story, we know that we are listening to the last gasp of the gothic hero's narrative, complete with its clear overtones of sexual corruption and resultant nausea. In the story of his disastrous marriage and life with Bertha, his affair with Céline Varens, the French opera dancer and mother of Adèle, and his liaisons with the other unnamed and frightfully foreign women, Rochester forces the reader to confront the legacy of aristocratic sexual license and British xenophobia.[20] He has indulged his passions the way Byronic heroes do, and now, like a latter-day Manfred, he stands accused and guilty before the young British virgin who is the only woman worthy to be his mate. He, however, is not worthy of her, and so the narrative traces how his vindication will occur. Rochester, in short, will have to be punished for participating in the British bourgeoisie's worst fears about the corrupt and sexual aristocracy. Rochester's sexual fall, however, haunts him both symbolically and literally, for the residue of that crime lives right above his head. Mad and lewd, Bertha exists as a reminder of Rochester's class-based greed and lust. Jane does not know that her real enemy, the gothic antiheroine, will have to be destroyed in such a way that Jane—the heroine—can never be suspected of wrongdoing. Such a task would be daunting to anyone except the gothic feminist. The contrivances of the narrative allow Jane to marry a tamed version of Rochester after Bertha commits suicide, and the convolutions of the plot are so strong—the sheer weight of its action is so compelling—that we seldom notice Jane's role—passive, of course—in the disaster.

The prolonged courtship of Rochester and Jane—the middle section of the text—consists of a series of approach-avoidance episodes in which each tries to discern how easily the other will be to dominate. Rochester initially appears to have the upper hand, both as an experienced man of the world and as Jane's much older employer. But, like Jane, Rochester also presents himself as the innocent victim of fate. He blames his mistakes, and they are many and many more than Jane herself knows at this point, on "circumstances," not on the "natural bent" of his heart. He tells Jane that he "turned desperate" and "degenerated" when his choices failed to work out, and he further confesses that he is still desperate: "since happiness is irrevocably denied me, I have a right to get pleasure out of life: and I *will* get it, cost what it may" (119–20). The costs, as we know later, will be paid by Bertha, who has her brains dashed out as a result of her mad jump from the roof of Thornfield. But what is most interesting in this relatively early exchange between Rochester and Jane is that Rochester, like Schedoni before him, sees himself as the innocent victim, not the victimizer of Bertha or Céline or any

---

20. Comparing and contrasting the perspective of the possessed with that of the dispossessed, Jane with Bertha, began with the publication of Jean Rhys's novel *Wide Sargasso Sea* in 1966. A number of critics have discussed the two novels and explored the issues raised by the contrast, notably miscegenation, colonialism, sutee, and Orientalism. See, for instance, Gayatri Chakravorty Spivak, "Three Women's Texts and a Critique of Imperialism," *CI* 12 (1985), 243–61.

of the other women he has used, abused, and discarded. Gothic heroes are anachronistic in their sexual libertinism. Their flagrant and active sexuality continues to function as a residual reminder of their aristocratic heritage, the right they possess to the pleasures that can be found with "foreign" women (read: sexually active and therefore corrupt and corrupting).

But if gothic heroes have an aristocratic past, so do novels, particularly gothic novels, as a genre. Part of the female gothic agenda concerns just this struggle to wrest away the novel and its "manly" hero from an aristocratic heritage that is sexually corrupt and alien to a newly emerging class of bourgeoisie.[21] The sentimental novel tradition chooses to tame the aristocratic hero by feminizing him, while the female gothic novel chooses to make the hero safe for the middle-class world by ritualistically wounding him. Emily Brontë plays with both of these options in *Wuthering Heights*, and so finally does Charlotte in her creation of Rochester and St. John Rivers. In fact, the rigid binary constructions we see in all the Brontë novels remind us of the doubling device as it was used in Radcliffe's works and as it originated in the fairy tale. The doublings of Jane and Bertha, Rochester and St. John, Bertha and Helen, Jane and Rosamund, Jane and Blanche, Diana and Mary Rivers, the Reed sisters and the Rivers sister, John Reed and St. John—the list is virtually endless—ultimately all remind us that finally we are reading allegory, psychodrama, and at times barely concealed dream work from the mind of one very lonely motherless woman in search of the perfect fantasy family.

That Jane persists through an unpromising childhood and lives to write her own tale are testimonies to Rochester's statement about Jane when he learns that she had survived so many years at Lowood: she is tenacious of life. Gothic feminists are tenacious of life because they have a mission and a sacred duty: they are creating androgynous middle-class families inhabited by strong women and safely tamed men. Jane is drawn to Rochester not simply because he is the manly and admiring father figure she never had but because he provides the wealth and class status for which she so clearly hungers. The merger of Rochester's class with Jane's moral goodness and

---

21. I am alluding here to Lord Chesterfield's letters to his son in which a "Novel" is defined as "a little gallant history, which must contain a great deal of love, and not exceed one or two small volumes. . . . A Novel is a kind of abbreviation of a Romance; for a Romance generally consists of twelve volumes, all filled with insipid love nonsense, and most incredible adventures." The origins and nature of the novel, hotly debated and continually unresolved, have been explored most recently and most fully by J. Paul Hunter, *Before Novels: The Cultural Contexts of Eighteenth-Century English Fiction* (London: Norton, 1990); Geoffrey Day, *From Fiction to the Novel* (London: Routledge, 1987); and Michael McKeon, *The Origins of the English Novel 1600–1740* (Baltimore: Johns Hopkins University Press, 1987).

purity represents the dream animating the female gothic project: that the aristocracy will be painlessly absorbed by the bourgeoisie and that the bourgeoisie will be controlled by strong women and their wily little daughters. The daughter in this scenario absorbs the patriarch, consumes his power, and emerges like a sort of Athena, an all-powerful goddess who has destroyed the patriarchy even as she has inscribed herself as the new matriarch. *Jane Eyre* presents the final and definitive version of this ideology for nineteenth-century consumption.

We turn now to an examination of the three key gothic scenes in the text, the three episodes that have forever inscribed *Jane Eyre* into popular consciousness. I refer, of course, to the discovery of Bertha in the attic after the aborted wedding scene, Jane's magical reclamation of an estate and family, and finally her "mysterious summons" to return to Rochester as his bride and redeemer. Each scene replays stock gothic topoi, but Brontë has reinvested this familiar gothic terrain with a power and passion that virtually rewrite these conventions in new and strikingly original ways. At least the text has had this sort of engaging and engrossing effect on its readers since its publication. Jane as idealized bourgeois heroine manages to triumph over a woman coded as "colored," as well as a variety of corrupt aristocratic women—most notably, Mrs. Reed, the suspiciously tall Blanche Ingram, and the excessively beautiful Rosamund Oliver. By seizing an estate and a fortune through no ostensible efforts of her own, Jane becomes a middle-class heroine gaining the aristocratic status that she has ostensibly shunned. In rejecting the aristocracy in the sexual arena and mimicking their values in the financial area, the novel clearly displays a conflicted ideology. I suggest that the text is riven throughout by these conflicts, but the reader experiences the story only as Jane's self-narrated and self-constructed vindication. We hear, in other words, only her side of the story. When Jean Rhys attempted to point out this imbalance in perception, she gave us a considerably different Bertha, a victimized woman who tells her own very different narrative in *Wide Sargasso Sea*.[22]

In presenting Bertha, however, Brontë plays on the stereotypes that have

---

22. Feminist critics have recently focused on analyzing the postmodern retelling of the novel by Jean Rhys. For instance, see Michael Thorpe, "'The Other Side': *Wide Sargasso Sea* and *Jane Eyre*," *Ariel* 8 (1977), 99–110; Elizabeth Baer, "The Sisterhood of Jane Eyre and Antoinette Cosway," in *The Voyage In: Fictions of Female Development*, ed. Elizabeth Abel, Marianne Hirsch, and Elizabeth Langland (Hanover: University Press of New England, 1983), 131–48; Peter Grudin, "Jane and the Other Mrs. Rochester: Excess and Restraint in *Jane Eyre*," *Novel* 10 (1977), 145–57; and Joyce Carol Oates, "Romance and Anti-Romance: From Brontë's *Jane Eyre* to Rhys's *Wide Sargasso Sea*," *VQR* 61 (1985), 44–58.

plagued gothic antiheroines from their inception. Bertha reminds us of all those lustful, ravening aristocrats who populated the texts of Charlotte Smith, Charlotte Dacre, and Ann Radcliffe, except that she is rather more far gone than even the mad nun Sister Agnes (in Radcliffe's *Mysteries of Udolpho*). Coding the aristocratic female body as sexually excessive was a convention that fed its bourgeois audience's worst prejudices about both women and the aristocracy. Bertha is associated in Rochester's mind with "vices," "giant propensities"; she is "intemperate and unchaste," "gross, impure, depraved" (269–70). Bertha's crime apparently has been to enjoy the sexual aspects of marriage a bit too much for her husband's tastes. As such she is constructed by Rochester as an animal, bestial, a Byronic hero-ine run amok, indulging her appetites until she has lost all vestiges of civil-ity and sanity completely. Confined in the attic of her husband's home, she contents herself with midnight forays around the mansion. On one occa-sion she lights Rochester's bed on fire, with him in it just to make her point. On another occasion she bites and tears away the skin from her brother's neck, thereby suggesting that women who have indulged their sexual pas-sions are actually cannibalistic, vampiric, and in need of constant surveil-lance. Furthermore, she seems to have no respect for her brother or for the sanctity of the patriarchal family. On another midnight sojourn she tears Jane's wedding veil in half, warning Jane in not very subtle terms what she has to look forward to on her wedding night.

Bertha enacts in all these episodes the revenge of the gothic antiheroine on her avatar, the gothic feminist. She promises through her violent actions to warn as well as punish her more docile sister by standing as a living object lesson in the consequences of sexual excess and pain. The gothic antiheroine is wounded and finally exterminated by the conclusion of the text, but what is important in *Jane Eyre* is that Brontë rewrote Radcliffe's Signora Laurentini and Dacre's Victoria as almost cartoonish figures when she cre-ated Bertha. The excessive, hyperbolic, carnivalesque body of Bertha con-fronts the composed, privatized, repressed body of Jane as the two women struggle for possession of the man and his estates. That the bourgeoisie tri-umphs in its claims of superiority over the aristocracy should hardly sur-prise us. Gothic feminist texts have existed precisely to present just this sort of ideology, and in the success of *Jane Eyre* we can see how thoroughly the middle class has convincingly apotheosized itself.

The first climactic denunciation of Bertha occurs in her activities the night before Jane and Rochester are to be married. Bertha invades the bride's bedroom and wakes her from yet another particularly troubling dream about dead babies. When Bertha confronts Jane in her virginal bed, she stands as a silent accusation, a living embodiment of something vestigial buried by the more powerful energy that the bourgeois Jane represents. Jane describes her later to Rochester as "a woman, tall and large, with thick and dark hair hanging down her back. I know not what dress she had on: it was white and straight; but whether gown, sheet, or shroud, I cannot tell." The woman alternately clad as bride, bedmate, or dead is a particularly appropriate representation of the vocational possibilities held out to women in the gothic universe. The triple woman figure, called by Robert Graves the "white goddess," is also a stock figure in mythologies and always represents the control women have over birth, reproduction, and death. When Rochester presses Jane for details, she provides the following: "I never saw a face like it! It was a discoloured face—it was a savage face. I wish I could forget the roll of the red eyes and the fearful blackened inflation of the lineaments. . . . [T]he lips were swelled and dark; the brow furrowed; the black eyebrows widely raised over the bloodshot eyes. Shall I tell you of what it reminded me?. . . Of the foul German spectre—the Vampyre" (249). The animalistic, vampiric, foreign qualities of Bertha code her as sexually predatory and dangerous, while her opposite stands embodied in Jane: the small, white, childlike girl-woman who deserves to be Rochester's wife because her sexual needs will be moderate, temperate, and unthreatening. What Bertha actually represents for the gothic hero is his fear of impotence before the sexually voracious antiheroine. Rochester hates Bertha because he could not satisfy her sexual demands. Bertha, in other words, is punished in the text for Rochester's sexual failures. Such would appear to be the (il)logic of this particular relationship, yet another unhappy marriage in the gothic universe.

When the wedding of Jane and Rochester is interrupted by Bertha's brother, Richard Mason, we recall an earlier version of the same incident in Radcliffe's *Italian*. In both episodes there is a slightly veiled agenda, that is, the intense female fear of male sexuality. It is as if the heroine can barely summon the courage to get herself to the altar, but then, praise the lord, there is an impediment that makes the marriage, both desired and dreaded, impossible. Jane's ambivalence is evident when she tells us that all she can remember about her trip to church is the memory of rooks circling over "green grave-mounds." Again, we are in the terrain of *Bewick's Birds*, but this time with Jane clearly intended as the sacrificial victim, her body being offered up to insure the continuance of a corrupt and bigamous (read: polygamous) aristocracy. In defense of his actions Rochester leads the wedding party back to his estate for a public viewing of his prize catch, the sexual wife. This scene is as gothic in its inspiration as is the earlier scene in which Jane spends a whole night sponging blood from the wounded Mason's neck and arm (186). Ritually wounded by his sister's teeth, Mason in that chapter is the frustrated and anachronistic embodiment of residual familial and kinship ties. In this chapter he successfully represents his sister's interests against a usurper, sent by Jane's long-lost uncle Eyre. The patriarchy closes ranks here to protect both women against Rochester's bigamous desires, reminding us that gothic sons always stand together against the sexual dominance of and control by the totemic father.

When Rochester presents Bertha for public viewing, he participates in an exhibitionistic idyll. Shielded behind multiple screens and deep within further recesses, Bertha is caged like a rare and extremely dangerous animal: "In the deep shade, at the further end of the room, a figure ran backwards and forwards. What it was, whether beast or human being, one could not, at first sight, tell: it grovelled, seemingly, on all fours; it snatched and growled like some strange wild animal; but it was covered with clothing; and a quantity of dark, grizzled hair, wild as a mane, hid its head and face" (257–58). This description differs significantly from the description Jane had given of Bertha only twenty-four hours earlier to Rochester. There Bertha's hair was long and dark; now it is grizzled like an ape's. Then she had worn a white sheath; now she is a wild animal seemingly covered with a coat of fur. Her demonization, her abjection, her objectification—all are motivated by Jane's intense guilt and shame.

In the presence of her intended's sexual history, Jane is overcome with sexual nausea. Or rather, she sees in Bertha her own projected sexual passions for Rochester, which she can only experience as animalistic and shameful. Bertha the mad wife is the gothic residue clinging to the tradition of bourgeois women's fiction. She is the embodiment of the subterranean depths from which it arises; she is the gothic mother gone mad in her captivity. She reminds us of the imprisoned mother in Radcliffe's *Sicilian Romance*. Or rather she suggests what that woman might have become had she been better fed and stronger. When Jane flees from Rochester's house to seek her fate, she is fleeing Bertha as much as she is running from a taboo relationship with him. But in the Bertha-Rochester-Jane triangle, we see the final working out of the female gothic fantasy of mommy-daddy-me. As an orphan Jane has been forced to see every relationship she has entered into as a substitute for the missing familial idyll she never had. In the Rochester-Bertha dyad she rewrites her parents as "gothic," strong, large, sexually powerful, and needy. Later she will rewrite them far differently in St. John Rivers and his two sisters. By the conclusion of the novel, she will finally be strong enough to confront the reality of her loss and return to a chastened version of her father, Rochester the blind and crippled. But before that happy day arrives, Jane, like all gothic feminists, must make her fortune.

In the second gothic set piece, Jane's successful claim on her uncle Eyre's estate and her suddenly discovered kinship to the Rivers siblings, we can see the rewriting of a standard gothic trajectory we saw first in Smith's *Emmeline*. The gothic feminist heroine needs an estate to prove her worth and value on the marriage market she pretends to condemn. But because she needs to appear above the financial dealings of placing herself on the market, she needs the estate to drop effortlessly into her lap. And that is exactly what happens to Jane. Her long-absent uncle leaves a will bequeathing his impressive estate to her and her alone. At the same time she is led as if by magic to the only living relatives in England she would like to have—Diana, Mary, and St. John Rivers. In a rewrite of the first half of the novel, Jane wins the love of these three siblings, even having to fend off a marriage proposal from her male cousin, the pious and seriously spiritual St. John (a doubled version of the odious cousin John Reed). When Jane inherits her estate she splits it four ways, giving three of her portions away to her "good" cousins. On its surface this act appears generous and selfless, but consider that it smacks of another very different motivation. Having been unable to gain the love and affection of a family freely, Jane now is in a position to buy a ready-made family, the Rivers, who stand in symbolic stead of the odious Reeds.

The final gothic set piece concerns the "mysterious summons" that calls Jane to Rochester on the night that she rejects St. John's final and most threatening ultimatum: marry me or else. Jane hears that mysterious cry for help as if written on the wind, and what is most interesting here is that in the melodramatic tradition it is the "cry of the mother" that always initiates the heroine's call to duty and resolution.[23] In this text the anguished cry of the mother is enunciated by the hero, ritualistically wounded by his mad wife in her insane attempt to kill both her husband and her rival. Although we know Jane has left Thornfield several months earlier, Bertha does not know. She lives in a decidedly different mental universe, and it would appear

---

23. Peter Brooks discusses the "cry of the mother"— *"voix du sang"*—in his *Melodramatic Imagination* (45). What he calls "melodramatic rhetoric" characterizes the style of all the female goth-icists: "Its typical figures are hyperbole, antithesis, and oxymoron"; "Nothing is understood, all is over-stated"; "the melodramatic utterance breaks through everything that constitutes the 'reality principle' [and] . . . [d]esire triumphs over the world of substitute-formations and detours, it achieves pleni-tude of meaning" (40–41).

that in setting Thornfield afire she is attempting to rid herself of her rival for Rochester. In Jane's narrative we have reached the point at which the female bodies turn on each other, the *homo clausus* body of Jane rejecting and abjecting the carnivalesque, hysterical female body of Bertha. In setting the fire, Bertha enacts Jane's projected desire, for Bertha is ultimately as ephemeral as she is allegorical. Bertha has always represented a split-off element or component within Jane's own psyche, and now, finally, Jane is ready to extinguish her. As she had earlier eliminated the part of her personality she called "Helen Burns," her tendency to masochism and her adherence to the self-defeating sentimental codes of conduct, now she is ready to destroy her attraction to the hyperbolic gothic codes that Bertha embodies.

But how do we know that Jane has a "Bertha" within her that she fears and finally destroys? Consider her strange tendency to debase herself in her dealings with her second father substitute, St. John Rivers: "I fell under a freezing spell. When he said 'go,' I went! 'come,' I came; 'do this,' I did it. But I did not love my servitude; I wished, many a time, he had continued to neglect me." Desperately needing his approval the way a needy child clings to a father, Jane reveals herself in this situation to be what she is: starved for attention, love, and approval from the "bad father"—cold, absent, unreliable, or punishing. Winning his approval she finally admits is impossible; he is, after all, not her father but merely an unsatisfactory substitute. Recognizing the futility of her efforts, she admits that to please St. John she "must disown half my nature, stifle half my faculties, wrest my tastes from their original bent, force myself to the adoption of pursuits for which I had no natural vocation" (351).

This tendency to debase herself before an ambivalently loved and hated authority figure is matched in Jane's character by the opposite tendency— revolt. We are within the parameters of passive-aggressive behavior when Jane herself confesses to the tendency as she attempts to explain herself: never in her life has she "known any medium in my dealings with positive, hard characters, antagonistic to my own, between absolute submission and determined revolt." She admits that she cultivates submission up to the "very moment of bursting, sometimes with volcanic vehemence, into the other," that is, "revolt" (352). But if Jane revolts against both the Rivers' class oppression and Rochester's phallic mastery, she chooses to submit to St. John until the "mysterious summons" allows her to revolt and flee from him. The "mysterious summons" would appear, then, as a species of self-talk, the voice within her own head that tells her she has reached a point in her relation with the cold daddy beyond which she will not and cannot go.

When Jane returns to Thornfield, she learns that Bertha has set the estate on fire and been killed in a mad leap from the battlements. Compared by many critics to an act of suttee, Bertha's suicidal jump as Rochester approaches her can more accurately be seen as a carnivalesque acting out of intense and destructive emotions aimed against authoritarian power structures, this time the patriarchally marked estate. When Jane learns that Bertha is now "dead as the stones on which her brains and blood were scattered" (377), we know that we have arrived at the final obsessive description of the state of Bertha's head. In the earlier two descriptions of Bertha's hair and body, the emphasis was on her vampiric, animalistic, subhuman qualities. Now we see that head totally reduced to inanimate matter, "brains and blood," splattered like so much refuse on the pavement on which Jane trods. Jane has won a ferocious and hard fought victory here over a rival, a triumph that allows her quite literally to tread on the physical remains of her competitor/alter ego. We are reminded of Victoria's pitiless murder of her nemesis Lilla, and we recognize that it is rare in women's literature to see two women poised in such a life and death struggle, the ultimate beating fantasy, for a man and his estate. *Jane Eyre* the narrative as told by the vindicated "Jane Eyre" allows Jane the victory without the appearance that she had anything to do with the event. Her hands are clean.

The final moment of apotheosis, the marriage of the "rehumanized" Rochester to the triumphant Jane, is one of the most hotly debated of "happy endings" in literary history.[24] Rochester has been crippled and blinded in the fire set by Bertha, so his wounding, like the one experienced by Richard Mason, occurs at the hands of Bertha, the ravening bacchanalian maenad. But Jane is not daunted by this symbolically "castrated" husband; rather, she rejoices: "'I love you better now when I can really be useful to you, than I did in your state of proud independence'" (392), further declaring that she fancies her beloved more as a "sightless Samson," a "Vulcan," or a "royal eagle, chained to a perch" and forced to "entreat a sparrow to become its purveyor" (379, 389, 387). The imagery from *Bewick's Birds* has come full circle. The cormorant that was the hungry and angry heart of Jane has now become a meek and mild sparrow. The sexually demanding gothic antiheroine has been replaced by the docile and undemanding child

---

24. The "castration" of Rochester is a hotly debated topic in the critical history of the novel. Richard Chase originally defined the issue in "The Brontës: or, Myth Domesticated," in *Forms of Modern Fiction*, ed. William O'Connor (Minneapolis: University of Minnesota Press, 1948), 1, 2–13. Adrienne Rich takes up the issue in a seminal essay on the subject, "Jane Eyre: The Temptations of a Motherless Woman," in *On Lies, Secrets, and Silence: Selected Prose, 1966–1978* (New York: Norton, 1979), 89–106.

bride. The sexually voracious patriarch has now become a repentant shadow of himself, eager, nay grateful, to be led around by his new bride.

   Jane Eyre presents in a dramatic and powerful manner the melodrama of gender and ideology that has animated the female gothic project. An orphan, friendless, misunderstood, and underappreciated by all her peers, wins her vindication and bests the patriarchy at its own game. And best of all, she gives every indication of having done nothing much at all. The passive-aggressive behavior that lies at the heart of the gothic feminist is in this text writ most plainly for all to see.

IV

Critics have persistently faulted Charlotte Brontë's final novel, *Villette,* for its "unreliable narrator" and its "odd structure," but finally *Villette* is puzzling as a novel because it is an example of a late female gothic written in a culture that no longer understood the codes or believed in the conventions.[25] Like an anachronistic religion with very few followers, the female gothic novel exists at this point in literary history as a vestige, a memory, a dying discourse system. The journey to Europe, the struggle with an evil abbess figure in a convent school, the visit to a confessional, the descent into Walraven's strange gothic castle, the mysterious nun who appears and disappears at moments of crisis in the text, the nocturnal ramble through a surreal landscape populated by doubles—all of these are stock gothic devices that have come loose from their moorings in the female gothic genre. Lucy Snowe, Brontë's final heroine, is "unreliable" because she was attempting to conceal her gothic ancestry; Brontë as her creator was attempting to erase gothic traces in a novel that was trying with great difficulty to sell itself to a new market, one that was interested in more realistic textual visions. Lucy "lies" as a narrator because she is ashamed to be a female gothic heroine caught in a gothic novel

---

25. *Villette* has received considerable critical attention during the past decade, attesting to its growing importance within the Brontë canon. Again, contemporary feminist criticism of the novel began with the publication of Gilbert and Gubar's "Buried Life of Lucy Snowe," in *The Madwoman in the Attic,* 399–440, although Kate Millett's discussion of the novel in *Sexual Politics* brought the text to greater public consciousness. More recent studies include Sally Shuttleworth, "'The Surveillance of a Sleepless Eye': The Constitution of Neurosis in *Villette,*" in *One Culture: Essays in Literature and Science,* ed. George Levine (Madison: University of Wisconsin Press, 1987), 313–35; Janet Freeman, "Looking on at Life: Objectivity and Intimacy in *Villette,*" *PQ* 67 (1988), 481–511; and Francesca Kazan, "Heresy, the Image, and Description; Or, Picturing the Invisible: Charlotte Brontë's *Villette,*" *TSLL* 32 (1990), 543–66.

presented to a culture that no longer tolerates such nonsense.

It has been conventional for many years to explain the central conflict in the novel as one between "Reason" and "Imagination" for control of the psyche of Lucy Snowe, surely the heroine who is Brontë's closest self-portrait.[26] But if female gothic novels are usually concerned with epistemology, class struggle, inheritance, power, and property, *Villette* is no different except that its author is the most self-conscious and controlled female gothic novelist working in the tradition. She was most probably introduced to Wollstonecraft by her feminist friend Harriet Martineau, while we know she read Austen, Radcliffe, and Shelley—and she learned from all of them. Her final heroine journeys into the European gothic convent and does battle with the gothic antiheroine (who more than remotely resembles Charlotte Brontë's real-life nemesis Madame Heger) for the male love object, the source of property and wealth in their society (who also more than remotely reminds us of M. Heger, idealized professor and taboo father-lover).

Villette, like the other works in the Brontë canon, finds its structure in the rigidly binary repetition of images and events. Thus, *Jane Eyre* consists of four parallel scenes in which the heroine comes into conflict with an authority figure, while *Wuthering Heights* repeats with eerie precision the triangulated love relationship of a Catherine with both light and dark heroes. In a similar manner, *Villette's* structure lies in the repetition of visual encounters between Lucy and her small coterie of acquaintances. Very early in the work, however, we become aware of the increasing uncanniness of this persistent emphasis on vision.[27] When Lucy and the Brettons attend a concert, Lucy sees their group reflected in a mirror and says, "for the fraction of a moment, believing them all strangers, [I] thus received an impartial impression of their appearance. But the impression was hardly felt and not fixed, before the consciousness that I faced a great mirror . . . dispelled it" (262). This sense of seeing oneself as another is one of the experiences that Freud lists as uncanny in his essay on the subject. In fact, George Eliot's observation that there is something almost preternatural about *Villette* can

---

26. See, for instance, Janice Carlisle, "The Face in the Mirror: *Villette* and the Conventions of Autobiography," *ELH* 46 (1979), 262–89, as well as the more recent discussion of the novel in Diane Long Hoeveler and Lisa Jadwin, *Charlotte Brontë* (New York: Twayne, 1997), 108–33.

27. On the uncanniness of vision in novel, see the early discussions by Mary Jacobus, "The Buried Letter: Feminism and Romanticism in *Villette,*" in *Women Writing and Writing About Women,* ed. Jacobus (London: Croon Helm, 1979), 42–60; and Diane Long Hoeveler, "The Obscured Eye: Visual Imagery as Theme and Structure in Villette," *BSUF* 19 (1978), 23–30. All quotations from *Villette* are from the Oxford edition, ed. Margaret Smith and Herbert Rosengarten (Clarendon, 1984), with page numbers identified in parentheses in the text.

be traced to this sense of the uncanny, which Freud defines as the familiar becoming unfamiliar through its recurrence and repetition. This "compulsion to repeat" is evidenced by Lucy's continual attempts to reinterpret the same characters as if they were different when in fact they are always the same.

In *Villette* we have moved from a world in which women were taught that they could not trust their emotions or sense impressions to a world in which this conflict is allegorized before their very eyes. Whether to see herself and the other women around her as "mirrors" or as "lamps," that is, as passive or active "Others" to men, forms the central dilemma in this text. When Lucy views the paintings of Cleopatra or "La Vie d'une Femme" under the tutelage of M. Paul or when she witnesses the performance of Vashti in the company of Dr. John, she is actually enacting her culture's attempts to define and reify women as active or passive objects within the male-dominated scopophiliac economy. Lucy wars with both options for women, rejecting them as equally dehumanizing and degrading. But her final image—herself as an old woman writing the narrative of all her rejected choices—is hardly reassuring. Lucy delivers what Carlyle would recognize as an Eternal No in this novel, just as Brontë's death shortly after the novel's completion suggests her own escape from the demands required to continue to wage the battle of life we call marriage and motherhood.

In Charlotte Brontë's last novel, her heroine can see her head and heart writ large in other characters acting before her. That she ultimately chooses to reject all of these characters and what they offer her will concern us later. But first let us examine Lucy's choices in the novel and notice that each one is a particularly literarily induced option. Each of the characters in *Villette* appears to have sprung from either a tired gothic novel or a gaspingly exhausted sentimental one. Lucy Snowe appears as a would-be postmodern author in search of six dissolute and uncooperative characters. The conflict facing Lucy, however, first appears most blatantly in her attempts to understand Dr. John and M. Paul, both of whom represent the "masculine" extremes that Lucy must name and then balance within her own psyche. Lucy, like other female gothic heroines, appears to be a victim of her own bifurcated vision throughout the novel. This bifurcation causes her to polarize people and places in a manner that reflects her own internal polarization. Thus, Graham becomes Dr. John (embodiment of REASON) or Isidore (sentimental wooer of the flighty Genevra); Polly becomes Paulina (sentimental motherless heroine becomes sentimental child bride); Mr. Home becomes the Count de Bassompierre (the bourgeois father becomes an aristocrat through magical sleight of hand); the Bretton house in England becomes La Terrasse (British property is transferred to European soil and the Norman invasion is nullified); and Madame Beck's *pensionnat* becomes the nightmarish Rue des Mages (the gothic convent becomes the gothic castle, reminding us of both *Udolpho* and *The Italian*).

As character and narrator, Lucy must mediate between and clarify these extremes, but she is unable to do this as long as she herself is governed by a radical distinction between her "life of thought" and her "life of fancy." In the course of the novel, however, both modes of perception—mimetic and projective—are proven inadequate if not dangerous, when one is not counterbalanced by the other, whereas both modes of perception have their particular visual agents or external manifestations in this, her most allegorical novel. The physical eye that sees external appearances conveys the mimetic, rational mode, while the inner eye penetrates to the hidden and emotional qualities of things. Significantly, this dichotomy is explored in Brontë's critical opinion of Jane Austen: "Her business is not half so much with the human heart as with the human eyes . . . what sees keenly . . . it suits her to study, but what throbs fast and full, though hidden, what the blood rushes through, what is the unseen seat of Life and the sentient target of death— *this* Miss Austen ignores; she no more, with the mind's eye, beholds the heart of her race than each man, with bodily vision sees the heart in his heaving breast."[28] The attempt to contrast herself favorably with a supposedly inferior literary rival is a standard move (and evidence of anxiety) in women writers. But surely it is significant that Brontë casts the rivalry in terms of visual power because seeing into the heart of the patriarchy has been the central concern of the gothic feminist from the earliest writings of Wollstonecraft. And now Brontë tells us that she has been privileged to bring us face to face with the heart of darkness itself. We read *Villette*.

Lucy begins the telling of her narrative—as all female gothic heroines begin—in a simplistic belief in external appearances as the means to truth. When Polly Home arrives at the Bretton household, Lucy looks at her luggage and asks, "Of what are these things the signs and tokens?" (7). She proceeds to watch and observe Polly in order to begin to understand this new object on her horizon. In fact, to this early Lucy human beings are purely objects of literal appearance. She never betrays her emotions; she has been so successfully socialized that she has learned that the display of emotion in

---

28. Brontë's comments on Austen's fiction can be found in *The Brontës: Their Lives, Friendships, and Correspondence*, ed. T. J. Wise and J. A. Symington (Oxford: Clarendon, 1932), 3:99.

a woman is as unseemly as it is redundant. During the emotional farewell to Polly's father, which surely recalls Lucy's own loss of her parents and guardians and her own repressed fear of abandonment, Lucy prides herself on her learned characteristic behavior: "I, Lucy Snowe, was calm" (26). Brontë structures the work so that we see the gradual thawing of a frozen psyche that has been dominated by her masculine faculty of reason and its corollary, a reliance on physical vision as opposed to that vision which is tempered by the emotions. Throughout the first half of this novel, Lucy continues in the stance of an objective observer and is content with inhabiting the "watch-tower of the nursery, whence I . . . made my observation" (92). Even after her involvement in the school play, Lucy retreats into a corner where "unobserved I could observe . . . all passed before me as a spectacle" (175).

Like the early Lucy and Lucy's first double, Miss Marchmont, Madame Beck is also wounded by abandonment and has escaped into a disengaged stance toward life. Like the young Lucy, Madame Beck also epitomizes strict adherence to external appearances, for she shuns all emotional involvement with her world as thoroughly as does Lucy. When Lucy first arrives at the *pensionnat,* madame studies her face for clues to read her character. Lucy remarks that to madame she is "an object of study: she held me under her eye: she seemed turning me round in her thoughts" (93). Madame Beck's "spying" and "espionage" are tolerated remarkably well by Lucy, largely because madame is using her eyes in the same way the early Lucy surreptitiously used hers. The gothic heroine and her nemesis, the gothic antiheroine, are doubles for each other. Both para-noid, both voyeurs, both obsessed with spying and being spied on— Brontë presents explicitly what we have suspected from the beginning. The heroine and her "stepmother" are versions of the same woman, one is merely a younger version of what she will become if she survives the gothic game we call life.

The physical eye has its limitations insofar as it leads Lucy to stultify her emotional life. Her disaffection with the physical senses reaches its climax during the long vacation when Lucy is left alone in the school to tend a retarded child, a cretin whose physical situation eerily mirrors Lucy's own emotional infantilism. Lucy has so neglected her emotional development that it is imbecilic compared to her highly developed rational faculties, and she breaks down under the strain, experiencing a vision of "ghastly, white beds" that turn into "spectres" with "wide gaping eyeholes" (198). Her sin-gle-minded endorsement of reason has led her to this crisis, one we might add that smacks of a fearfully powerful sexual repression. The blank beds that Lucy fancies stare at her are, in fact, the gothic feminist's worst nightmare: the ambivalent fear of being an old maid. And this is the dilemma for the gothic feminist: she fears sexuality as much as she needs it. She lives in a body that she wants to control completely, and yet she knows that her body, let alone the body of a man, is not controllable. She fears the empty bed even more than she fears the marriage bed.

Lucy embraces her rational faculties throughout the first half of the novel in her love for Dr. John, the embodiment of the reasonable British Protestant. But loving Dr. John proves futile for Lucy. Instead of bringing her happiness and unifying the faculties of her split being, Lucy experiences only frustration. When Polly asks Lucy, "'Do other people see him with my eyes?'" Lucy replies, "'I never see *him*. I looked at him twice or thrice about a year ago, before he recognized me, and then I shut my eyes; and if he were to cross their balls twelve times between each day's sunset and sunrise, except from memory, I should hardly know what shape had gone by.'" When Polly is puzzled by this statement, Lucy amplifies and states her knowledge of the inadequacy of mimetic perception alone: "'I mean that I value vision, and dread being struck stone blind'" (532).

By denying her emotions, Lucy has in effect blinded herself in order to win the approval of Dr. John. But Lucy's emotions will not be so easily rejected; instead, they emerge symbolically in the repeated episodes of the spectral nun. The first time the nun appears, Lucy has retreated to read the innocent letter she has received from Graham Bretton. She self-consciously places herself in a gothic ambience reminiscent of Radcliffe's Ellena or Emily reading by a flickering candle. Lucy tells us to imagine her, "[t]he poor English teacher in the frosty garret, reading by a dim candle guttering in the wintry air, a letter simply good-natured—nothing more" (305). But this deflation of the gothic staple, the letter furtively read by candlelight, is suddenly regothicized with the abrupt insertion of the phantom nun. For the the scene to be appreciated, it needs to be cited in full:

Are there wicked things, not human, which envy human bliss? Are there evil influences haunting the air, and poisoning it for man? What was near me? . . . Something in that vast solitary sounded strangely. Most surely and certainly I heard, as it seemed, a stealthy foot on that floor: a sort of gliding out from the direction of the black recess haunted by the malefactor cloaks. I turned: my light was dim; the room was long—but, as I live! I saw in the middle of that ghostly chamber a figure all black or white; the skirts straight, narrow, black; the head bandaged, veiled, white. Say what you will, reader—tell me I was nervous, or mad; affirm that I was unsettled by the excitement of that letter; declare that I dreamed: this I vow—I saw there—in that room—on that night—an image like—a NUN. (306)

This description of "an image" is qualified even further by the word "like." This is not a nun, but it is something like a nun. Notice further how uncannily similar the imagery and emphasis on the head is to the repeated descriptions we had of Bertha Mason. The bandaged head actually recalls the wounded Bertha come back from the dead, determined to do battle with her nemesis, the gothic feminist. But the nun is linked to Lucy's frustrated love for Graham, just as the nun is tied to Lucy's letters from him. But what is the connection? Why does something like a nun appear in such a literarily charged atmosphere, almost as if she were an avatar of the aborted gothic letter tradition itself?

The particular nun who supposedly haunts the *pensionnat* Beck is a woman who was, according to legend, buried alive in a vault under the Methuselah pear tree "for some sin against her vow" (131). Later we learn that M. Paul's beloved Justine-Marie entered the convent when her marriage to Paul was prevented for financial reasons, that she died and that Paul is now the guardian of a girl named Justine-Marie who could very well be his natural daughter, born of his aborted affair with the first Justine-Marie, perhaps another wayward and sexual nun. The uncanniness of women duplicating each other, daughter replacing wife and mother, that haunts the text of *Wuthering Heights,* is played out here with even more self-conscious seriousness. When Dr. John attempts to question Lucy about the nun he asks, "'Was it a man? Was it an animal? *What* was it?'" (310). To the rational Dr. John, the nun can only be a "spectral illusion" or an "optical illusion" (312, 321). The mad or bleeding nun—a persistent image within the female gothic tradition—recurs here as almost a parody of herself.[29] But perhaps Brontë is trying to explore and at the same time explode the gothic inheritance for women. Perhaps she is conveying her sense of the gothic as a dead end, a barricaded and empty hall of mirrors inhabited only by memories of past fascinations that no longer have meaning for women in an industrialized and successfully professionalized world.

The second appearance of the phantom nun occurs after Lucy has decided

---

29. The spectral nun in Villette is the most dramatic and blatant example of gothic residue in the text. See discussions of the nun in E. D. H. Johnson, "'Daring the dread Glance': Charlotte Brontë's Treatment of the Supernatural in *Villette*," NCF 20 (1966), 325–36; and Christina Crosby, "Charlotte Brontë's Haunted Text," SEL 24 (1984), 701–15.

to give up her infatuation with Graham and bury his letters under the Methuselah pear tree. This act appears to encode the gothic as the literally buried residue of a forsaken passion, a necessary renunciation if the woman author is to move on to a higher form of creativity and composition. But before she can move to that higher level of repression or regression, Lucy confronts once again the nun: "the moon, so dim hitherto, seemed to shine out somewhat brighter: a ray gleamed even white before me, and a shadow became distinct and marked. I looked more narrowly, to make out the cause of this well-defined contrast appearing a little suddenly in the obscure alley: whiter and blacker it grew on my eye: it took shape with instantaneous transformation. I stood about three yards from a tall, sable-robed, snowy-veiled woman. Five minutes passed. I neither fled nor shrieked. She was there still. I spoke. 'Who are you? and why do you come to me?'" (370). Lucy is the only one to speak and she assumes that she can discover a meaning (who? why?) in the visitations of the nun. She is compelled to read the nun as a text or a tradition that has meaning, whereas we learn by the end of the novel that the nun has no meaning apart from Lucy's compulsions to read her as a real personage with personal significance to her. Lucy appropriately describes the nun as having "no face—no features; all below her brow was masked with a white cloth; but she had eyes, and they viewed me" (370). Again, the paranoia encoded in the watching eyes suggests that the gothic tradition is as self-referential and self-parodying as any in the literary canon. The nun who stares at Lucy is a version of Lucy staring at Emily or Ellena or Victoria. The ghost who haunts Lucy is the ghost of a dead or dying literary tradition, hoping to survive for yet another generation by feeding on the paranoia and fantasies of another group of women writers.

The third and final appearance of the nun occurs as Lucy and M. Paul are walking together and he declares his intentions to pursue Lucy as the doubled female version of himself: "'we are alike—there is affinity. Do you see it mademoiselle, when you look in the glass?'" (460). Their conversation shifts to the legend of the nun, connected as it must be for M. Paul with his dead fiancé Justine-Marie. The story of the nun and the act of believing in her function as a connection, a conduit between the two would-be lovers. Their potential love is constructed over the dead body of the legendary nun, the dying gothic tradition, and the memory of the sacrificial Justine-Marie, the woman who quite possibly indulged her passions, gave birth to a daughter, and paid the price with her life. As Lucy and Paul muse on the nun's reality, Nature speaks as it always does at climactic moments in Brontë novels:

Yes, there scarce stirred a breeze, and that heavy tree was convulsed, whilst the feathery shrubs stood still. For some minutes amongst the wood and leafage a rending and heaving went on. Dark as it was, it seemed to me that something more solid than either night-shadow, or branch-shadow, blackened out of the boles. At last the struggle ceased. What birth succeeded this travail? What Dryad was born of these throes? We watched fixedly. A sudden bell rang in the house—the prayer bell. Instantly into our alley there came . . . an apparition, all black and white. With a sort of angry rush— close, close past our faces—swept swiftly the very NUN herself! Never had I seen her so clearly. She looked tall of stature, and fierce of gesture. As she went, the wind rose sobbing; the rain poured wild and cold; the whole night seemed to feel her. (461)

The bell rings and the nun appears. One is tempted to observe that there is something vaguely Pavlovian about the appearances of the nun. She is born like a force of nature; she springs full grown from the branches of a tree. She is more than human; she is inhuman. She is something; she is nothing. In the sheer multiplicity of images of the nun—alternately an ambiguously empty or full signifier—Brontë suggests the fate of the female gothic novelistic tradition. In the parodic birth of the nun from the trees, we can actually see the death of the genre. There is no nun, of course, only an effeminate man cross-dressing as a nun in order to court Genevra, and this deflation would appear to be Brontë's final send-up of the gothic brooding nun. But the fact that the nun is a man and an effeminate one at that suggests Brontë's subtle critique of gendered constructions of "masculinity" and "femininity." Combine de Hamel's cross-dressing with Lucy donning a partly male costume above the waist for her own performance in a school play, and we have the crux of Brontë's "androgynous" vision.

Just as men can dress like women and women can dress like men, Brontë suggests, so must our emotions be balanced by the claims of reason and fact. The mind and emotions are ultimately part of the gender masquerade, like changeable costumes one puts on and takes off depending on one's needs and situations. Gender is as amorphous and transformational in this novel as clothing is. And just as soon as Lucy rejects or is rejected by Dr. John, she finds herself drawn to his polar opposite, M. Paul, an avatar of the feminized gothic hero and the embodiment of Lucy's repressed emotions. M. Paul first coaches Lucy's character transformation in a literal manner when he directs her performance in the school play. He declares, "'Has your flesh turned into snow and your blood into ice? I want some fire in it, some life, some soul!'"

(159). But M. Paul's emotionalism is equally dangerous, because extreme. An early endorsement of the purely projective, emotional form of perception leads Lucy into the flames of vision that Brontë associates with M. Paul, that is, voyeurism and fancy.

In Lucy's visits to the art gallery and the theater, we can see Brontë's most careful delineation of woman as object or woman as mirror, woman as the lamp by which or the mirror in which man seeks to see himself enlarged or reflected. In the first instance, the viewing of the painting of Cleopatra, Lucy confronts a representation of the gothic antiheroine, fleshly, carnivalesque, wanton, and embarrassing: "It represented a woman, considerably larger, I thought, than the life. I calculated that this lady, put into a scale of magnitude suitable for the reception of a commodity of bulk, would infallibly turn from fourteen to sixteen stone. She was, indeed, extremely well fed: very much butcher's meat—to say nothing of bread, vegetables, and liquids— must she have consumed to attain that breadth and height, that wealth of muscle, that affluence of flesh. . . . She had no business to lounge away the noon on a sofa. She ought likewise to have worn decent garments; a gown covering her properly, which was not the case" (250). Lucy herself is repulsed by this representation of woman in the flesh and cools her eyes by making a hasty retreat and viewing instead "little pictures of still life" (251). The still life is precisely what Lucy is after for herself, but before she realizes that, she is led by M. Paul to a four-paneled visual tableau: "La vie d'une femme." Each one of these scenes presents a model young woman at a crucial stage in her life. In the first, "Juene Fille," Lucy notes that the young girl is leaving the church, missal in hand, "her eyes cast down, her mouth pursed up—the image of a most villainous little precocious she-hypocrite." In the second picture, a bride prays before being led to the slaughter, and in the third, the young mother, we see a woman struggling with "a clayey and puffy baby with a face like an unwholesome full moon." In the fourth and final picture, a widow and her daughter survey a military monument to their illustriously dead husband and father. Lucy tells us that the entire panorama presents woman as "grim and gray as burglars, and cold and vapid as ghosts. What women to live with! insincere, ill-humoured, bloodless, brainless non-entities! As bad in their way as the indolent gipsy-giantess, the Cleopatra" (253).

In this sweeping condemnation Lucy has effectively rejected both options held out to women by her society. She is repulsed by the carnivalesque and blatant sexuality of the Cleopatra as thoroughly as she is by the domestic idyll (sexuality safely contained and disciplined) in the bourgeois home. She is, as was Catherine I and Jane Eyre, in the grip of "neither-norism" or

"double surrogation" with a vengeance. If Lucy rejects these iconic representations, however, she also rejects their real-life counterparts, for Ginevra
the coquette appears to be a domesticated Cleopatra while Paulina Home-
Bretton (Bretton as Home, the British embodiment of the domestic ideology) models uncannily the conventional woman's life choices. Lucy has
nothing but contempt for all of these women. But where does that leave her?

In the next voyeuristic set piece, the performance of Vashti on stage as
suffering woman incarnate, Lucy is confronted with yet another female representation, this time of a slightly veiled gothic antiheroine, another carnivalesque female body emoting wildly on stage for public consumption. As
she observes the performance of Vashti, Lucy muses that, "Pain, for her, has
no result in good; tears water no harvest of wisdom: on sickness, on death
itself, she looks with the eye of a rebel. Wicked, perhaps, she is, but also she
is strong; and her strength has conquered Beauty, has overcome Grace, and
bound both at her side, captives peerlessly fair, and docile as fair. Even in the
uttermost frenzy of energy is each maenad movement royally, imperially,
incedingly upborne. Her hair, flying loose in revel or war, is still an angel's
hair, and glorious under a halo. Fallen, insurgent, banished, she remembers
the heaven where she rebelled. Heaven's light, following her exile, pierces its
confines, and discloses their forlorn remoteness" (322–23). In the presence
of this show of female power, this performance of epic female rebellion and
suffering, anger and retribution, what does Lucy do? She looks at a man, her
escort Dr. Graham, for his reaction: "In a few terse phrases he told me his
opinion of, and feeling towards, the actress: He judged her as a woman, not
an artist: it was a branding judgment" (325). We can assume that Graham
condemns as a whore any woman who would make a spectacle of herself on
the stage. But cannot we also hear in these terse comments Brontë's own
condemnation of herself as an author who has made an analogous spectacle of her own suffering, her rejections, her abandonments throughout her
novels? The fact that someone shortly yells, "Fire!" and clears the theater
does not deny the denigration and ambivalence that Brontë has displayed
here toward female passion and suffering, the two wellsprings she has tapped
in her own artistry.

Just as Lucy plays the voyeur throughout the novel, so is she continually
finding herself the object of M. Paul's prying eyes. When she tries to hide
herself in order to grieve over her loss of Dr. John, she suddenly becomes
aware that "two eyes filled a pane of that window; the fixed gaze of those two
eyes hit right against my own glance; they were watching me" (289). This
type of voyeurism pervades the novel, while Lucy in particular suffers most

acutely from paranoia about being the object of invisible spying eyes at her own moments of pain. She dreads and consistently encodes her own victimization and spectralization; she is the child being beaten (by Madame Beck, by Dr. John, by the nun, by life), and everyone is watching her sufferings and humiliations. In her "l'allée deféndue" she realizes that even here she is not free from madame's prying eyes and that even "the eyes of the flowers had gained vision" (142). It is M. Paul, however, who is described as having a "habit to wear eyes before, behind, and on each side of him" (290), and who prides himself on the discoveries he has made about the other teachers by spying with a glass from his window. He tells Lucy, "'I watch you and the others pretty closely, pretty constantly, nearer and oftener than you or they think'" (455).

M. Paul's espionage, however, is quite different from the rationalistic surveillance carried on by Madame Beck and the even more frightening presence of Père Silas as Jesuit inquisitor. When Lucy is driven to visit the Catholic confessional and is further lured into Madame Walraven's gothic abode, we know we have arrived at the fairy-tale fantasy animating this very ambivalent gothic text. We never hear the confession that Lucy gives to Père Silas after her disastrous stint as caretaker for the cretin, but that unheard confession functions much like the unheard confession at the beginning of Radcliffe's *Italian*. Those unspoken words are not buried; instead, they haunt the text, motivating most of the action from that point forward. We know that Lucy was strangely seduced by her visit to Père Silas, so much so that she vehemently resists him throughout the rest of the text, and indeed, frames her sense of herself as a writer in opposition to the priest's power over her: "Did I, do you suppose reader, contemplate venturing again within that worthy priest's reach? As soon should I have thought of entering a Babylonish furnace. . . . The probabilities are that had I visited Numero 10, Rue des Mages, at the hour and day appointed, I might just now, instead of writing this heretic narrative, be counting my beads in the cell of a certain Carmelite convent on the Boulevard of Crècy in Villette" (228). But, we might legitimately ask, how would Lucy's life have been much different? Lucy the old woman writing the text we know as *Villette* is a virtual Protestant "nun" whose only claim to superiority over the Catholic variety would appear to be her novel's "heretical" quality, and as several critics have noted, "heretical" means "able to choose." I would claim that Lucy is no more able to choose being the old maid writing her novel than she was able to choose fleeing from Père Silas. Lucy is a character in the grip of a variety of compulsions, but all of them center on her need to say no, to be negative, to reject and deny, to judge and censor, to remain frozen in the face of life's demands to participate in the warm blood of procreation and generation.

In that other gothic set piece, the visit to Madame Walraven's gothic abode, we witness a return of the repressed, a sudden appearance of the deadly and devouring mother come back to life to claim the young and vital young virgin for sacrificial purposes in the underworld. The exchange of fruit between the two women derives from Little Red Riding Hood, while the identity of Madame as "Malevola," the wicked witch, recalls all those phallic mothers who have tried to consume young gothic heroines since the time of Radcliffe. It is in the gothic underworld of Malevola that Lucy hears from Père Silas the tale of the first Justine Marie, M. Paul's lost and lamented beloved, a bleeding nun who quite possibly died giving birth to their daughter, Justine-Marie Sauveur. But the most uncanny scene in this very gothic abode occurs when Lucy waits in the entryway for madame to appear, and she does, apparently stepping through the picture of the dead nun: "I was attracted by the outline of a picture on the wall. By-and-by the picture seemed to give way: to my bewilderment, it shook, it sunk, it rolled back into nothing; its vanishing left an opening—arched, leading into an arched passage, with a mystic winding stair; both passage and stair were of cold stone, uncarpeted and unpainted. Down this donjon stair descended a tap, tap, like a stick; soon, there fell on the steps a shadow, and last of all, I was aware of a substance. . . . Well might this old square be named quarter of the Magi— well might the three towers, overlooking it, own for godfathers three mystic sages of a dead and dark art. Hoar enchantment here prevailed" (487). The woman with the stick, the phallic mother, looms here as the final manifestation of the beating and abusive maternal presence, Mrs. Reed come back again, very old and very ugly. What is most uncanny about the scene, however, is its extreme self-consciousness. This is a stylized presentation of the gothic universe, and as such it suggests Charlotte Brontë's final take on the horror of maternal politics. Malevola the phallic mother in league with Père Silas the crafty Jesuit, barren substitute parents bartering and selling their relations, stand finally in Brontë's imaginative universe for the degradation and prostitution of the family in Victorian culture. Lucy flees from them, but as I have suggested, she was compelled to construct them as cartoonishly evil figures in order to justify her flight.

The final impetus of the novel concerns Lucy's discovery of her own nature and emotional character, and this she is unable to accomplish alone. She needs a "masculine muse" figure to assist her in understanding herself, and she finds him in M. Paul. But M. Paul actually does succeed in helping Lucy uncover the emotionalism that she has successfully hidden from the other characters. We first see M. Paul when he is called upon to interpret Lucy's face and she observes, "The little man fixed on me his spectacles . . . he meant to see through me . . . a veil would be no veil for him" (81). Whereas Dr. John has seen Lucy as an "inoffensive shadow," M. Paul perceives that she is a "Little cat, sweet, alluring little flirt, . . . with a wild light in your eyes" (396). M. Paul goes so far as to define Lucy as "'one of those beings who must be *kept down*. . . . Other people in this house see you pass, and think that a colourless shadow has gone by. As for me, I scrutinized your face once, and it sufficed'" (191). Both views of Lucy, of course, are mistaken and both bear a strange similarity to the virgin/whore dichotomy operating vaguely on the margins of this genre. We are told that Dr. John is wrong about Lucy's character because "He wanted always to give me a role not mine. . . . He did not at all guess what I felt: he did not read my eyes" (395). M. Paul's vision of Lucy is also mistaken, but only in being extreme, for whereas Dr. John denied Lucy the potential for emotional growth, M. Paul sees only her emotional and passionate nature, which she has hidden from others and herself.

M. Paul's vision errs because he projects his own emotionalism onto Lucy. An interesting encounter reveals Lucy's growing fear that M. Paul will discover more than she would like about her repressed character. In a symbolic effort to prevent him from further discoveries, Lucy accidentally causes M. Paul's spectacles to break, a symbolic blinding reminiscent of Rochester in *Jane Eyre* (the Brontë père had been virtually blind at the time Charlotte began writing *Jane Eyre*). M. Paul responds to the destruction of "his treasures" by cursing Lucy as a "traitress! You are resolved to have me quite blind and helpless in your hands" (412). The blind and helpless Rochester being led by the maternal Jane is the immediate association. M. Paul's vision is also described as "near-sighted," while his need for glasses "served him as an excuse for all sorts of little oversights and short-comings" (414). One of his amusing distortions of vision occurs when he transforms Lucy's innocuous pink dress worn to the concert into a "scarlet gown" (418). Lucy is distraught over this misrepresentation and wishes M. Paul could "take me for what I was." To do this she longs to "burst on his vision, confront and confound his 'lunettes'" (445).

But it is M. Paul who bursts upon Lucy's vision and breaks reason's stranglehold on her emotions. When M. Paul is ready to express his affection for Lucy, he bases it on an affinity that he sees in their eyes: "'when you look in the glass . . . [do you not see that] your eyes are cut like mine?'" (460). But M. Paul is not only studying Lucy's physical eyes. He plays the self-confessed Jesuit inquisitor as he studies her eyes in order to "gaze deep through the pupil and irides into the brain, into the heart, to search if Vanity, or Pride, or Falsehood, in any of its subtlest forms, was discoverable in the furthest recess of existence" (440). In contrast to the emotional blindness that loving Dr. John causes Lucy, M. Paul's love and guidance are represented as "collyrium to the spirit's eyes; over the contents, inward sight grew clear and strong" (477). M. Paul's love reveals and clarifies internal visual perception so that Lucy is able to see "beauties I never could be brought to perceive" (480). Lucy as the last of her breed—the nineteenth-century British gothic feminist heroine—has finally found the ideal father-lover-teacher-priest. In unifying all four of those roles in one man, roles usually split among contending males, Brontë expresses the dream of middle-class women: that they will love and control the social and personal forces that contain and discipline them. In loving the priest-manqué, Lucy embraces and feminizes the religious establishment. In loving him as both father and lover, she introjects the family and the threat to the family, while in the teacher she seizes control over the socialization and education processes. By feminizing all of these institutions, the female gothic project has reached its end point. But it is for Lucy at least a dead end.

Just as Lucy's adherence to rationalism led to her nightmare visions during the long vacation, so does her more recent endorsement of emotion lead to her confused and irrational perceptions during the midnight fete. Lucy's emotions are heightened by the drug that madame administers as a sedative, so that instead of producing the desired effect, the drug unleashes Lucy's long-buried emotions. After taking the drug, Lucy's "Imagination was roused from her rest, and she came forth impetuous and venturous. . . . 'Rise!' she said. 'Sluggard! this night I will have *my* will; nor shalt thou prevail. Look forth and view the night!' was her cry" (562). Lucy is led almost magnetically to the park and within the park she becomes engaged in trying to locate the huge stone basin filled with cool water, a pool in which the "moon supreme" was brilliantly reflected (562). Lucy states, "My vague aim, as I went, was to find the stone-basin, with its clear depth and green lining" (568). This pool, a "circular mirror of crystal . . . [with] the moon glassing therein her pearly font" becomes the final image of reconciliation to which Lucy has struggled throughout the novel.

The challenge to reconcile her faculties lies within the park, but instead of finding harmonious unification of those faculties at the fete, Lucy is plagued by the "dream-like," "half-certain" character of everything she sees

(567). Upon first arriving at the park, Lucy finds herself seated behind the Brettons and under the intense gaze of Dr. John's "full, blue, steadfast orb.... why did he ... study me leisurely?" (571). In a symbolic action that has motivated her throughout the novel, Lucy keeps her head down so as to protect "my secret; my identity" (571). She succeeds in concealing her identity from Dr. John, but leaves the Bretton group at the fete with the same feeling that she experienced while living with them earlier in the novel—frustration, nonacceptance, and the need to repress and hide her emotions. Lucy next encounters the doubled family of the Brettons—the Walraven/ Beck/Père Silas enclave. If Lucy had not been accepted by the Bretton/Home group, she is even less at home with this darkly doubled family.

The climax of the novel would appear to be the confrontation with M. Paul's ward, the young Justine Marie. But just as Lucy's new emotionalism cannot be repressed, neither can it be trusted in the culminating and most dramatic epistemological moment of the novel: understanding the significance and identity of Justine-Marie, with whom both the spectral nun and M. Paul's deceased fiancé have been associated. This young woman embodies the emotionalism and imaginative fancy that Lucy has tried to suppress. Lucy now confronts in Justine-Marie an aspect of herself, long hidden: "I had seen this spectre only through a glass darkly; now was I to behold it face to face. ... my life stood still" (579–80). Justine-Marie encodes the gothic feminist's desire to be both daughter and wife to an idealized father-lover figure. As symbolic residue, she is both the product of incest and the practitioner who loves the father. Lucy confronts, in other words, her desire to be both daughter and wife to M. Paul; hence the scene's confused combination of repressed and supercharged emotion. I cite the climactic passage in full:

> It is over. The moment and the nun are come. The crisis and the relevation are passed by. The flambeau glares still within a yard, held up in a park-keeper's hand; its long eager tongue of flame almost licks the figure of the Expected—there—where she stands full in my sight! What is she like? What does she wear? How does she look? Who is she? There are many masks in the Park to-night, and as the hour wears late, so strange a feeling of revelry and mystery begins to spread abroad that scarce would you discredit me, reader, were I to say that she is like the nun of the attic, that she wears black skirts and white head-clothes, that she looks the resurrection of the flesh, and that she is a risen ghost. All falsities—all figments! We will not deal in this gear. Let us be honest, and cut, as heretofore, from the homely web of truth. *Homely*, though, is an ill-chosen word. What I see is not precisely homely. A girl of Villette stands there. (589)

Note again the repetition of the physical description, nay, the compulsion to repeat it. Lucy wants to read Justine-Marie as the phantom nun. She wants to be able to tell us that Justine-Marie dressed in a nun's habit and that this confrontation will allow her to solve the riddle of her life, just as Charlotte Brontë would like to be able to resurrect yet one more time the gothic subtext that has crept quietly out of the woman's literary tradition. But it is not to be. Justine-Marie is just a "bourgeoise belle" (580), and surely the repetition of the word "homely" reminds us of the antithesis of Freud's definition of the uncanny. In the embodiment of Justine-Marie as professionally feminine, we can see that the triumph of realism has been reified before Lucy's and Charlotte's startled eyes. Charlotte writes her incestuous fantasy as text and thereby safely distances it from both her consciousness and ours.

The dark glass that Lucy imagines herself looking into stands as a reflection of her unbalanced perception and is a contrast to the clear pool that reflects the moon. Lucy has been allowed to enter the temple of Truth and lift the veil, but she does not interpret correctly. Jealousy and "Fancy" mislead her. Ironically, she embraces a lie while vehemently declaring it to be her "good mistress" (583–84). Lucy's experience with misleading and inadequate visual perceptions throughout the novel should have prepared her to be suspicious of external appearances. She has been taught painfully that a man who looks as kind and wise as Dr. John can be insensitive, but Lucy has not learned her lesson well. At this point of misinterpretation, Lucy denounces "All falsities—all figments! . . . Let us be honest and cut, as heretofore, from the homely web of truth" (580). Truth, however, is as elusive and deceitful as the senses with which we attempt to perceive it. Lucy may denounce falsities, but she has consistently been their victim because she has not unified her sensibilities; she has not perceived with both her eyes and her heart. Robert Heilman has observed that feeling is placed above seeing or Reason as an avenue to truth in *Villette*, but such is not the case.[30] Brontë is asserting that there must be a conjunction between feeling and seeing. Instead of endorsing one above the other, Brontë asserts that both are necessary, not only for balanced perception but for normative gendered consciousness as well.

---

30. Nina Auerbach argues that the spectral nun has no relation to Lucy's search for identity in her "Charlotte Brontë: The Two Countries," *UTQ* 42 (1973). For an essay that argues the opposite and presents one of the most influential readings of the Brontës' use of what he calls "the new gothic," see Robert B. Heilman, "Charlotte Brontë's 'New Gothic,'" in *From Jane Austen to Joseph Conrad*, ed. Robert C. Rathburn and Martin Steinmann, Jr. (Minneapolis: University of Minnesota Press, 1967),

Lucy returns to the school for her final confrontation with the spectral nun, surely the most self-consciously antigothic moment in the text. This time Lucy recognizes the delusion her emotionalism has led her to embrace. She realizes that the only life in the nun is the life that she, the perceiver, has bestowed: "so was all the life, the reality, the substance, the force . . . I shook her loose—the mystery!—And down she fell" (587). But Lucy's final renunciation of the extremes of both rational perception and excessive emotionalism comes only after M. Paul proves his love. He questions Lucy: "'Must I show and teach you my character? You *will* have proof'" (601). Thereupon he presents Lucy with her own school, an ideal embodiment of both love and work that represents the goal she has struggled toward throughout the text. Lucy tells us, "I lifted my happy eyes; they *were* happy now, or they would have been no interpreters of my heart" (602). The inner, emotional condition is finally reconciled with and reflected in external appearances. When Lucy asks M. Paul, "'Do I displease your eyes much?'" she is reassured that to him she is beautiful. Lucy can now declare that "what I might be for the rest of the world, I ceased painfully to care. Was it weak to lay so much stress on an opinion about appearance? I fear it might be—I fear it was" (603).

Unlike Jane Eyre who leads the blinded Rochester to an understanding of internal vision, Lucy guesses and gropes her way in the dark until she is led by M. Paul—her masculinized inner faculty—to a proper assessment of herself and her place in the world. She is able to accept her external appearance and her emotions only as they are approved by M. Paul, the perfect lover-father. Lucy realizes that she misinterpreted the riddle of her life and the people most concerned with its meaning. In the process of writing her story, Lucy relives her mistaken perceptions and, as a type of artist, exorcises the past in a new and created vision. If Lucy is Brontë's "supreme psychological achievement," as Laura Hinkley claims, it would appear to be because of what critics have perceived as Lucy's capacity for psychic growth and balance.[31] She has finally learned, through the symbolic sacrifice of M. Paul, to accept instruction from others in harmonizing her faculties. In this manner she has matured before our eyes. By tracing the journey of progressive self-realization, Lucy—like Jane Eyre before her—is both a character and her own creator. She is another exemplar of the female gothic artist who creates

---

118–32. Other critics who situate *Villette* within its gothic ambience include Rosemary Clark-Beattie, "Fables of Rebellion: Anti-Catholicism and the Structure of *Villette*," *ELH* 46 (1986), 821–47; and Robert Newsom, "*Villette* and *Bleak House*: Authorizing Women," *NCL* 46 (1991), 54–81.

31. Laura Hinkley, *The Brontës: Charlotte and Emily* (New York: Haskell House, 1945), 297. More recently Karen Lawrence has argued that Lucy constructs herself as the embodiment of "lack," a

her own reality in an ambiguous and ultimately unknowable universe. In Lucy's ability to unify the mimetic and the projective, reason and the imagination, the sentimental and the gothic, past and present, appearance and reality, she becomes the supreme novelist, the heroine of her own self-created universe.

But Lucy is not as triumphant as her self-constructed tale would lead us to believe. The levels of irony and pessimism in this novel run deep. We are certainly within our rights as readers to view Lucy as even more physically and psychically regressive in her behavior than is Jane Eyre. Lucy rejects marriage and children and retreats into an all-female school, reminding us of the convent returning once again to absorb the female gothic heroine. And it appears that Lucy needs M. Paul not as a husband or even a father substitute but only as a "masculine muse" figure, an all-wise instructor and guide who leads the heroine to a proper appreciation of her place in her small universe and then magically disappears.[32] In her determined retreat from marriage and domesticity, in her need to kill off M. Paul despite her father's pleas to save him and provide a happy ending to the novel, Brontë existentializes the gothic feminist.

Charlotte Brontë places Lucy, her final accomplishment, in an ultimately ambiguous and unknowable universe. In allowing Lucy to survive M. Paul's death, she suggests what we have long suspected: female gothic heroines would like to be self-sufficient. Lucy in her part-female, part-male costume was finally more fully realized than she could have known at the time of the school play. Lucy, like all gothic feminists, finally embodies the dream animating the middle-class woman's project: the creation of an ideology that promises female self-sufficiency, a parthenogenetic heroine who lives in and

---

"cypher" who refuses to explain herself fully even in her own autobiography ("The Cypher: Disclosure and Reticence in *Villette*," in *NCL* 42 (1988), 448–66. On the same subject, see Patricia E. Johnson, "'This Heretic Narrative': The Strategy of the Split Narrative in Charlotte Brontë's *Villette*," *SEL* 30 (1990), 617–31; Syd Thomas, "'References to Persons Not Named, or Circumstances Not Defined' in *Villette*," *TSLL* 32 (1990), 567–83; Mary Ann Kelly, "Paralysis and the Circular Nature of Memory in *Villette*," *JEGP* 90 (1991), 342–60; and Luann M. Fletcher, "Manufactured Marvels, Heretic Narratives, and the Process of Interpretation in *Villette*," *SEL* 32 (1992), 723–46.

32. See Irene Tayler's *Holy Ghosts: The Male Muses of Emily and Charlotte Brontë* (New York: Columbia University Press, 1990) for the fullest discussion of M. Paul as "the muse triumphant" in *Villette*. Robert Bledsoe overstates my sense of the passive-aggressive nature of the gothic feminist when he observes, "Lucy Snowe is the quintessential gothic passive-sentimental protagonist: infinitely pitiable, but not lovable, not mature, and not triumphant, except to a reader who shares her own sentimental orientation towards nostalgic stagnation. Unlike her main character, Brontë was in the process of moving on" ("Snow Beneath Snow: A Reconsideration of the Virgin of Villette," *WL* 1 [1980], 220).

through herself and no one else. Lucy does not need even the residue of a wounded male figure leading or protecting her. She steps into the modern world as her own person, or at least as the semblance of the modern independent woman, the "feminist." Single, parentless, childless, the proprietor of her own school for girls, she has achieved the gothic feminist dream. She has become a "mother" without sullying her own body. She is a "teacher" who can "mother" her students without the ultimate and terrifying responsibility that real mothers face in the real world. She has escaped or at least elided the demands and pitfalls inherent in the flawed female body. She is, quite simply, all mind. She embodies Charlotte Brontë's "supreme psychological achievement" because Lucy is finally pure psychic energy set free from the trammels of that most gothic of nightmares, the female body.

Afterword

I always try to rationalize my nightmares.
—GRAHAM GREENE

Two of the most potent and conflicting images of female power in the classic Hollywood cinema occur in *Gone with the Wind*. The first is when Scarlett O'Hara, starved and desperate, retreats to the shambles of a garden behind her plantation, digs up a dirty carrot, ravenously consumes it, and quickly vomits. On her vomit she swears an oath: that she and her family will never be hungry again, no matter what she has to do. But what Scarlett has to do fairly quickly is dress herself up, masquerade as a femme fatale in the plantation's curtains, and vamp her erstwhile suitor, Rhett Butler, in order to get the money she needs to save the family estate. The first scene is a deeply stirring and authentic moment in the film because it taps into a powerful scene of female victimization and strength, while the second vignette is camp, masquerade, ludicrous in its parodying of the professionally feminine woman, cunning, shrewd, and yet all too dependent on masculine largesse and favor for her survival. The second scene, in fact, would appear to reverse and deny the power of the first, suggesting the fantasy that lies just below the surface of much cultural work about women. Women may appear to be weak, but their strength, cunning, courage, and sheer persistent willpower always see them through the worst gothic scenarios constructed for them by men.

By the time Scarlett O'Hara vamped her way to economic and social success in the Hollywood blockbuster *Gone With the Wind,* it was clear that the masquerade of the gothic feminist had entered the cultural mainstream so seamlessly that its origins and history were not even considered, let alone scrutinized. As Raymond Williams has noted, such has been the fate of popular culture in Britain, and, we might add, America. For Williams, the Education Act of 1870 in Britain created a new mass-reading public, "literate but untrained in reading, low in taste and habit. The mass-culture followed as a matter of course." But, as Williams points out, the other decisive period in the history of culture was between 1730 and 1740, when a new middle-class reading public first appeared and "the immediate result was that vulgar phenomenon, the novel."[1] Whether in novels or films, women have cast themselves or been cast as both victims and victimizers, a spiral that oscillates wildly because their contested gendering, with all its attendant complications of power and status, appears to be the real issue.

Seeing women as only the object of the all-powerful "male gaze" fails to account for the persistence of a "female gaze"—in novels and films—that objectifies women just as thoroughly and ambivalently. When Mrs. Danvers fondles Rebecca's fetishistic nightgown on her mistress's empty bed, we are eerily reminded of the nun's costume in *Villette* left behind as a joke played on poor Lucy's credulity and chastity. In both instances women are left with the enigma of the costuming of femininity—the props of the masquerade—but with no real role, no real power apart from the scripts that the patriarchy has already decreed and institutionalized (Lucy Snowe as virgin; Rebecca as whore).

I have attempted to explore in this volume some of the reasons why and how women writers have been complicit in constructing limited roles and self-destructive poses of femininity for other women, their readers, to embrace. To cite T. W. Adorno, when people are the beneficiaries of "free time" through the advances of a machine culture, they "first inflict upon themselves (and celebrate as a triumph of their own freedom) precisely what society inflicts upon them and what they must learn to enjoy." Middle-class women in large numbers were "free" for the first time of the drudgery of domestic obligations, and yet an examination of the female gothic novel suggests that the claims of the family and the bourgeois home haunted these women, consumed them with ambivalence, and engaged them in a life and death battle for their survival. This is clearly a paradoxical situation, and by way of explanation we can appeal to another of Adorno's observations: "Phantasmagoria comes into being when, under the constraints of its own limitations, modernity's latest products come close to the archaic. Every step forward is at the same time a step into the remote past. As bourgeois society advances it finds that it needs its own camouflage of illusion simply in order to subsist. For only when so disguised does it venture to look the new

---

1. Raymond Williams, *Culture and Society: 1780–1950* (New York: Columbia University Press, 1983), 306.

in the face. That formula, 'it sounded so old, and yet was so new,' is the cypher of a social conjuncture."[2] In other words, just as bourgeois women began to envision a life for themselves that was free from the home and its overwhelming demands, they were compelled to look back longingly and ambivalently at the ravaging patriarch and his power base. Only in the female gothic fantasy could they return to the full trappings of the situation with all its potent illusions: that women were contained and commodified by the home and family, that they were haunted by the very people who had created and enslaved them, and that they loved and hated those people in about equal measures.

So exactly how did the confluence of sex, sense, and sensibility that we call the female gothic come to have such cultural power? As I have argued throughout this book, as well as in my other writings, notions about gender in Western Europe radically altered sometime during the middle to late eighteenth century. Men sought to become androgynous, to imbibe the best that was thought to reside in the feminine soul. But analogously women also sought an androgynous quality, sought to absorb those qualities most highly prized by their society—reason, control of the emotions, and control of the body. They tried, in other words, to become the "honorary men" that Wollstonecraft advised them to be if they were to survive and prosper. If women were "naturally" volatile, emotional, and prone to excess, then they should learn that excising those qualities and aping masculine virtues was their one sure path to social and cultural acceptance (indeed, survival).

Wollstonecraft died giving birth to Mary Shelley, who almost died giving birth. Radcliffe, Austen, the Brontës—all were childless, although Charlotte Brontë died from complications related to her pregnancy or pseudopregnancy, an issue that has never been resolved. If the male Romantic poets were fearful of the female body, if they fetishized and hystericized its difference only to absorb a transformed version of it, women writers suffered an even more intense dread of the female body. A tomb, a stinking mass of death and decay, a site of vulnerability and horror—we have seen all of these attitudes toward the female body presented in female gothic writers. The dream of rising above the corrupt body, the dream of becoming masculinized—all mind, all reason—these are the core ideological fantasies that animate and motivate what I have identified as the masquerade of gothic

---

2. T. W. Adorno, "Free Time," in *The Culture Industry*, ed. J. M. Bernstein (London: Routledge, 1991), 168; *In Search of Wagner*, trans. R. Livingstone (London: New Left Books, 1981), 95–96, quoted in Clery, *The Rise of Supernatural Fiction*, 9–10.

feminism. The tragedy implicit in subscribing to such thinking is that self-hatred and self-deception become endemic in women, causing them to despise an identity that they cannot alter in any meaningful manner. If contemporary feminists like Shulamith Firestone, Andrea Dworkin, and Catherine MacKinnon suggest in their writings that they hate their flesh, they can only impotently rail at the unchangeable ontological conditions of material existence. There is no escape except through the grave, and we have left too many female gothic heroines there already.

Gothic feminism arose from the strange historical nexus of the French Revolution, sensibility, gothic romanticism, and hyperbolic melodramatic discourses of meaning and performance. British women as writers sought for the first time in fairly large numbers to define for themselves how they experienced the social, political, and economic upheaval that occurred between 1788 and 1853. They feared that economic disinheritance would befall women swept away by the newly emerging industrial base, and as an escape they imagined a world where the wily little woman would triumph through her skillful use of femininity as manipulation and guile. Gothic feminism taught women that pretended weakness was strength, and that the pose, the masquerade of innocent victim, would lead ultimately to possessing the master's goods and property. Gothic feminists believed that the weak and meek deserve to inherit the earth and that women's best defenses were a beguiling demeanor and a sweet smile. In the melodrama that is the female gothic novel, women authors constructed for themselves an alternate locus in which gender and ideology could interact to form a new world.

In this alternate world, "femininity" was self-consciously constructed as a pose of innocent, asexual victimization for effect. "Masculinity" was constructed as violently lustful, ravening, ferocious, dangerous, and evil. The civilizing effects of the innocent woman on the evil man were spelled out time after time in every melodramatic permutation imaginable. Gothic feminism finally was an ideology that aimed to do nothing less than civilize the world, making middle-class society safe for women who feared their bodies as much as men did. The dream that concludes these works—escape from the decay of the world of the female flesh into a realm of pure masculinized mind—lives on today in the writings of several contemporary American feminists, as well as in the male-authored cyberpunk novels that celebrate the human as a species of computer. And I would claim that this is an ideology that will continue to lure both sexes because it is a dream that will never, indeed can never, be realized.

Index

Printed in the United Kingdom
by Lightning Source UK Ltd.
123809UK00001B/231/A